CROSS ROADS
OF THE
JAVA
SEA

DECORATIONS BY ALEXANDER KING

CROSSROADS OF THE JAVA SEA

BY

HENDRIK DE LEEUW

GARDEN CITY, NEW YORK
GARDEN CITY PUBLISHING COMPANY, INC.

PRINTED IN THE UNITED STATES OF AMERICA BY

TO MY PARENTS

*LET US, A SMALL NATION, BE GREAT WHERE
WE CAN BE GREAT*

EMMA, QUEEN REGENT
KINGDOM OF THE NETHERLANDS

PREFACE

To those students of strange tribes and customs in tropical countries, the Netherlands-East-Indies present a fertile field for research. For centuries these lands, also known by the more romantic name of Insulinde, have been ruled by the Dutch. The Dutch have shown, in their rule, not only ability in economic development, but also humanity to the various natives and subject races under their charge. They confirmed the natives in perpetual possession of the richest lands, sacrificing material considerations, while spending large sums for the establishment of hospitals and of thousands of schools, affording technical education and scholastic training to millions of natives.

During the years that I have lived and worked in the Netherlands-East-Indies, I have come to the conclusion that no nation under the sun can boast of greater achievements in these lands than that small nation situated on the banks of the Zuider Zee.

Now as to what prompted me to write this travel narrative: the first book, I believe, by a Dutch-American pen, on the islands, Java, Sumatra, Borneo, Celebes and Bali, since Wallace wrote his famous book on Malaya in 1868.

My grandfather, himself keenly interested in all matters ethnographical and geographical, used to take me as a boy on his weekly jaunts to the Ethnological Museum in the Zoological Gardens in Amsterdam, which housed one of the finest collections of ethnological material in the world. I believe that there the foundation was laid of my ethnologi-

cal and geographical appetite, that later on was to culminate
in a desire to visit the Far Eastern lands.

Amsterdam had been for centuries the great Officina
Centralis whence flowed East Indian trade and it was here
that Council Seventeen of the East India Company swayed
its sceptre. I was born in a house that for a few hundred
years had stood in the centre of this activity, in an odour of
spice so to speak, a stone's throw from the house of Jan
Pieterszoon Coen, the first Governor General of the Indies,
and a few minutes' walk from that of Rembrandt van Ryn.
It was necessary only to open the quaint Dutch shutters of
our house for the scents of fragrant spice to fill my nostrils
and make me long even more for a sight of those strange
lands whence these treasures came.

After the good education that is so characteristic of that
of most young Dutchmen, and for which I owe a lasting
debt to my parents, and after having made a special study of
history, ethnology, anthropology and philology, that included a thorough speaking and reading knowledge of English, French, German, Spanish, Malay and Javanese, I
started my roving, almost restless career.

It was not unlike that of a certain Arent de Leeuw, a
voyager, explorer and chief engineer, who in 1623 visited
Dutch New Guinea and of whose exploits a fairly good
record and chart is kept in the Royal Dutch Archive at the
Hague. My itinerary did not confine itself within the
bounds of the East Indian Archipelago. My logbook shows
early visits to Canada, the United States, Central and South
America, Africa, India, China and Japan, whilst my activities
were concerned with trade in spice, rice, coffee, tea, and other
tropical growths and plantation work, occasionally broken
by an expedition of a more scientific nature into Borneo,
Celebes, Sumatra or New Guinea.

In pursuit of this career I came into closer contact with numerous tribes and strange native peoples, learning of their habits and customs and so enriching my ethnological and geographical knowledge.

When I finally came back to my adopted country with a wealth of material, it was my intention to write a History of the Malayan peoples. My friends, however, urged me to write, as a prelude, a travel book of the Archipelago, describing my adventures and incorporating therein the strange customs and other interesting data of the various native tribes that it was my fortune to visit.

Among the great number of books which I have studied relevant to this part of the world few appealed to me. Many appeared to be the usual travel narrative, entirely devoid of scientific background. Many were the days spent delving into old records, in libraries of the Batavia Society for Arts and Sciences, in Batavia, Java, and in the libraries in Bangkok Siam, Singapore, French Indo-China, Amsterdam and Leiden. I was anxious to produce a travel book from which one could learn something. Once started, I wanted my work to give a good picture of the places, their peoples and customs, together with a liberal mead of personal incidents for the purpose of enlivening material that otherwise might seem too academic or serious.

If I were to write down the names of all the individuals and institutions that have been so generous in their assistance to me, it would consume too much space, so it must suffice to name a few. First of all—the officials and staffs in those universities and libraries where I have done my research work. An extra word of thanks is due to the officials and staff of the New York Public Library, who did all they could to assist me in my work. Books that were lacking in other libraries of the world I have been able to find in this marvelous institution.

Of great help to me have been the papers and proceedings of the Batavia Society for Arts and Sciences; The Colonial Institute of Amsterdam; The Royal Dutch Geographic Society of Amsterdam; Koninklyk Instituut voor Taal; Land en Volkenkunde van Nederlandsch Indie; Journals of the Linschoten Vereeniging; the Hague; Royal Asiatic Society; Koninklyke Akademie van Wetenschappen; Great Britain Imperial Institute; Smithsonian Institute; Royal Academy of Arts and Sciences and many other learned Societies.

I also owe a word of thanks to Sir Henri Deterding, Director of the Royal Dutch Petroleum Company, for his letter on Borneo; to Ir van den Broek and Administrator Pan, both of the Billiton Tin Company for their kind assistance; to the United States Rubber Plantations, Ltd., for their excellent material; to Professor Krause, whose publishers have so kindly consented to let me use his photographic material; to Assistant Resident I. Jóngejans of Djambi, Sumatra, for the use of his material, and further to all of those whose names I cannot remember at this moment.

As I said at the outset, I wanted this book to be somewhat more than a travel book. I wanted it to become a written record, the first one appearing in the English language in America, of the most important islands of the East Indian Archipelago. I decided that its value would be enhanced if I incorporated a bibliography of those books that I believe any student of Far Eastern matters would need. I hope therefore that *Cross Roads of the Java Sea* will find a place in most libraries of the world, among travel-minded people, and among those who look for more than travel-talk in a travel book.

I have contributed to a great number of American and foreign magazines and scientific publications. Some of the material I have used again with permission of the Editors.

I wish to acknowledge the kindness of the following publications:

The Antiquarian, The Sportsman, Scientific American, Musical America, Geographic Society Bulletin, Dance Magazine, Travel Magazine, Sportsman's Digest, The Nomad, Engineering and Mining Journal, Journal of Chemical and Metallurgical Engineering, Medical Journal and Record, Rubber Age, Oil Weekly, Drug Markets, etc.

Now, in looking back over this preface, I made a startling discovery, that I hasten to rectify. It has been said that writing a preface is like sending out Christmas Cards. One usually finds that one has forgotten as many as one has sent. The same pertains to acknowledgments in this preface. To my great sorrow I found that I had overlooked to give thanks to my dear friend Paul R. Milton for an indebtedness, which is much more difficult to acknowledge. I am under obligation to him, not only for steadfast encouragement, but also for his judgment and understanding in criticising and correcting my manuscripts and ironing out various defects. Without him my task would have been very hard indeed.

HENDRIK DE LEEUW.

Member American Society of Agricultural Engineers
Member Royal Dutch Geographic Society
Fellow American Geographic Society
Member The Java Institute

CONTENTS

I
BORNEO

Java, Celebes and Bali present glistening rocky coastlines to the beating of the seas; Borneo is low and dank. The sun beats down on Java, Celebes and Bali and makes people kind and cheerful; in Borneo it makes them primitive and often ferocious. It is healthy to travel in those other islands; in Borneo there are moist heat, malodorous jungle and fatally dangerous insects to contend with.

Yet Borneo magnetically lures the explorer, the pioneer of world industry and the traveller, for behind the curtain of its impenetrable jungles guarded by erstwhile cruel tribes lie hidden riches of every kind as payment for the endurance of hardship and sufferings.

The multitudinous tribes of Borneo are not half-known; its natural wealth has been only superficially tapped, along the seaboard; it has not even been completely explored geographically.

But the comparatively slight inroads of western civilization have worked miraculous changes in the outer aspect of Borneo's coast. And to a large extent it is possible to visit Dyak tribes and discover that, despite their stern life, they have qualities of gaiety and humanity. For the people of this vast island lack the highly developed civilization of Java and Bali; they do not compare at all favourably with the Toradjas and Minahasians of Celebes. But they are, in a distinctly different way, every bit as interesting. It is amazing to see how much diversity there can be among blood brothers.

My first view of Borneo was in the morning from the deck of the Royal Packet, of the K.P.M., en route from Surabaja to Bandjermassin. This is a twenty-four hour trip, and the course across the water gives no hint of the astonishing sight that is to loom up ahead. On the deck of the packet it was cool, yet the low dark green—almost black—coastline ahead looked like a steaming wall; forbidding and impassible.

Then we came shortly to Bandjermassin, barely stopping there, and steamed right on down the coast. It was on our left all the way: muddy, poisonous-looking, making navigation dangerous for ships that come too close. Thus we passed the Straits of Laut, whence the town of Pulu-Laut, where the Dutch East Indies government maintains its own coal mines, is visible. Soon Pulu-Laut, dingy-looking, was left behind, and in the evening we came to Balik-Papan, Oil City, the seat of the "Bataafsche" or Royal Dutch Petroleum Company. This is a big town, laid out in European fashion, noisy even at that hour, and positively the last sort of place any one would expect to find stuck incongruously on the Borneo coast. The circular spread of its lights made a coronet of bright sparkles about the harbour.

Here I went ashore, feeling out of place in a town that bustled with European industry, when I had been mentally preparing myself, in a vague sort of way, for plunging at once into a jungle.. I recalled then the fantastic stories that float about the world concerning Borneo: the unreliable stories of Dyak cruelty; of people of aboriginal habits who live in trees; of the jungle-man Daah, and so on.

Naturally I had expected some sort of town, but nothing like this, with its wide boulevards, its trolley-line, its large and in spots palatial European quarter at Klandassan, its clubs, hotels, factory life and industry. Here everything relating to oil is produced. The oil itself is pumped into Balik-Papan from outlying points—one five-inch pipe-line running the sixty-eight miles from Sanga-Sanga—and turned into gasoline, paraffin, sulphuric acid, candles and a horde of other by-products. In a tin factory are manufactured the red cans with the Shell insignia on them, familiar to all Eastern travellers. The refineries themselves, according ill with the scrupulously clean look of the rest of the city, make Balik-Papan one of the very largest centres in the world, what with its employment roll of over twenty-three thousand men. All this busy life, so strange within a few miles of the real jungle, goes on about a fine natural bay, across which is Pantjur, another settlement founded and developed by the

Royal Dutch Petroleum Company. In the course of a short number of years this growing town has been built on what was formerly thick, damp and swampy jungle terrain, and undoubtedly the driving force behind this enterprise was the Napoleonic spirit and imagination of Sir Henri Deterding, the Managing Director of the Royal Dutch and Shell enterprises.

Among the twenty-three thousand workers, an official of the company told me, there are over sixty different nationalities of the East, all toiling daily side by side in unusual peace. The number is made up largely of Klings, Sikhs, Javanese, Malays, Chinese, Bugis, Hindus, Dyaks, Bataks, and hosts of others. The Sikhs, fulfilling the destiny that seems theirs all over the East, are policemen, and being universally respected and feared, preserve order. They, in combination with the inability of most of these racial divisions to understand one another and thus be capable of conspiring, maintain an almost strikeless economic existence. This is reflected in the huge annual oil production of the Balik-Papan refineries.

But the wonders of Balik-Papan, consisting after all in their incongruity at the fringe of one of the world's most impressive jungles, are soon exhausted. I boarded a small coastwise steamer, heading for Samarinda, the much more native town on the delta of the Mahakam river, the Mississippi of the Dyak country.

The coast on this trip offered, virtually without difference, the same prospect as my first view of Borneo. Marshy strips extended far out into the water, while low vegetation marked the beginning of the jungle wall, which a little further back towered up to tall majestic trees, bound together thickly with creepers and vines. On the entire scene the sun beat steadily and hotly, and at spots an almost visible vapour steamed up from the forbidding panorama.

The island of Borneo, geographically, is the third largest

island on the face of the globe, after New Guinea and Greenland, with an area of some 360,000 square miles, and owes most of its fame to the stories of headhunting which emanate from it. It is, of course, in the stronghold of the world's headhunting preserves. The Philippines are to the north, Java is to the south, Sumatra and the Malay Peninsula are to the west, while the Equator neatly slices the island in two equal parts. Control of about two hundred and thirteen thousand square miles of the compact, almost bayless, island rests in Dutch hands, the English having dominion over the rest. Certain portions of Borneo are quite unexplored by white men, and the geography of these tracts can only, in reality, be guessed at from clues given by what Dutch and other explorers thus far have noted.

The central portions are very mountainous, and it is there that the four main waterway systems have their fount, working down to lower levels and thus to the ocean, where the detritus carried from the highlands forms large and swampy deltas. The completeness of the jungle territory in the east has caused most of the native population, and European pioneering, to be concentrated in the west. And there where the people are is where most of the history of this "heart of darkness" has occurred.

A Portuguese (what would historians have done without those courageous adventurers?) named Antonio Pigafetta was the first white man to leave written record of his visit to Borneo, and there is reason to believe that he was among the very first of any whites to visit the island, for he came there with Magellan in 1521 and stopped at the town of Brunei. But he called this place Burne, and applied the name not only to the comparatively small native principality, but also to the whole island, though it is probable he had no real idea of the magnitude of the place.

Whence derives the name Borneo is a more or less agreed

thing; it comes from this centre of native civilization, Brunei, which is variously written by Malay tribes as Brune, Brunai and Burnai. Certain Malay historians in their works refer to Borneo as Pulu Kalamantan or the island of Kalamantan, obviously based on Dyak usage.

It has subsequently been learned that the Chinese were frequent visitors to Borneo from the Sixth Century on, and a study of Borneo life and history shows many traces of Chinese influence. I will discuss these later on in their proper places, limiting this necessarily brief account of Borneo history to what is known of the autochthonous peoples.

They themselves possess absolutely no written trace of their existence, and thus we are forced to rely on Cantonese records of the Sixth Century, which mention repeatedly a place called Puni; since the Chinese still call Borneo, and particularly the town of Brunei, Puni, it is clear beyond question that there was considerable traffic between Canton and the island. In the Fourteenth Century the kingdom of Brunei was tributary to the Brahmans and Hindus of the Modjopahit Empire of Java and the Islamic peoples of Malacca on the shores of the Malay Peninsula; and so when Pigafetta called at Brunei in 1521, he found the King an active Moslem. This fact owes its existence also to a man named Alak ber Tata, a Bisaya, who became a great Islamic power in Brunei and squeezed tribute from everyone. He left his mark on the ruling house of Brunei, which thenceforward showed its threefold ancestry of Arab, Bisaya and Chinese roots, crossed with the native vitality and ferocity.

Of this long succession of rulers, the outstanding one was undoubtedly Nakoda Ragam, the Sultan Bulkiah, who spread civilization by the old accepted doctrine of sword and conquest. He subdued all of eastern Borneo and the Sulu islands, sent an expedition to Manila, and in general con-

ducted himself like a scourge. His wife, be it noted, was
Javanese.

From that point on, however, the power of the Brunei
empire waned through repeated and disastrous conflicts with
troops and expeditions from the Portuguese and Spanish
governors of the Philippines, culminating in the arrival of
the Dutch in 1600. But they did not stay long, considering
the place a nest of rogues and scoundrels, as no doubt it was.
But some Dutch did remain, and were there when the British
made their first contacts, during bloody struggles in 1704.
But the British too withdrew officially, leaving Brunei un-
officially occupied by stragglers who slowly and painstakingly
persisted in trading there.

In 1747 the Dutch East India Company was granted a
concession to trade in Brunei, of which it took immediate advantage by opening a factory. In 1785 the native sultan, by
one of those master treaties made famous by those old trading concerns, was dethroned, ceding all his possessions to the
Dutch and remaining himself as a vassal. This was the
stroke that gave the Dutch control of seventy per cent of the
island—which they retain to this day—enabling them, without contest from the British, to claim sovereignty over the
greater part of Borneo, leaving the rest to the consolidating
efforts of the English, who now find British Borneo, Sarawak, one of their richest possessions anywhere in the Empire.
One of the consolidating forces for them was Sir James
Brookes, who in 1841 proclaimed himself Rajah of Sarawak
—the only white rajah of history.

Not only Holland and England, but also the forces of
nature, have conspired to divide Borneo into several large
distinct parts: of oil lands and of jungle, of small western
flatlands and of towering mountain regions. The varying
character of these component sections has acted on Borneo's
personal history as a barrier to any real unity, governmental

or economic. Java, with a few periods of her history ex-
cepted, has always been a single unit; but not so Borneo.
The neighbouring island of Sumatra offers a like example.

These same natural difficulties have stood in the way of
development by the Dutch and English, and the marvels that
have been accomplished in the face of the heat, rarely less
than ninety degrees, and the feverish weather, have hardly
succeeded in tapping the vast reservoir of riches that is
Borneo. An island as vast as this, and inhabited by less than
two million people, offers all sorts of opportunities to colonial
governments with foresight as already, here, the Dutch and
English have shown themselves to be. When I say population of less than two million, I base the statement on what
censuses the authorities have been able to make, despite the
practical impossibility of finding all the island tribes. The
last official estimate of the total population was about one
million eight hundred thousand, the Dutch residencies having slightly less than one million five hundred thousand and
the British the rest.

This population is made up of four principal stocks: the
aboriginals, the Malays, the Chinese and the Buginese, present here as everywhere else in Malaya. The last named
inhabit the shores of the straits between Celebes and Borneo;
the Malays are scattered everywhere along Borneo's coastline, as are the Chinese, who centre wherever there is business. In places they have mingled with the Dyaks. The
aboriginals referred to are the Dyaks, the name itself, in
Malay, meaning "savage." They are not strictly a homogeneous people, but are divided into a multitude of tribes,
each with its own mead of power, and each with its own language and customs. The population is kept down, according
to Dr. Nieuwenhuis, noted Borneo authority, by malaria and
the ravages of venereal diseases, and not, as others have

advanced, by massacres, the climate alone, or the low state of local development.

An important one of the tribes is the Klemantans, a collective name for tribes who are thick in the south and west, and who seem to show close relationship with the Kenjas and Muruts, referred to below.

Most of them are found in the coastal regions in the northern and northeastern parts of the island, where, as a result, they are more civilized. As one goes inland, the tribes are discovered to be more and more of primitive types. The Mahakam river is thickly populated with Dyak tribes, and has always served as an artery of travel and warfare for the different Dyak peoples. The Bahan and Long Glat Dyaks, for example, originally inhabited the Apo Kajan region, the *habitat natalis* of all the Dyaks, whence they were driven by the bellicose Kenyas, who were themselves driven away two hundred years ago by the Hebans from Sarawak. The upper reaches of the Mahakam river are today inhabited by the little-civilized Bahans and Long Glats, and the Pnihings and Seputans, while the most powerful tribe of all is the Kayans, who are not nomadic, but who have built up a strong and enduring life of their own. The language they speak, while different in dialect with almost every tribal division, divides itself generally into the Dgaju in the south and east; the Olou Manjaan in the region west of the Barito river, and the Busoang in the west. Malay, of course, is the most widely used language on the coast and in the chief towns of Samarinda, Balik-Papan, Bandjermassin and Pontianak in Dutch Borneo—and Sarawak and Kuching in British Borneo.

Physically the Dyak tribes resemble each other very much, being all of medium height, skins varying from rich brown to light coffee, black or brown wavy hair, with a strong Mongolian cast of features. The notable exceptions to this rule are the Kenjas, who surprisingly have aquiline noses, instead of the wide-nostrilled, flattish noses of the others.

The geologist Molengraaff recounts the following legend, which presents the Dyak notion of their own origin and distribution over the earth's surface.

In the olden days there was war between fire and water, which rose to such a pitch that all the land was inundated and fire was extinguished. Every living soul was drowned, except those that took to the *praus*. These, after floating about for an extended period, decided to sacrifice the daughter of a chief by stabbing her to death. This they did, and at once, miraculously, the water receded. But, as it receded, it carried the different boats to different parts, and thus the people of Apo Kajan were scattered, and their language grew to vary, as it does to this day.

Such, in very general terms, are the people of Borneo with some of whom later, as I travelled up the Mahakam river from Samarinda, I came in much closer contact.

I<small>N</small> the small coastal steamer from Balik-Papan I arrived in Samarinda, its harbour filled and studded with little native craft, particularly *tambangans*, gondola-like affairs, but very narrow and frail-looking. On the muddy harbour

13

surface floated bunches of seaweed, clods of vegetation from upstream, all sorts of natural detritus borne down by the river current. Above the water, here and there, and clearly visible in the light of the waning afternoon, hovered thick clouds of *lajaps*, little insects whose presence in this way was supposed to presage rain.

We moored to a dock, and went off to town.

Samarinda has a future as the commercial city of East Borneo, though it is only since 1905 that any real exploitation was undertaken here by the Dutch, whose sovereignty was acknowledged in 1844. The Sultan of Kutei makes his home in Samarinda, though within a few days I went a number of miles up-river to visit him in his palatial establishment at Tenggaron, where he has his treasures in a wooden mansion. Among his more notable possessions, which include a wealth of diamonds, rubies and pearls, he has a collection of strings of beads, most amazing in every way, consisting of every conceivable kind of bead made in the world, and running in value up to some unheard-of sum. The old rascal showed them to me proudly, his brown and wrinkled face glowing, his hands fondling lovingly the strings upon strings of orna-ments.

He personally conducted me into his throne-room, which presented an altogether majestic aspect, with the dais and throne chair at one end of the long, low room. The effect was ruined for me, however, when I noticed an old and bat-tered orchestrion against the wall to the right of the throne. It looked very discouraged and out of tune. I did not ask the old Buginese, reckoned a true Dutch ally, to demonstrate.

But in Samarinda itself I found myself suddenly busy. The day after my arrival I had visited the local offices of the oil company, chiefly for social purposes, and learned that within the week two of their engineers were going up the Mahakam to do a little exploring and prospecting. It was amiably suggested that I go along, since I was looking for just this sort of opportunity. I agreed, as I had intended to go upstream, and I met my two future companions that evening. They were Dutch, of course, and were in the employ of the oil company. Their task in going up the river was to discover new mineral deposits, for which their profession of geological engineer fitted them. They were pleasant companions, I knew at once, and well acquainted with the interior of Borneo. It was indeed a stroke of luck that enabled me to accompany them.

Our first task was to obtain *praus* and men, and to facilitate this we dug up, through a servant of the company, a Dyak chieftain who would act as the *mandur*, or our head man. Accordingly he came to see us, and we beheld before us a stocky, muscular man who must have been between forty and fifty, but who at first glance seemed infinitely younger. Except his face, which seemed infinitely older. His name was Lukut, and we conversed in Malay, which he had learned in Samarinda. He came, he told us, from one of the smaller tribes from the very uppermost parts of the Mahakam region, yet he found it better, much to my surprise, to live in Samarinda, where life, at his advanced age, was much more comfortable. Besides, his wives and sons were no more, having been exterminated in a battle with smallpox and disease, many years before. His tone permitted us to infer that he in no way regretted this, and had, as a matter of fact, enjoyed himself much more since the battle than before.

He informed us—and we believed him—that he was a resolute soul, well equipped to cope with whatever might come up on the trip, and only too glad to be of service—for a consideration. He would, he said, go at once and assemble all the necessary paraphernalia, leaving us to send down to the river's edge what we thought we would need in the way of white man's things, meaning food, firearms, tents, clothes, and so forth.

Then he left us to congratulate ourselves on what he no doubt considered our immeasurable good fortune in having found him to guide us up the river to the haunts of Borneo's people.

The next morning we went down to a certain spot on the river's border where we found Lukut superintending the careful inspection of five river *praus*, while about him, in varying attitudes of standing, sitting and lying, were nearly fifty-five Dyaks: well built bodies nearly every one, and though all were smiling at us cordially, they looked ferocious enough.

Said Lukut: "These are the men who will go with us."

Said we: "That is splendid. Are they—trustworthy?"

Lukut looked offended. "Otherwise I would not have them." He squinted at us to see what effect his reply had made, and walked back to the *praus* and devoted himself to a personal inspection.

We arranged to start the next morning, allowing the rest of that same day for our necessary equipment to be brought, such as it was. We intended taking little, both because of our up-river voyage, and also because none of us needed much. Though a jungle such as I expected interior Borneo to be was more or less new to me, I felt I would have no need for the vast amount of baggage most people insist upon carrying into distant places. We were all three, however, careful to provide ourselves with stout puttees and various unguents, for protection against the armies of insects that fly around and make their home in and under one's skin, not forgetting the showerproof so-dry explorers' tents which I believe to have been of American make.

For each *prau*, therefore, we had ten paddlers, and a *mandur*, while Lukut, head *mandur* intended, he told us, to move about from one boat to another. The men we had were Kajan Dyaks and natives of the very section through which we were going to pass. This in itself eradicated many potential difficulties, for none of us spoke any of the Dyak dialects; this way we could converse in Malay with Lukut and do our best to pick up what we could as we went along with him. None of the Indo-Polynesian tongues offer any special obstacles to one with some gift for languages. They are all interrelated, and fortunately have none of the complicated grammar that makes Western tongues such infernally knotty things to pick up.

So, we started.

The three of us arrived at the *praus* while it was still dark, and found Lukut and his followers just bestirring themselves. But they took very little time, and by the moment that the sun had come up, with its effect of suddenness, they had eaten their rice, splashed their sleep-sodden faces with river water, and declared themselves ready for the first day's jaunt. We took our places, shoved off and sat back to watch the easy paddling motions of our men, that nevertheless sent the laden *praus* gliding over the grey water smoothly and speedily.

For many miles that first day the river flowed in a wide course, with a deep current, strong but not very swift. Of course as we progressed the almost imperceptible narrowing of the banks became noticeable, especially as compared with the delta from which we had come, where the main river divided itself into smaller streams constantly, until the sea was reached and the network of branches merged into the harbour and the shore.

Our narrow *praus* knifed their way through the water. As I sat aft I could watch the rhythmically moving bronzed backs before me, swinging steadily back and forth, almost without cessation, their voices from time to time joining in strange, flowing chants. The sun came down hotly; it must have been well over ninety, though a faint and fitful river breeze kept us actually from melting completely away. The first few days in that humid heat were a strain even on me, who had lived so long in the tropics. My friends seemed to mind it very little, though I noticed they perspired every bit as much as I did. But soon I grew accustomed to it, and although it felt just as hot, I was able to retain my energy. How it would have been to plunge through the jungle on foot, as initiation into the hidden charms of Borneo, I do not like to think. But when we did come, some days later, to travel on foot for miles, I found it not a bit worse than any arduous travelling I had done in Java and Sumatra, for instance.

As we sat bunched up in our *praus*, we had plenty of time to watch the banks slip by. Nearly all that first day they were monotonous. Low and poisonous looking, with only stunted trees to mark the edge, behind which seemed to stretch an interminably flat country. The year before there had been a disastrous drought, and we passed regiments of trees denuded of foliage, stretching gaunt, sun-blackened arms to the blazing sky.

But soon the view took on a different aspect. The banks grew somewhat steeper, and seemed to press in on us as we slid silently over the surface of the great river, near the right bank to avoid the strongest section—in midstream—of the downstream current. Now the trees were surrounded, smothered in vegetation. It was not a solid green, but a strange merging of seemingly hundreds of infinitesimally differing shades of green. The undersides of great heavy leaves, turning lazily in a faint gust of wind, would show momentarily an almost white green, and then disappear as suddenly. It was like seeing a great fish turn belly over near the surface of the water. Gigantic fern-like growths reached their nodding heads over the bank, at times dipping gently, like weeping willows, into the water. And among these were thickly scattered thousands of the Pohon biyou, a flower species, their rich orange heads emerging proudly from the dense masses of riverside growths, looking like huge fans in the hands of beautiful women at a ball. There were thick bushes of them, the brilliant orange hues standing out against the myriad green and greenish shades of their background.

Under the *praus*, as I looked over, I could see vast schools of crayfish, big and little. Here and there little sand-bars projected into the stream, and on their sides basked turtles; and gigantic freshwater shrimp scurried to and fro, in and out of the water. Here and there along the shores, where we passed small open stretches, we saw a few monkeys and apes, who glared at us in unanimous hostility. They seemed unafraid, and would cling to a branch and stare us down without any apparent fear of what we might do to them. We did not shoot.

Lukut pointed out, now and again, some snake darters, which he called, in his Dyak dialect, *Burung damdang*. These hung from the topmost branches of trees, curled like the letter *S*, and seemed not to move. From time to time, as we came exceptionally close to the shore, we could see literal swarms of centipedes, scorpions and tarantulas. The very undergrowth seemed to creep with them, while over the edge of the water where the vegetation disappeared into it, hovered numberless squadrons of huge mosquitoes, each carrying its deadly load of germs. In truth, the anopheles of Borneo are as dangerous, if not more so, than all the other poisonous denizens of the interior. During our several weeks' sojourn in the hinterland we found them certainly much more difficult to detect and avoid, notwithstanding our *klambuks* (or mosquito nettings) and native concoctions.

And now, as we progressed further upstream during the afternoon, the river narrowed even more. We glided along between the walls of dark green in the shadow of mighty trees, their boles hidden behind thick creepers and parasitical climbers, the area around the roots of the trees being choked with floral growths in brilliant and contrasting colours, like a hodge-podge garden. Above, waving gently to and fro in the puffs of faint river breeze, were the tops of the trees, plumed like giant green feathers.

About mid-afternoon we stopped at a riverside clearing which extended, man-made, some distance to an open space, somewhat overgrown and weedy, where there were some old Dyak graves.

This was my first opportunity to see, with my own eyes at this close range, what Borneo was like. So while the others snoozed, I prowled about, stepping nimbly among the treacherous underbrush.

Down at one side, about a hundred feet from the water, I found a cluster of huge lilac orchids, like those of Sumatra (*dendrobium superbum*). They grew strangely, so close to the trunk of a tremendous tree that they seemed to sprout from the very bark itself. Their pale beauty struck a surprisingly delicate note in the midst of the stark, crushing effect that everything else produced on me. There everything was big, of heavy, solid colours, with tree bound to tree by twining, writhing creepers, that seemed like fetters

chaining a vast horde of giants together. And in the midst
of this, like an oasis, the enormous orchids, pale and beautiful, nodded their drooping heads.

One of the boys came to call me back. It was time, he
said, to go on. At least, I gathered that was what he meant,
for he referred obscurely to something about boiling rice.
Later in the day I asked Lukut about it, who patiently explained that Dyaks compute time in units of the amount of
time necessary to boil rice. Thus a man might say: "*Ekeh
teh dueh telo krassa kakedjane,*" which, literally, means:
"His house is two or three times as far away as is necessary to
boil rice."

Again we started our silent smooth gliding between the
ever-narrowing banks, until our speed was considerably les-
soned by trees fallen into the river, which also accelerated
the current. Then we came to a stretch where the shores
were suddenly low and sandy; then rocky and brush-covered
again, until the sight of the constantly recurring dense green
of the jungle began to wear on us. We had all day seen no
one other than those with us, and Lukut said that it would
be impossible for us to reach a Dyak compound that night.
As I looked ashore, and saw frequently recurring spots where
decayed vegetation lay thick on the ground (the early stage
of coal formation) I wondered where we were to find a place
suitable for bivouacking. But Lukut found a place not far
along, just as the sun gave the first hint of plunging from
sight. The boys drew the *praus* up on a clear stretch, where,
marvel of marvels, it was dry and cool, now that the sun had
taken its glow and glare from the world.

Lukut stationed himself erect in the very centre of the
camping place and proceeded to give orders. Some of the
boys cut wood to build little lean-tos for us to sleep under.
Then, over these they stretched our *klambuks*, which would
also protect our more tender skins from the Agas-Agas, tiny

insects smaller than pinheads, but infernally annoying. Their
metier, I found, is to bite, burrow under the skin and breed.
The only way to be rid of them is to cut them out, or use
mercury. Their chief effect is one of severe itching and pain,
but not one of poison.

Our retainers cut firewood, made fires, began cooking
preparations and brought our duffle from the *praus*. In no
time we were eating rice and soup and turtle meat. The
fires threw fantastically dancing shadows on the vast screen
of the dark jungle beyond us. Twenty feet away the Dyaks
squatted and lay around three fires, dozing, talking, some
lying on their backs, weary from the day's paddling, and staring wide-eyed at the starless sky. Others already slept
soundly under the shelter of the palm-leaf lean-to they had
constructed in a few minutes, and a few cooked themselves
extra rations of rice.

Apart from all, though not far from the biggest fire, sat
Lukut, not mingling with his hirelings, or rather our hirelings. Dignity, despite his primitive appearance, sat well
upon him. His *tjawat* (bark loin-cloth) was still his only
garment, and his long uncombed hair hung down straight on
either side of his flattish, lined countenance. His dark eyes
stared at the fire, and he did not speak to the others. Nor
they to him, though they were careful not to get between him
and the flames, nor to raise their voices so loud as to disturb
his meditations. He still sat there, motionless, when I
turned in.

· But before that moment came, the incidents round those
camp fires gave me my first insight into the Dyak character,
particularly of these of the Kajan division. Their postpran-
dial snoozes over, each busied himself in one or another fashion until sleeping-time came: some wove rattan baskets as
supply containers, others cut new axe sheaths for themselves.
Now and then one would rise and consult Lukut, who would

38980

gaze with what seemed a scornful expression at the piece of handiwork, make some monosyllabic comment and then return his stare to the flames.

An hour or so after we had finished eating, one of the boys suddenly began singing: a song different from the monotonous chants they had used on the river to assist them in maintaining a rhythmic paddle swing. This was gayer, had even the elements of a recognizable melody—recognizable, that is, to Western ears. I tried to discover then, and on other occasions, what sort of music was used, how their scale compared with ours or with the Chinese. As far as I could determine it seemed nearer the Chinese than ours, all the intervals being of that strange indistinguishable kind we think of in connection with Chinese music. The melodies seemed scientifically constructed, but all were built on the repetitive principle, going on, like a cowboy song of the American West, from verse to verse interminably.

When the first boy had finished his short solo verse, the rest joined in, their strong virile voices blending beautifully in rudimentary harmonies. Then the first boy sang again, and so on from chorus to chorus. As they sang they worked, and seemed a contented and happy lot.

One by one, after a while, they dropped off, first rubbing themselves with the Broatali concoction to ward off mosquitoes, leaving Lukut the last one, to my view, awake, seemingly satisfied to do with fewer hours of sleep.

But no sooner had I composed myself under the *klambuk* for sleep, when a terrific din broke out. Like the mingled roar of a myriad throats, it poured in on us from every side. There were howls and screams, and wails and yaps. The uproar was finally identified as the usual nocturnal concert by multitudes of Borneo's wild dogs. These are short-haired, usually yellow-brown, medium-sized animals, with thin curly tails, erect ears and alert expressions. Every Borneo household has at least one of these noisy beasts. At length the din died away, leaving only some dogs, stronger lunged than the others, to give vent to spasmodic howls of fear, rage or joy. When they too had taken themselves away, we slept, our first night in Borneo's Nipa—Endless Jungle.

W E awoke early, naturally, to find that it had rained
during the small hours, though so well had our little
shelters been constructed that none of us was wet. Nor had
we heard the downpour, so it must have been slight. We

emerged from our lean-tos, and looked out. It often happens in this country that, after a shower such as we had experienced, the atmosphere becomes preternaturally clear. Every leaf, studded with raindrops, sparkles glitteringly in the morning sun, and seems large and very close. The scenery in the distance stood out as clearly as if we had been looking at it with binoculars. We could see tall trees in detail at great distances; the rise of a hill seemed but a step away. Yet the telescopic effect made everything softer, lent to the view an aspect of gentleness and beauty which made me forget the harsh monotony of the landscape as we had come up the river the day before.

After a quick breakfast we embarked and were once again on our up-river way. Perhaps the shower did it; perhaps the quality of the terrain changed; but everything looked much more beautiful. Rapidly the river narrowed, though after a certain point it remained the same width, at places not much wider than a creek, though considerably deeper and with a strong current. Lukut stood in the bow of the first *prau*, *mandau* in hand, ready to cut away, with one dexterous blow of the blade, any rattans that might have spanned the stream. On all sides now, thicker than before, the rattans climbed and crept their way from towering tree to towering tree, so that it must have been possible for a monkey to travel dozens of miles without touching foot to the ground. These, too, were the finest kind of rattan for export; it is really a shame that the natives, in gathering the fibres nearer the coast, have been so careless, since the best rattan, up-river, is still expensive to cut and transport.

During the morning we found ourselves paddling between much higher banks, for on either side of us were hills to the height of several hundred feet, covered densely with virgin forest growth. Among the trees now I saw, standing out dazzling white in the increasingly bright sun, the boles of *tapang* trees, much like our oaks, but with whitish bark.

Then we hit the *kihams*, or rapids, which made the river difficult of navigation from that point on. But the Dyaks knew perfectly how to maneuver the *praus* through. After each rapid was passed, the paddlers let out a deep-throated "Oo-hoooo!"

We swept round one bend and found ourselves in the teeth of a fierce divided current rushing from above a rocky island in the middle of the stream. Three times we went back, got up momentum and tried to get by. And twice we were halted. The third time we made it, and a triumphant "Oo-hoooo!" roared out from fifty throats. From there on it was a bit easier, though frequently some boys would swim ahead with rattans in their mouths, to a rock whence they could pull the *praus* up. Some of the boys rolled palm-leaf cigars, others took a few mouthfuls of *sirih*, and happily we went on.

Late in the afternoon we came to a Dyak *kampong*. A hard-beaten clearing extended from a row of houses (called *long-putih*) some distance back from the water right down to the bank. With a shout from our boys we swept alongside a thing that looked like a crude jetty, and debarked, waiting for Lukut to make our arrival official by announcing it. This he did, with many words but few gestures, to a group of armed men who issued at once from the largest house. After his speech they looked at us casually, not impressed as far as I could see, and then led us to the same house from which they had come.

The posts of the house were constructed from roughly hewn tree-trunks, and hardwood logs notched with steps served as ladders to the long veranda which ran along the whole front of the structure. As we neared it, I could see that tree bark was used for all walls, doors and partitions, and that most of the delicate lathwork on the floor was of thin bamboo strips. The whole affair was held together with rattan, which is as strong a means as could possibly be found. The veranda, in this as in all Dyak houses, was used for all household enterprises, while the insides are divided into two large sections, one for daily use and the other for sleeping, subdivided into numerous smaller apartments for individual and family use.

From the door of this building came a woman, about thirty-five, I judged, attired in an elaborate skirt-effect about her loins, but naked above the waist.

Without hesitation she greeted us in excellent Malay, her ability to speak it surprising me considerably. Her first question was the old standby question of all Polynesian tribes: *"Dari mana tuan?"* "Where do you come from?" But inside, after we exchanged salutations in that language, she told us that she had married a Banjarese, and that she was Chieftain of this tribe, by virtue of her father's premature death the year before. She had also, she said, been to Mecca on a pilgrimage, and had married the Banjarese purely for commercial reasons, in an effort to stimulate the trade activities of the people under her. She pointed out, in support of this plan, that Malays travel, for trade purposes, more readily than Dyaks, who will only under dire duress leave their home *kampongs* and the places near which their ancestors are buried.

She said, with evident pride in her dark-eyed side-glance at us, that the tribe had just completed an excellent crop, with which they were all extremely well pleased. It was partly due, she said in answer to our questions, to the use of the crop-time designator, which consists of a piece of bamboo planted in the ground after a special ceremony. It is then necessary for the stick to throw a shadow of a certain specified

length in a certain specified direction. At the actual moment
when the shadow appears, sowing is begun.

The name of this place, we learned, was Liong Kiliam,
and that it was the nearest Dyak *kotta* to Samarinda, which,
of course, we already knew. Our welcome was in every respect cordial and free from suspicion, though I was to learn
that the slight touch of civilization had softened these peoples in comparison to those we were to meet farther up the
river. We were to have our first taste of native life.

That first taste came that evening, when a *tudan* or
round dance was performed, by village girls only. Lukut
told us it would not start until the moon had come up, so
until that time we enjoyed a comfortable smoke while conducting a desultory conversation with the female chieftain,
who proved agreeable in every respect. It took nearly two
hours after sundown for the moon to appear, and when it
stood above the trees, fully visible, we passed down the village street, now very quiet, to a large open compound. With
us went Lukut, the chieftain and her Malay husband, who
said hardly a word throughout the time he was in our company. His wife, however, in her very good Malay, kept up
a genial, smiling, running commentary on the spectacle as it
proceeded.

Round about the compound were thickly massed the several hundred inhabitants of the village. The half, opposite
us, were in the full and bright glare of the moon, and those
on our side were in comparative shadow. Faces seemed to
our eyes expressionless, but exclamations breaking forth at
frequent intervals attested to the lack of boredom among the
audience.

The dance had already started when we arrived. A
dozen or more girls, perhaps averaging fifteen in age, and
attired only in brief skirts, had formed a circle, and were
holding hands. They moved round, lifting and dropping

their linked arms in smooth rhythm to the tempo of a chant-like song begun by the largest—and also the oldest, said the chieftain at our side. This song celebrated the deeds of past and gone heroes in short verses, coming back repeatedly to a brisker refrain in which all the dozen girls joined.

Then, from the spectators, another and somewhat older girl emerged. In her clear young voice she began another song, this time praising the doings of a certain young chieftain of past days who had won particular glory in a head-hunting expedition.

Many minutes passed, the girls continuing their circular motion, the two singers in the middle throwing back their heads and sending the mournful-sounding notes of their chants up into the face of the bright silver moon. As the dance progressed a dozen or so young men detached themselves from the crowd and squatted in a larger circle around the girls. The tempo of the chant increased, and the young men muttered among themselves, and from time to time one broke out in a short sharp laugh.

The young brown torsos of the girls wove to and fro, when suddenly the dance ended. The girls turned, frightened laughs on their lips, and stood quietly until the young men chose among them. These, leaping to their feet at the moment the rotary movement of the dance had ceased, each ran up and picked out a girl. Then, hand in hand, the dozen or so couples fled from the compound to the *lumbung, uma kalo,* a group of small, square houses raised from the ground on stilts. There they passed the night in company. . . .

In the morning after our own breakfast we watched a mob of at least a hundred men around the base of a few huge forest giants—the Tanggiran located some distance from the village—gathering honey. Some climbed to the top, driving the bees away with the suffocating smoke of a number of torches, and then threw the nests down on a large cloth spread around the tree on the ground. They then hung the nests to drip, obtaining about twenty-five pounds of pure honey from each nest. This tribe, and many others, make a business of honey gathering, selling both the honey and the wax, in addition to other jungle products.

The only native with whom, at this early stage of the game, I could converse freely was our amiable hostess. After watching the honey-gathering process for a while, I went off in search of her, and at length discovered her superintending the building of a new council house. Seeing me, and scenting another opportunity to air her Malay, she gladly left her task and together we went to her house, one larger than all the rest and mounted on high stilts.

In one corner of the large, general room we occupied were some earthenware pots, glazed, and decorated with dragons and other Chinese motifs. These, my friend told me, were called Tempajans, Djawet (also Balangas) and are venerated by the Dyaks as holy things. How such things, of obvious Chinese derivation and origin, came to Borneo, neither she nor any one else could ever tell me. But those that possess them are thus assured of success in all things, including rice crops, commerce, hunting, health and the avoidance of demons. When a man obtains one, the *balians* of his village hold a week's festival, culminating in a banquet dedicated to the holy pot. Then the vessel is smeared with the blood of a dog or pig once a year to keep fresh its potent qualities. This reverence smacks strongly of some sort of fetishism, dating perhaps from some remote time when these Chinese pots were used as the receptacles for the earthly remains of important men, leaving the ground for the lesser fry.

I sat with my friend, the chieftainess, in full sight of one such venerable object, and with it before my eyes listened to the many things she told me.

I managed by adroit maneuvering of the conversation to

draw her out on head-hunting: that strange and sinister custom which has prevailed in so many, but widely separated, parts of the world. In northern South America to this day, I understand, head-hunting among tribes is an established custom. I have seen little dried heads from there on sale in many cities of Latin America or in New Guinea, as souvenirs. But the Dyak, I found, did not collect the skulls of his enemies in order to preserve them as paper-weights, mantelpiece ornaments, or as bases for lamps.

The chieftain told me that really, in her comparatively enlightened opinion, head-hunting had been (it now no longer exists except in very remote and unreachable tribes) a most unheroic business. The Dyak warrior, head-hunting bent, never went out on his errand in a stand-up-and-fight frame of mind. He preferred to ambush his enemy by stalking him warily, and kill him with poisoned darts from a blow pipe (*sumpitan*). Having felled the luckless wretch, and ascertaining, still from ambush, that the victim was helpless or dead, he would creep out and sever the head with his *mandau*. Whites, curiously, were only rarely bothered when head-hunting was still in vogue; the art was waged only by neighbouring tribes on each other.

The principle of head-hunting is not, as I said, the search for quaint and bizarre mementoes. It is rather, this, that the Dyak wants possession of the murdered man's soul, which, according to Dyak beliefs, resides in the head and hair. By obtaining the soul, the Dyak then assures himself of a servant and slave when he departs for Apo Kesio, the Dyak Hereafter.

The servants can be obtained vicariously. For example, ferocious and well-organized head-hunts were wont to take place when a chief, without skulls to his credit, died and before doing so expressed himself ashamed and humiliated at the thought of entering Apo Kesio in solitary splendour.

Then his followers went out with their blowpipes and collected as many skulls as possible. In this case the souls belonged to the chief and not to those who gathered them.

An individual frequently went out on a solitary headhunt to demonstrate his bravery—by killing a man from ambush!

The influence on the people of the skulls was very great. When the skulls were brought in and exposed, it was confidently believed that all evil influence was driven out, and the row of heads hanging in ghastly symmetry from the roof beam of a large family house dispensed an aura of stability and benignity. A number of houses in some Borneo valleys had a row of heads; in some cases only one or two, all preserved from the recent days when Dutch authority made determined efforts to stamp out the practice. No effort was ever made, my informant went on, to preserve the heads, beyond cleaning them up. That is, cutting off the dangling flesh at the base of the neck and repairing other such defects, with the little knives Dyaks carry attached to their *mandaus*. Then the heads were hung up on the fore-gallery and left to dry and grin down in horrible benevolence, their souls meantime doing yeoman duty for those who had collected them and passed on to Apo Kesio.

All the heads I saw were shrivel-skinned, wrinkled and crinkled, the lank black hair falling over the dried-up eyeballs in disarray, and the whole set of features distorted in such a way as to make the faces almost unrecognizable as those of human beings, though some were quaintly and grotesquely decorated.

The chieftain told me that she has small regard for those who continue to bewail the passing out of the ancient and manly custom. She herself, having travelled and having tasted, if only fleetingly, of the more refined ways of other Malay peoples, would be perfectly content to go on to Apo

Kesio without such bloody slaves.   But, she felt herself constrained to add, there were many of the Dyak peoples who encountered the greatest difficulty in living up to their *adat* without the assistance of servants in Heaven.

"But," she finished, regarding me with a quizzical smile to show that she understood my feelings in the matter, "you can tell your people at home that head-hunting is dying out. It will soon—" and very unexpectedly she sighed, as if at the passing of an ancient glory, however distasteful to her personally— "be no more."

As a matter of fact, nowhere did I find signs that active head-hunting was ever carried on, except in a few of the tribes most distantly removed from contact with the Dutch and English.

HERE in Liong Kiliam I managed also, still from our
hostess who never wearied of giving us information,
to learn something in my own way about Dyak religion. Of
course, many eminent ethnologists, scientists and travellers,

such as Nieuwenhuis and Molengraaff, also Elthout, Hose and McDougall, have excellent records of some aspects of it, but I was anxious for first-hand information.

The Dyaks are, as might be expected, animists, and their beliefs are founded, as accurately as I could learn now, and check up later, on two fundamental dogmas. First, that everything in nature, large and small, whether man, animal, plant life, or mineral object, has a soul. Second, that these same souls possess the power to leave their present habitats and settle in others more congenial to them. This point, unformulated, may be compared to fetishism.

The Dyak, however, is not fanatic, and does not live in fear of the spirits, embodied and disembodied. He is broadminded enough to make deals with the spirits, and pictures his Hereafter like his own surroundings and the spirits of the dead like himself. The clouds are, in his eyes, the domicile of spirits, and those spirits he endows with all human attributes.

This animism is the belief of every Dyak tribe, and is rejected by only a very few converted Christians and Mahometans, and some Hindus. At some time in the past, Hinduism seems to have made considerable progress in the island, having, it is my own belief, been brought there indirectly by Javanese, and not by Hindus from elsewhere. Traces of the Javan influence are noticeable also in names of towns, Bandjermassin, for example, meaning "Salt Gardens." In certain parts of the Borneo interior there are ruins of Hindu temples, their Sanskrit inscriptions having been translated by that eminent Dutch Sanskrit scholar, Kern. These temples have never been replaced by anything else, for the animism of the Dyaks does not call for temples or priests, or, in fact, any sort of ritualism at all. The nearest thing to any sort of formality in their religion is—or was—head-hunting, which might be considered a sacrificial custom in its anxiety for souls.

Superstition and a kind of demonology play a larger part in the Dyak life than even the vaguely understood doctrines (to dignify them by that term) of their animistic beliefs. Monkeys and dogs are held sacred, birds and deer are used as sources of omens, and our own men, when seeking to learn if such and such a day was propitious for continuing the journey, consulted the *pelaki*, chicken thief, a small wild bird. Many other birds are believed efficacious for such purposes, including the falcon, carrion bird, spider hunter, woodpecker, and rhinoceros hornbull.   Their term for omen birds in general is *bali flaka* (derived from the Sanskrit). (Cf. Lat. *falco* and Ger. *Falke*.)

They employ black magic, sometimes with and sometimes without the assistance of a medicine man, to bring death to their enemies. For this, the sorcerer betakes himself to an open, deserted field, but no one must watch and the sky must be clear. Two short poles are placed in the ground and between them in a hole is laid a small wooden effigy of the object of the enmity. Some water and loose earth, representing blood, are tossed in the hole with the effigy, and the flight of falcons, always plentiful, is closely watched by the magician. Should the birds fly a certain way, death will come as desired. If not, wait for another day. It can be seen that with sufficient money in the possession of the omen-seeker, and patience on the part of the sorcerer to sit out in the sun, this method can never fail in the long run.

It was comparatively easy for me to learn of the simpler and more forthright superstitions of the Dyaks, but some of the more recondite customs and beliefs may not be ferreted out so easily, since a curious reluctance to speak attacks these people when the questions strike them as too pointed. But I did, little by little, sometimes arousing the anger and suspicion of my interlocutors, find out a good deal. The female chieftain, who in the few days we stayed at Liong Kiliam, told me so much, barely hinted at the full extent of their credos.

From a hint here, a sentence there, I managed to learn something about their really evil spirits, the ones they fear the most. It seems that the really and enterprisingly bad ones are *bali djaka* or, the worst human corpses. The word "worst" is used here advisedly, because the Dyaks believe that a person who is good is never wounded or hurt but, no matter how violent his life, will die a natural death. Therefore, one who dies from some one else's violence to his person, or by suicide, head-hunting, torture or other cruel death, becomes the home of *bali djaka*, vicious demons. To have a member of one's family die by any method which indicates that he was evil is a cause for saddened but philosophic resignation.

But even more feared than the violent death of an individual is the demise of a woman in childbirth. This fear by itself is easy to comprehend, in view of the united belief among all Polynesian peoples that the true and fundamental purpose of existence is to breed children. A barren or sterile woman is held in great contempt and disgusted pity, and for those who are able to breed, the strictest obligation to do so is in force. They have not yet arrived at the conclusion of civilization that too many children—when several may be weak or puny—is bad. Nothing must stand in the way of a successful delivery, and, by a most natural consequence, it follows that the spirit of a woman dying in childbirth was afraid. Such is the anger and awe of other Dyaks when such an untoward event occurs that they are apt to visit their wrath on the cause of it. The sufferings of women in delivery fills them with great amazement, and for all this agonizing commotion to take place, only to end in death, is in their eyes a crime toward the universe and mankind.

The Dyaks, further, believe in witches, werewolves, and vampires (or *Antoe-Hoetangs*). The river is not only the path of good departing spirits; it is also considered the path by which evil spirits return to their native *kampongs* to spread wickedness and disease. They are convinced that it is no feat at all for a bad spirit to assume any shape at will, and so, when leaving the confines of a forest, no Dyak ever forgets to ask the forest ghost for his soul. He does not know but that his soul has been snatched away from him. For should his soul have been thus purloined, he will become ill and die forthwith. There are other witch spirits that are believed to steal souls, mangle the bodies of their victims, decapitate them in the night, bearing the heads away to torture somebody else, returning before morning to rejoin the severed members.

Against this multitude of invisible and terribly supernatural phenomena, the Dyaks have an equal multitude of protective omens and preventatives, such as crossed sticks, puppets, amulets, and so on, not to mention a million little things they are not to do, like the *Pemalis* of the Toradjas, described later on.

Our stay at Liong Kiliam was nearing its close when, our affable chieftainess told us, a burial would take place of a man who had unfortunately died during our arrival, which made the village *lali* (taboo). We extended our stay by one day to witness the ceremony.

We discovered then that the deceased was an old chief, long removed from power because of senility. He had been lying on a large litter in an isolated house, attired in full war regalia. At the ceremony, such as it was, they placed him in a rude coffin and carried him to the sepulchre (his body not being taken out through the door, as the latter was only used by the living, but the side wall being removed to make it possible for the corpse to be carried out this way), a small structure on high stilts, where his spears, knives, *mandaus* and blowpipes were placed by his side. I was especially interested in seeing them erect a pole by his bier, for on the pole was an old, dried human scalp: the best substitute for heads, indicating souls, to accompany the ancient warrior to Apo Kesio. His nails, on both hands and feet, were gilded, and altogether he appeared very dignified.

We were unable to wait to attend his actual funeral, but as we embarked in our *praus*, a strange, depressingly resonant sound floated down to us from the inland side of the river where the funeral was taking place. This was the *titih*, the Dyak death bell, made of four metal pieces, and struck in sequence, producing a clock-like, dolorous noise. It is beaten only when death has come: first, when some one has died, second, at the placing of a body in its coffin, next during the transportation of the coffin to the graveyard, and last when the grave is sealed.

Its mournful pealing pursued us on the surface of the river, for soon we were on our way again, swaying up the current in our *praus*, with the brown brawny backs of our paddlers, led by Lukut, moving in rhythmical swing before us.

On the shore stood our friendly chieftainess, her right arm raised in a salute of farewell; perhaps we would see her on the way down. A few feet behind her stood her merchant husband, and behind him were a group of five armed men, the waterfront guard that had first greeted us. Then we shot round a wide bend and Liong Kiliam was as if it had never been, for all around us towered the green masses of the endless jungle.

THE cool damp, pale grey veil of the morning mist still hung, in swiftly disappearing shreds, over the water when we resumed our journey into the heart of the Dyak country. Though slightly wider near Liong Kiliam, the river almost at once became narrower than it had been so far, and then we came to a rapids or *kiham* that must have been about two hundred feet through. The black jagged edges of huge rocks lifted their ugly heads above the foaming water. It was impossible to go through.

At the orders of Lukut, the *praus* were unloaded, and the contents carried by our sturdy fellows along the shore. The *praus* were likewise borne up to a point where the river was again smooth enough for us to paddle. Very soon there came floating downstream, past us, a bamboo chicken coop containing a young live chicken. It peeped distressfully as it rolled by swiftly toward the rapids. Lukut observed, a frown creasing his face, that this indicated the outbreak of some contagious disease way up the river. This method is adapted to warn others of dangerous neighbourhoods.

The middle of the afternoon became terribly warm, but we had hopes of reaching Ma Mehak Tebui, the next village, before long. Suddenly, when not far from it, though it was not yet in sight, we heard a very melodious rhythmic noise. When we swept in view of the *kampong*, the sound seemed to come from one of the larger structures. We came to the landing place, but a guard told us the village was *lali*, which meant, Lukut told us, that we would have to go on without stopping, or in other words, "no trespassing."

Why? we demanded to know, being weary of the heat for that day. Because, he said, *lali* meant that everything was sacred in the village: no one could enter the *kampong* because a rice feast (*tugal*) was in progress. This, we said in effect, was a confounded nuisance. We would see the chief. Accordingly, after an interval, the chief came. Without preamble, we offered him a present of a collection of beads to let us come in and stay. The chief, for which I admired him at once, did not hesitate. He let us in. I shot a triumphant look at Lukut, who, however, neither by sign nor word indicated what he thought.

In a large hut placed at our disposal we deposited our things, and then without delay went in search of the source of the strangely melodious sound. We traced it to the main community house, and so we entered. Once inside its long, dim and lofty interior, the sound was not so dulcet. It was overpowering.

There was a long row of rice blocks, on which pairs of young girls were alternately pounding rice. The construction of the rice blocks is such that the rhythmic pounding makes a surprisingly musical click-clack. Hence its enchantment at a distance, and likewise, its overpowering quality close by.

The rice feast, or *tugal*, plays a very important part in Dyak life, as the success of rice crops means the success of life until the next harvest. From every door, as we walked about, we saw palm leaves hanging, while in the ground in front of almost every house were stuck little crude puppets, intended to drive away the evil spirits. Other houses had the front walls roughly decorated with *naga* (dragon) motifs, a custom obviously derived from the olden times of Chinese influence in the island.

During these festival times, while the girls spend days pounding up the harvested rice, the men consult the chiefs for advice on sowing. The chiefs in turn consult the omens, and finally hit on the day for sowing. The chief, as a result, plants a wild sour fruit in a certain spot, and the sun is carefully watched to see if it sets at a certain spot against the horizon. Then sowing begins. But should the cry of a bird, the *burung pemunak*, be heard just as the sowing is about to begin, it must be delayed for three days. Should one of the sowers see a milliped, or a certain kind of snake, one day of rest is entailed.

During the sowing, none of the men may bathe, but a rest period of seven days follows, and on the tenth day everyone may bathe again.

The days of rest are occupied by housework, the making of masks for the feast dances and other preparations. The most important of all rice feasts is that which takes place when the rice is harvested. It was such a feast that we arrived to see. The same occasion is used for name-giving for children, offerings to the spirits in the house of the chief, and also for the consumption of excessive quantities of palm wine, not to forget the festival of *blako ontong*, or wedding.

The festival of *blako ontong*, one of which took place during our five-day in Ma Mehak Tebui, is most interesting.

This celebration is a pointed request to the Radja Balawang Bulan, the all-highest of spirits, to bestow his benediction on the young couple. As soon as the sun had disappeared below the horizon the bride was fetched from her dwelling by an honour guard of seven girls, all, like herself, dressed in *saois*, short *sarongs*, leaving their young bodies bare from the waist up. . . . At the same time a squad of seven young men went to get the groom. They were dressed in full war togs, with berets of chicken skin on their heads, and in their hands were spears. From separate directions the bride and groom were brought into a large house, while the *balians* (medicine men) began to beat their drums and to chant a eulogy to the couple in nasal monotonous voices. The couple met in the centre of the room, where the girl presented her future husband with a *mandau* as a symbol that she expected him to be courageous and give her his protection. Then they sat down, side by side, on a rattan mat.

The group of seven *balians* against the wall began to sing a weird-sounding song, at which everyone present seized a short bamboo stick and began to beat insanely on the walls. This terrific uproar was intended to drive away any malevolent influences intent on the house and its occupants. This din lasted several minutes, after which the guests spread their offerings on the floor in the centre before the couple. These included seven full-grown chickens, seven packages of rice, seven pieces of sugar cane, and a multitude of other things, but seven of each in every case. Two fires were lit as soon as the couple had had time, according to custom, to cast appreciative eyes over their gifts, and the *balians* took up anew, but equally weirdly and monotonously, the song. Then all the guests rose, went outside, and formed a circle about a pole in the middle, to which was tethered a small buffalo. Their finger tips touching, they began a dance consisting only of a few steps forward and backward, at the same time emitting series of harsh and discordant yells. This dance is called the *Bigal*, and is found among nearly all Dyak tribes. The married couple were still there but their eyes now gleamed more intensely as the leaping firelight played on the distorted features of the yelling guests.

Then began the worst. The younger men pulled out their *mandaus* and subjected the snorting, terrified buffalo to cruel slashes and cuts, so that soon it staggered and fell, breathing heavily, blood gushing from its many wounds. The guests then darted in and smeared themselves with the blood. Although buffalo blood was used, human sacrifice would certainly have been more in keeping with the temper of the people. The *balians* consulted a rattan covered with rice, dough, and gold-dust and discovered by this means that the all-highest approved the match.

All this had taken hours. The fires were now subsiding. Men drunk with *toewak* or palm wine lay against the wall, sprawled in slumber. The couple were then led away to their new house, escorted by the seven girls and as many of the male guard as could stand up with certainty. The noise subsided. Groups went off to their own houses. The *balians* gathered up their drums and other paraphernalia and departed. At length all was quiet, except for a lot of snoring. The wedding had been a big success.

The Dyaks have practically no moral standard in the sense of restrictions on conduct based on moral grounds. Dyak youths and girls have the same privileges in every respect, and consequently the fullest liberty prevails. Absolutely no penalty obtains against sexual intercourse before marriage, and thus the young people of Borneo have every opportunity to indulge in their desires. This indulgence begins early, since the girls as a rule reach puberty at the age of twelve, the boys somewhat later. They are all tattooed as soon as possible, a procedure which means real suffering for the girls, since they are tattooed more extensively than the men.

Some of the tribes have the awful custom of piercing a ring of metal through the glans penis indicating real martyrdom. It is claimed by some scientists that this was insisted on by the wives who feared their husbands would practice pederasty. Perhaps these fears were justified, for despite— or more probably because of—the great sexual freedom, sexual abnormality exists in many forms. Masturbation is widely practised among women, the girls using a contrivance called the *balak*, a piece of waxed wood, similar to those employed in Bali.

Despite the fundamental belief, common to all Polynesians, that children are the purpose of life, the Dyaks believe that the sexual desire is one which should at all costs be satisfied as are hunger and thirst. Hence the lack of restraint, and hence also the custom in some regions of providing their native visitors of elevated rank with a girl for the night. In other tribes husbands care very little whether or not their wives give themselves to other men, reserving to themselves the right to demand children. Contraceptive methods are crude and far from dependable, and hence doubtless the growth of abnormal means of satisfaction, since the normal method so frequently brings children, entailing a long period of abstinence to the woman.

Again, and contradictorily, a girl who becomes a mother before she becomes a wife is disgraced. It then devolves upon her father to name the transgressor, who must then marry her. Should he deny his part, he has to undergo the ordeal of the spirit, which takes place in the open *kampong,* where the accused has to dip his forefinger in molten wax. Should the finger show damage of any kind, the owner thereof has no choice. He marries the girl forthwith. But should his finger show no evidence indicating his fatherhood, the girl has the right (an ironic touch!) to name up to three others who, she thinks, might be the father of her child!

After marriage, however, most Dyak tribes, with the notable exception of those referred to above, expect and demand complete virtue. Harsh penalties are imposed, which in some places leads to husband and wife conniving at the ruin of another man. The wife will beguile the visitor into submitting to her charms, and the husband, at the crucial moment, will step in and learn all—also profiting by the penalty imposed. I had not thought to find the badger game in the Borneo jungles!

W<small>E</small> stayed five days in this village, where we found our
first Christian Dyaks, products of the Laham mis-
sion. They were held in a sort of secret contempt by the
others, though many seemed waiting for the converted ones

to show visible signs of better destiny, at which, without doubt, everyone would have rushed to the mission to learn the secret.   Needless to emphasize, the missions have a much more difficult time in Borneo than anywhere else in my knowledge in Malaya, not only because of the low cultural state of the Dyak tribes, and the attendant animistic beliefs, but also because of the hardships consequent upon any extended journeys into the hinterlands.   Once the outposts of progress, as Conrad has called them, where the trading companies have their stations, have been left behind, travel is extremely arduous.

Many times the founding of missions has been attempted in the deeper interior, where the Dyak *kampongs* are many, but the type of individual suited to missionarying is not the type to endure the life in such places.   Heat and sickness have carried off many people, whose courage must be admired as much as their comparatively fruitless persistence.

The Catholic mission and school at Laham, in spite of these difficulties, has existed for many years now: almost as many as the Dutch have officially ruled Dutch Borneo and have had their military posts there.   But the results are not startlingly successful.

Throughout Borneo, whose people are in many subtle ways resentful of Western influence, I found little real impress of outer civilization.   Nowhere, certainly, is there such evidence of Dutch power in Borneo as there is in other islands.   The Dyaks, outside of the coastwise towns, pursue their own untouched existence, with the two major exceptions of better markets for their surplus jungle products and the gradual dying out of head-hunting.   Still the Dutch maintain government civil officers way into the interior.

As we proceeded up the river, fighting our way past more and more dangerous rapids, the *kampongs* became somewhat more frequent, the people more natural and less in touch with the outside world. Although they are not yet invariably friendly, they have at least gotten over any unreasonable fear of white men. But they have not the ready knowledge of the coast—nor the appreciation of commerce—of our friend the chieftainess far down the river. Our own men were splendid, in every way good to have with us.

Their eyes darted everywhere along the narrowing banks, seeking plants, wild fruit, anything with which to garnish the main dishes at meal times. The second day from Ma Mehak Tebui, Lukut spotted a wild boar at a point by the left bank. He barked out a command; the men slowed and directed the *praus* toward the animal. It had crossed to get at the wild berries hanging low over the opposite bank, its beady eyes had lit upon us, and it was now frantically trying to regain its way to the top of the steep bank. Twice it attempted to climb up, and I expected it to vanish crashing through the undergrowth, but twice it fell scrambling back.

The *praus* picked up speed, trembling like jumpers under the strain of being forced at top speed through the water. The men bent over and paddled as one man; wild boar cutlet is a delicacy in the Nipa. Several stood ready with spears in hand, their eyes following the erratic, terrified movements of the darkly coloured beast. Within a minute the first *prau* was almost on top of the boar. Lukut stood up, tense, and then with all his strength, and deadly aim, buried the head of the spear in the boar's back in a wonderful throw. The boar plunged, and emitted a gurgling squeal. It continued its course through the water, turning its bull neck frequently to snap its fierce tusks at the spear shaft. Blood spurted in dark crimson jets from the wound, and ran down the animal's glistening sides. Ordinarily boars are not the best swimming animals, and this one, exhausted and leaving a trail of its life on the rushing stream, soon fell back. The *praus* caught up with him, again Lukut plunged another spear into him.

The boys gave a yell of triumph. A second *prau* shot alongside, and eager hands hauled the huge dead boar, dripping
with blood and water, up over the gunwhale, to be nicely
carved up later when we bivouacked.

After considerable more paddling we came to Laham
where the Capucine mission and school was located.

As visitors or explorers do not often come to Borneo's
interior, the Catholic father would under no circumstances
permit us to leave until we had tasted some of the fruit of
his hospitality. So we stayed.

This, of course, was just as much to my own liking,
though my friends chafed at the delay. It gave me the opportunity to mingle more with the people, for by now, what
with my constant practice in the settlements we had stayed at,
and with the boys in the *praus*, I could make fairly decent
shift to speak the Mahakam dialect with some facility. Lukut seemed relieved at no longer having to stand about with
me and ask what he no doubt considered useless and idiotic
questions. I went about myself, and found everyone perfectly disposed to tell me all I wanted to know, though frequently it was difficult for me to get my meaning over.

Almost my first impression here was seeing the great
pride of Dyak fathers in their children; though they were
not so proud of their sons as of their daughters—as girls here
have commercial value, the father receives the bridal sum. I
came upon one father, an elderly fellow, walking steadily up
and down the gallery of his house, coddling a tiny baby in
his arms. Another father, talking to me one day, interrupted
himself to call my attention to four tall, strapping young fellows, all his sons. His gaze rested on them with paternal
self-satisfaction.

A word or two here about Dyak customs of name-giving
to children is appropriate. As with all other Dyak prece-
dures, this depends also on the signs of weather and omens.

Not only that, but it depends on the child. The Kajans, for example, tickle a baby's nose with a feather to see if it sneezes. If so, it is at once given a name. If not, the ceremony is postponed until such time as the child sneezes at the feather.

Some tribes in northern Borneo will not name a child until after its initial bath, while the tribes of the south and east leave the name to pure hazard. Seven unmarried male relatives are necessary for this process, which demands that each of these seven choose a short rattan stick and stick it upright in a large bowl of rice. Then the senior guest takes the bowl of rice in to the mother, who haphazardly chooses one of the sticks. The child is then given the name of that relative who planted the stick in the bowl. By the same token the same gentleman becomes foster-father to the baby.

Laham is quite a large settlement or *kotta*, even for the Mahakam Dyaks, and thus I had the chance to attend a session of the native court. Special days of the week are put aside for the sittings of this court, which consists of a judge and either three or seven older men of the settlement. Here let me point out again the esteem in which the mystical power of the number seven is held. It was used, the reader will recall, in the marriage offerings previously described. When the judge could, he always had seven men sitting with him, not to make decisions, but merely to advise on points calling for Solomon's wisdom. The sessions of the *kotta* are popular and are, really, as entertaining as a play. The Dyaks love legal cases and arguments, and are as pleased as punch over any opportunity to take themselves to court. They have lawyers, each of whom has in front of him a number of puppets. When one lawyer wins a point, the judge indicates this with a nod of his head, and the winning lawyer takes one of his opponent's puppets. Frequently the zeal of the attorneys leads them to seize puppets when they have not really won them, and free-for-alls result. But the session I attended, and most others, I was informed, are conducted peacefully.

In my wanderings about the village, one day, I inadvertently got into the village death house or morgue. Its dark interior at once made a dismal impression on me. Then I caught sight of a coffin, open, in the centre of the long room, between four centre-poles. With a start, as my eyes became accustomed to the dimness, I made out the figures of the widow, dressed in white according to the custom of Dyak mourning, and two children (other mourning customs make relatives wear bark till it drops off of old age).

The corpse was of a man of about fifty. He was dressed in full war regalia, of elaborate head-dress and special *abet,* or loin-cloth. Beside him, on the wide bier, lay his daily girdle and his arms—his feet on a big gong. There was a string of beads round each ankle and a white bead on each closed eyelid, the idea being that in this way he would be able to see his way to heaven. The creepy atmosphere of the death house affected me unpleasantly; I tiptoed out, without having disturbed the widow and children in their silent grief.

But it so happened that the next night was the funeral ceremony, following a big festival dinner. The ceremony consists chiefly of protracted wailing by everyone, led by the *balians,* who chanted interminably.

We did no wailing at all, and stayed only until the repetitive chanting got on our nerves. As we went down the street, I looked back. A huge fire was leaping and playing, throwing gaily dancing shadows on the walls of nearby houses. But the faces of those about the fire were not gay. They riveted their gazes on the burning wood, and their bodies swayed in slow rhythm to the eulogistic but dolorous singing of the *balians* on the other side of the fire. The deceased was well sped on his way to Apo Kesio.

It was here in Laham that we had one of the memorable

experiences of the trip. It began innocently enough with our receiving an invitation from a man whose acquaintance we had made while going about talking to the people, who had a large and populous family on the inland side of the town. We went over and soon we were sitting on the gallery of his house, eating delicious dishes.

The first was *tambilok,* he told me (I had to take his word for it), something fried and well spiced. This was followed by pieces of something else floating in a sour egg sauce, and then by slices of *kudjang*—a dish whose tastiness I have not yet forgotten. After the food, and when we had managed to digest it successfully, I asked him what the various dishes consisted of.

He explained the *kudjang* was an herb which grows wild all over the Dyak lowlands, and I saw that it largely replaces the potato. Then, before telling us what the other dishes had been, he led us outside to a huge tree. With his *mandau* he delivered a swift, slicing blow on the bark, displacing a whole section. We were just quick enough to see a mass of white worms, wriggling and tangled, before it dawned on us that the preliminary dish had been made of their bodies. In a daze we heard my friend's undisturbed voice continue to explain that the other dish—the one which I had commented favourably on—was made from a three-foot water snake, red with black stripes and as thick as a man's arm.

The first effect of this edifying information was not bad. We hastily smoked cigarettes. But when we got back to our hut, we could stand it no longer. We were, in a word, ill. And how! . . .

Rumours of a head-hunting party were, one day, confirmed; the next day refuted. But we stayed on, particularly as Lukut said he could not guarantee the behaviour of the boys until the rumour was definitely squashed. So we stayed on, and went on a fishing party.

The Dyaks regard fishing not so much as a sport, nor as the world's best excuse for laziness, but as a serious business. The night before they spent gathering *tubah*, the root of a rhizophore shrub growing in the marshes by the river. This was placed in the *praus* to be used the next day, mixed with water and beaten up. Then the remains of branches and stems were removed, and the whitish fluid left in the boats. In the morning we went up-river a small distance, coming almost immediately to a small tributary. A net was strung from shore to shore, weighting its bottom side with stones so that, when complete, the barrier left absolutely no loophole for even a minnow to escape.

Then the *praus* divided in two squads, and each began working up and down the patch of water, throwing the *tubah* water over in handfuls. Then we sat for half an hour while the Dyaks got ready with harpoons, nets and spears and many other weapons. The poison distributed itself quickly and soon the fish began coming up to the surface, some leaping clear of the water as if to escape death by that means.

The little fish were the first ones to come up, and there was little excitement. But soon they began to get bigger. Harpoons were used freely. One *prau*, filled with *balians*, encouraged the rest with chants and concerted yells. Large slippery bodies were dragged gleefully over the gunwales; little fish were netted by the hundreds. This went on for at least two hours, the quantity of fish seeming not to end. At the end of this time, the head-man commanded the fleet back to the village, where the entire catch was divided equally among every household. I found that they try to avoid catching more fish than they need, for other than slicing up the meat and baking it, they have no means of preserving it. The poison of the *tubah* does not harm the meat for eating purposes, but accelerates its decomposition.

Most of the species were more or less familiar to me,

with the exception of one they called the *ikan sumpit* (*ikan*: fish; *sumpit*: blowpipe). It is not unusual in shape or colour, but its peculiarity lies in the fact that when it rises to the surface it ejects a swift jet of water at insects, flies and mosquitoes, killing them for food. It exercises this faculty with speed and accuracy, reminding one of the Javanese chameleon, which has a preternaturally long tongue to flick out at its tiny prey.

The blowpipe I have referred to frequently; it is a type of weapon found among primitive peoples in almost every tropical part of the world. I say tropical because the success of a blowpipe lies not in the force with which the little darts are ejected on their missions of death, but in their bearing poisoned tips. It is well known, of course, that poisons are more easily found in natural and luxuriant growths, which in turn, are more plentiful in hot regions than in temperate or cold ones.

I tried to find out how and whence they acquired the poison for their daggers and darts, and learned they used vegetable poisons of the Siren and Ipoh. The Siren grows on mountains and hilltops, and is like an oak, with a diameter of at least six feet. The Ipoh however is a creeper, its stem not exceeding one inch in diameter.

Both yield a fluid, which oozes from the tree or creeper through an incision and is collected in bamboo cylinders, assuming a yellowish hue after coming in contact with air, resembling somewhat the mysterious Upas tree.

The fluid after being boiled with a few other growths is the one in which the darts and dagger points are dipped. The *sumpitans* consist of bamboo tubes about a yard long, with cork mouthpieces. The darts are inserted in the charging end and the mouth is applied to the cork. Healthy lungs then send the dart on its deadly mission with a faint pop. I have seen those tiny arrows sail many hundred feet.

THE fifth day of our stay in Laham a *prau* full of up-river Dyaks, Kenjas, arrived and pooh-poohed the rumour of the head-hunting party. It appeared that nothing was known of it, except that a group of Dyaks from still another tribe had been out hunting wild buffalo or deer. How the rumour started we never learned, but in this way Lukut was satisfied to proceed.

We paddled on up the river. Its jungle-like shores never changed in aspect, and I thought that no man would care to do this alone. The river became still narrower, with rocky jumbled bottom and more numerous cataracts and rapids. Native settlements were more frequent up here; coal deposits could be seen in the broken country, likewise indicating the presence of oil in large quantities. Suddenly and inexplicably the river widened out. The actual main stream did not become wider, but instead of high narrow banks, the water extended into the forest, whole long stretches of trees standing in water like people frozen stiff in the act of wading. The colour of the water became a strangely transparent brownish yellow, and we could see the tree roots beneath the surface.

The next day we passed a *kampong* where, indicated by the banana peels hung at the entrance gate, contagious disease had broken out. Lukut refused to let us stop. We kept right on, and later in the day were caught in our first rain storm. The grey water turned the day into dusk. It seemed not to consist of drops, but to be one solid mass of water coming down without an interval. It was impossible for us to stop anywhere along this stretch of the river, since the forest edges made the finding of any solid land out of the question in this downpour. We paddled along, getting soaked to the skin, and several of the boys dropped their paddles to bale out the water that was filling the *prau* bottoms. It was incredibly dismal. I could see nothing, hear nothing, outside of the hissing fall of the million tons of water, except the monosyllabic exclamations or commands of the paddlers. Lukut took us close to the right bank, and then, without saying a word, kept peering toward the shore. This he continued for about an hour, rarely shifting his stance, the water pouring off his brown statue-like body as if he were standing under a shower-bath. At last he barked an order, we shot toward the invisible (to me, at any rate) bank, and came upon a short stretch of solid land that seemed to spring at us out of the endless grey surroundings. We leaped from the *prau*, the boys took out all the supplies and equipment, and behind Lukut we ran up the bank. Amazing man, he must already have known of what he found: a ramshackle tottering structure, evidently the beginning of a *kampong* now deserted.

We crowded inside, it was large enough, but I expected that our combined weight would send us all crashing through the floor to the ground beneath. There we stayed, soaked and cramped, the rest of that day and all that night. The roof leaked, the whole structure creaked if there was any violent movement. We were miserable, and everybody cursed in his own language. The happiest—or rather, the least miserable—were the paddlers, who removed their loin-cloths, dried them on a smoky fire we took the risk of building, and then were soon dry. We, in our western clothes, had a worse time of it.

But in the morning the sun shone again, blindingly, intensely—as usual. I had thought I should never, after the way it had made me pour out perspiration, be glad to see it again. But I was. The jungle all about dripped from its wetting. As the sun crept higher and blazed more fiercely, the vast reaches of unbroken jungle steamed. But we were dry, and everybody was more cheerful.

The settlements we came to here were far from pleasant places to stop; they were poor and the people were largely hungry. In almost every one of the few we stopped in now, at once upon disembarking we were besieged by beggars, the women far out-numbering the men among them. Their feeble voices cried out for alms, for food.

We asked the chief of one such place why they did not move down-river, where sowing land was more fertile, where the rains and *bandjirs* (floods) were not so unhealthful and damaging. He replied, with sullen frankness, that his tribe feared the Malays and the attitude of the stronger down-river Dyaks. Lukut further informed us that up-river was likewise impossible for these Dyaks, for there, at the head-waters of the Mahakam, and beyond, where the country was better, there were a great number of very strong and belli-cose tribes, who likewise would not have new peoples moving in on them.

We hurried on, and then had our first major accident: one of the *praus* got smashed to a pulp in the rapids. A black jagged rock ripped the bottom completely away. We at once thought it would be necessary to divide its human cargo and freight between the other two, but not so Lukut. We stopped at the first convenient place, and the boys set to work calmly. Twenty of them set off into the jungle, shouting gladly, laughing with joy at this surcease from the gruelling paddle-work. In a moment we heard their axe-blows resounding through the forest, ending with a triumphant crash as the jungle giant measured its length on the ground. More axe-blows as they sheared away the branches, and soon they came dragging the tremendous log to the shore.

The whole lot of them then set to work, with axes, knives and other implements. Soon they had the inside hollowed out and smoothed, the rough edges taken off, and a sharp graceful prow cut. They coated her with a paint made from herbs they gathered on the spot, and thus had her ready for launching. A shout of joy greeted the new vessel as it floated beside the bank. Lukut stepped carefully in it, tested it care-fully for balance and weight, explaining that if it tipped to the left, that would have been a bad omen. But it tipped slightly to the right and therefore all was well.

It was that same day, I distinctly remember, that I saw my first nose ape (*nasalis larvatus*). We were passing an open stretch, when Lukut pointed it out. I looked and saw the man-size animal with its ludicrous countenance. It has a flat face, exactly the opposite of the orang utang, one of the other ape species of Borneo, but from this flat red-yellow face there juts out a long thin nose which droops slightly at the tip. Its eyes are round and bright like brown metal buttons, and its body is slim and grey. The male of the species only is graced by this astonishing proboscis; the female's face is merely flat with a slight nose effect. These nose apes travel in groups of twos or fours, and move majestically or lazily along through the tops of the highest trees, coming down but infrequently. (When captured they turn melancholic and cannot get used to captivity.)

There are a vast number of monkey species in Borneo, including the loris, which sleeps all day and prowls all night, and is so lazy it often lets itself be killed before it will make a move to escape. There is also the flying ghost monkey, a tiny greyish-white monkey which flits through trees with incredible lightness and speed, and which it is almost impossible to catch sight of. And among Borneo's *most charming* little animals is the Saāt, which also sleeps by day and prowls by night, and which attacks its prey snorting and grunting like a pig. It has litters of three or four young, and gives out a penetrating odour that infests a wide range of territory. This ejectable fluid is secreted in two glands beneath the tail, and is given out when the beast is angered, precisely like the skunk. Which odour is worse is hard to say.

WE had now been up-river eleven weeks. My friends had to return, and much to my own keen regret I could not go on alone. Beyond us stretched the vast and almost impenetrable reaches of interior Borneo where the average tourist does not come, and of which not too much knowledge exists.

This is all to say nothing of the incalculable riches of the country. I just referred to the presence of the coal and oil up the river, most of it not even touched by the feelers of Dutch pioneering. So great are the stores of wealth along the coast, that there has not been time enough to push up into the country and establish commercial and industrial centres there. The chief difficulty is, of course, the navigation of the Mahakam in craft large enough to make the whole thing pay. The lower tribes have become wealthy, as I have pointed out, by trading in all sorts of products with the people in Samarinda and Bandjermassin. But the people of the remote interior have as yet no inkling of what can be done through exploitation of the products of this curious country.

And not only is it wealthy in natural resources—it is also a mine of ethnological information. There have been but a small number of books written about Borneo, and only a few of those tell anything other than about the tribes which have so far been touched by white men repeatedly. Among these few are the excellent works of Molengraaff, Nieuwenhuis, Elshout, or Hose and McDougall, the latter two for British portions of Borneo.

In comparison to the existing knowledge about Java, for instance, a large portion of Borneo is untouched. In the foregoing pages I have written the record of a trip up the Mahakam (although I am not the first one who visited these parts), with as many of my observations included as space permitted. In my descriptions of the Dyak tribes I have preferred to be general rather than confine myself to one particular tribe. But obviously there is more to say. My notebooks still bulge with material—material, I am proud to say, much of which is as yet unrecorded. But there is not room for it all in a book which attempts a picture of Mother Insulinde's five greatest jewels.

I can conceive, and concede, that the foregoing picture of arduous, hot, and dangerous travel in Borneo may not appeal to everyone who reads this. Nor do accounts, on the other hand, of Polar expeditions, succeed in thrilling others. But here is an important point: in Borneo exists one of the greatest patches of the earth's surface that is still for a great part unexplored. Some of its central territory is today largely a matter of guesswork. It is even a little too soon for the aeroplane to come in, for a man lost there is a man never found. But I expect that within ten years the plane, by reducing to a few hours a journey which it took us hot days to travel, will help solve the great mystery of Borneo's unknown regions where the Dutch have not yet penetrated.

Our journey down was of course much easier than the way up. But we stopped at night only long enough to eat and sleep. My friends were in an infernal hurry, and since I could not go alone, I couldn't complain. We visited again in this fashion several of the *kampongs* we had already been in. Our welcome was invariably cordial, and I found this a country I could grow to like. It is infernally hot, it is pestiferous, it is dangerous—how dangerous we can't say—but its vastness makes an undeniable impression. And besides, the people, at least most of those I met, are disposed to be friendly. Perhaps if we hadn't kept our revolvers so well hidden we might not have been so well received.

We reached Samarinda in less than half the time it had taken us to go up the river, and in the moment of my first view of the town from the water, the first inkling came to me of my future plan: to return to Borneo for a real expedition up-river. Head-hunters and all, I would see what these people were like, or if there was still more to learn than many before me have so intelligently recorded.

On the same jetty from which we had started out we parted from our boys and Lukut. We distributed gifts among them and won exclamatory good-byes. Lukut was more dignified. He said that he would be glad to repeat this voyage. It was a thing that gladdened his heart, he said, to go as we had gone. We should find him, he added, always ready.

I can see him now, his brown creased face staring thoughtfully at me as he speaks; his words courteous but short, his gestures sparing. I often wondered what kept him in Samarinda, for I knew he came from up-river. It could not be economic pressure; who knows what escapade he concealed behind his present?

We left him standing by the edge of the river he lived on, the sun beating down on his stalwart, uncovered figure, his black eyes watching us vanish into the limbo of civilization, as big a mystery to him as his life is to us.

II
JAVA

VERY soon after May 30, 1619, Jan Pieters Zoon Coen
wrote an exuberant letter to the East India Company
in Amsterdam, the most significant part of which was: "The
foundation of the so-long-desired rendezvous has now been

laid. A great part of the most fertile soil and the sea rich in fish of India is now yours." [1]

The home of this optimistic and astute man still stands in Amsterdam, the chief city of Holland. Curiously enough, I was born in the house in which my relatives still live, not a stone's throw from that of Jan Pieters Zoon Coen. He wrote the letter from which the first sentence of this part is a quotation, describing the taking by the Dutch of Jacatra, which is now known on the maps of all nations as Batavia, the capital of Dutch East India. The name "Batavia" was bestowed upon the strategically located settlement at a later date.

But this was not the first contact of Java or the archipelago with Europe. In 1511 a troop of Portuguese, then the leading navigators and adventurers of the world, landed on the Malacca Peninsula. Eleven years later, 1522, another Portuguese band landed at the mouth of the Tji Liwung, the river on which the modern city of Batavia is situated. The leader of the band sagaciously obtained a trading concession from the nearby ruler of Pakuwang Padjadjaran. The settlement there was called, in Javanese, Sunda Calapa, and in 1527, it fell into the hands of the Bantammers, the inhabitants of western Java. These apparently having little regard for local tradition and preference, called the community Djajakerta. This it remained until the Dutch came there roughly one hundred years after the advent of the Portuguese. The Dutch had even less respect for local custom and pronounced "Djajakerta" as Jacatra.

The first visit of the Dutch to Java was not, naturally, that of Coen, but took place on June 23, 1596. After a voyage which began on April 2, 1595, Cornelius de Houtman, as

---

[1] In old Dutch: Het fondament van het soo lange gewenste rendezvous is nu geleyt.   Een goet deel van het vruchtbaerste landschaap en de visrycxste zee van Indien is nu uwe.

agent or supercargo, a courageous voyager, came there with a fantastically small squadron, consisting of the four-hundred-ton *Mauritius*, Jan Molecate, master, the four-hundred-ton *Hollandia*, Jan Dingmans, master, the two-hundred-ton *Amsterdam*, Schiltinger, master, and the fifty-ton *Duifken* (*Little Dove*)! This imposing array of armed ships anchored in the harbour of Djajakerta, which the unaccustomed Dutch tongues called Jacatra, and for five days de Houtman and his zealous followers terrorized the natives. Examples were made of leading native figures; the Inquisition was emulated in most worthy fashion, though without the stamp of religious fervour. De Houtman and his men were animated simply by a desire to impress upon the nearest Javanese the necessity of being hospitable. They succeeded, bloodily. And then returned to Holland with cargoes of extraordinary loot: batiks, metal work, precious stones—and with word of the fabulous wealth of treasures to be found on this island garden. Just what the Portuguese were doing while de Houtman was engaged on his five days of terrorization is not made clear in history. They probably remained discreetly behind the walls of their trading post at the mouth of the river.

When at last the Dutch had stopped at Java, they worked fast, but it is curious that for nearly a hundred years Dutch war and merchant vessels sailed on past the full six-hundred-and-sixty miles of Java to the Malacca Peninsula and the Moluccas, the Spice Islands. Why they did this is an insoluble mystery.

But before the factory was built in 1612, the year 1602 had been highly significant in East Indo-Dutch affairs. In that year all Dutch trading companies in Amsterdam which traded in the Far East banded together to prevent unfair competition. This organization, later to play the part of almost absolute ruler in the Insulinde archipelago, was named the V.O.C., *De Vereenigde Oost-Indische Compagnie,* the United East India Company. It received a patent, or charter, from the government for twenty-one years, and it was capitalized, with almost unlimited powers, at six million, six hundred thousand guilders, a sizable sum even for these days of elastic credit.

Jan Huygens van Linschoten, who had spent many years in the Portuguese service, pointed out in his *Jan Huygens' Book* the importance of a small part of Java's north coast—Sunda Calapa or Djajakerta, lying at the mouth of the Tji Liwung.

The first settlement of the Dutch was at Bantam in 1603, and the V.O.C. obtained the right to build a stone fort. Great rivalry between the British and the Dutch ensued; Pangeran Aria Rana di Manggala, the Sultan, capitalized on it. The Dutch looked about for another fort location, and hit upon Jacatra.

So, in 1610, there resulted a contract between the President of the *loge* at Bantam and Widjaja Krama, Regent of Jacatra, giving the Dutch permission to build a *loge* fifty fathoms square at the mouth of the Tji Liwung. In 1612 a stone house arose at the mouth of the river, followed later by a second, Mauritius, under Governor-General Pieter Both.

It was through the V.O.C. that Jan Pieters Zoon Coen later became Governor General of East India, after having worked himself up in the employ of the company from a clerkship, and assisted at the definite capture of Jacatra in 1619. For the next two hundred years the Dutch company, backed by its own practically unlimited resources and influence, and the home government fought the native rulers of Java, finally conquering it from end to end. In 1811, through a series of international conflicts centring in Europe, Java fell into the hands of the English.

Sir Stamford Raffles became Governor General of the

former Dutch East India, and performed wonders for it. He spent five years in command there, during which time he built up settlements, extended the influence of European ways, and began the excavation of the Barabudur, the great Hindu monument in Java. He was also the author of a book on Java, which to this day stands as one of the most complete and authoritative works on the island and its people.

But on August 19, 1816, a new treaty was negotiated between England and Holland and Dutch East India was restored to Holland. This was followed by a treaty in 1824, Sumatra, with the exception of the Sultanate Atchin that remained independent, being ceded to the Dutch. This latter, after a treaty in 1871 and wars until 1904, was also completely ceded to the Dutch.

As soon as the news reached Batavia, the Dutch colours went up over Java, some parts of Borneo (while other parts are unsubdued and some even unexplored), parts of the coast of Sumatra (also largely unmapped), Bali (finally subdued in 1906), Lombok, the Moluccas, Celebes, et cetera.

The Dutch East Indies present a situation today comparable to that of the colonies of Spain when that country was the mistress of dominions and territories liberally spread over two continents. In natural wealth and potentialities, the colonies of Spain in North America, South and Central America and the West Indies far exceeded the mother country. So with Dutch East India. Java itself, is larger by far than Holland. But Java is not all of the Dutch East Indies by any means. The archipelago consists of Borneo and Sumatra to the west and north of Java, while there are groups of little islands off Java, not to mention a tiny unimportant dot in the ocean north of Java with the diverting name of Boompjes. To the east of this, more than a hundred miles, is a large group of small islands. Close by Java on the east are Madura, Bali, Lombok, Flores, Sumba, Sumbawa, Aru Islands, some of which were, at a prehistoric time, connected above water with Java. Further east and somewhat to the north are Celebes, the Moluccas and Halmahera.

Properly speaking, Java, the centre and focus of Dutch East Indian matters, lies off the main current of eastern ocean traffic. But it is on the main route between Asia and Australia, situated as it is near the vast Strait of Malacca, with the romantic-sounding Java Sea to the north, and the Indian ocean, of dread portent, on the south. Despite this, it is only during the last ten years that Java has received really serious attention from travellers in search of strange and fascinating places. Java is such a place. Today many steamship companies distribute attractive folders depicting the joys of sojourning, however briefly, in Java. In a way I rejoice, because this means that many riches of culture and hitherto hidden knowledge will be brought to light and limitless commercial expansion made possible. But in another way, it is saddening, for I have come to know—and to love—this part of the world, and it is only natural that I should resent the advent of a Western civilization that will blight, instead of maintain; that will standardize, instead of differentiate. Countless books will be written about Dutch East India, in whole or in part, during the coming years. But there are comparatively few today. Of magazine articles there have been many. This book, therefore, may be called a "travel book" but my own idea of it is something a little more. It attempts not only to describe many typical and characteristic things, but also to get at the reasons behind them. It is not enough, I think, to say that I saw the dancing girls of the Sultan at Djocjakarta do a ceremonial dance of such and such a description. I believe that one is entitled to know why they do it just that way.

But first to locate Java a little more accurately. Geologically, it owes its appearance above the water level to a fold in the earth crust known as the "Sunda fold." The peak of the fold forms a central northern alluvial plain, where, as a result, rice and sugar grow almost without encouragement. Statistically, for the benefit of those who read the Almanac in their spare moments, Java is six hundred and sixty miles long, maximum breadth one hundred and thirty miles, and supports a population of some fifty-one millions, of which figure only some two hundred and fifty thousand are whites. This results in a population of seven hundred and seventeen to the square mile, which is considerable.

In consequence of the past and present activity of its one hundred and nine volcanoes, of which thirteen, no less, are still igneously active, Java has a soil of the greatest natural fertility. It is packed with luxuriant vegetation of bright solid colours upon which shines a sun of sometimes immoderate heat. East Java is hilly; high volcanic plains fill the west; limestone mountains abound in the south; and the aforesaid alluvial plain takes up the narrow nothern strip. The fiercest of the volcanoes, which I shall describe later, is the Merapi; the highest, achieving well over ten thousand feet, is the Smeru, and the most remarkable, for reasons to be elaborated later, is the holy mountain, Bromo.

Apart from the sheer forceful attractiveness of its natural garden-like beauty, Java hides among its hills and volcanoes the ruins of a once-powerful civilization. On the Dieng plateau rear the mighty ruins of the Barabudur, one of the largest and most beautifully imposing of Hindu monuments known to man. In every recess of Javanese life and thought lurk vestiges of questions to intrigue the visitor and to prod his mind with surmises about the titanic religious upheavals that tore the East into rival camps centuries ago; with astonished guesses as to the extent of gospels spread with the sword in wars and conquests that dwarf our Western ideas; and last of all, with amazed conclusions as to the worth and validity of a civilization which is and has been practically untouched by European invasion and has gotten on quite well indeed.

Old Jacatra, now for many years Batavia, is the *medulla oblongata* of Dutch East India. No longer is it a Javanese city, but a modern Dutch one. But the Dutchman is a different man away from home. His blue eyes twinkle more readily in the heat; his natural energy replenishes itself admirably on frequent draughts of Pahit or Dutch gin in the afternoon siesta; his active personality accommodates itself with amazing facility to the easier modes of life in a city which trembles on the brim of a centuries-old tradition and legend—and volcanoes.

THERE is little of old Batavia, once called Jacatra. The chief relics are the Stadhuis (City Hall) built in 1707, the Portuguese Buitenkirk (outer church) on the Jacatra road built in 1695, and the Amsterdam tower. Beside the old town gate lies a brass cannon of antique construction, half-buried in the mud. A legend has sprung up about this cannon: that when it is united to its mate at Surabaja the end of Dutch rule will come.

Properly, the modern Batavia is divided into two separate cities. Batavia is the business section, with Kotta, the lower town, a combination of past and present; Weltevreden is the residential section, while newer suburban additions have been made in recent years in new Menteng, Meester-Cornelus and Gondangdia. In former times division between Batavia and Weltevreden was made by a sort of canal of stagnant water, called the Molenvliet, which caused abundant cholera and fevers. The canal is still there, and is still used for washing clothes. Today the population exceeds three hundred thousand natives, forty thousand Chinese and thirty thousand whites.

Weltevreden is magnificently built, presenting to the eye a blending of soft light tones contrasting with the vividness of the vegetation. Gardens, hedgerows, clusters of trees, abound, making the wider streets a pleasure to walk in. Every home is well-nigh hidden from its fellows by luxuriously planted and cared-for gardens. The temperature fluctuates in the year from 66 to 97 degrees Farenheit, and refuge from the higher temperatures may be found in the race club, founded by Sir Stamford Raffles in 1812, a French Club, a German Club, the Royal Batavia Society, and in the excellent swimming offered near Tandjong Priok.

One of the visitors to Batavia during my time there was the late Vicente Blasco Ibañez, the Spanish novelist, on a world tour. We discussed Mata Hari, the glittering, tragic figure whose trial and execution as a German spy in 1917 by the French involved high officials on both sides of the fence. She had been born in Holland, but had married an English officer with whom she went to Java. On her return she had parted from her husband and become a dancer. Her public and private behaviour has not yet ceased to scandalize the world, though she has now been dead for more than twelve years. Ibañez, in writing *Mare Nostrum*, had been accused of basing his story on the life of the pseudo-Javanese dancer. This had excited his interest in her, though it is perfectly true that he never knew anything about her until after he had completed his novel.

Thus, when he found himself in Java, he asked me many questions. We all knew something of her, since her name had been a by-word in Europe for years prior to her death. He voiced the belief that she had been born in Java, and that was largely taken as the truth until later research of her career published in an American magazine proved this not to have been true.[1]

Coming back for a moment to historical background, there is the head of Pieter Elberfeld which today grins down upon passing people from a point in lower Batavia. An inscription in old Dutch states: "As a reminder of the executed traitor, Pieter Elberfeld, none shall be permitted to build on this spot in wood or in stone or to plant there from this day forth forevermore."

Pieter Elberfeld was a Jacatra half-caste who was inspired by a fierce hatred of the Dutch—a manifestation of the inferiority complex instinct in the Eurasian of today. In 1722 he conspired with certain native princes to massacre the whites, overthrow the current native ruler and place one of the conspirators on the throne. In return for this Elberfeld was to become High Priest of Java.

Unfortunately Elberfeld had a niece who had fallen in love with a young Dutch soldier. She got wind of the plan and told her lover. The authorities immediately imprisoned

---

[1] W. Adolphe Roberts, "Mata Hari—The Fabulous Dancer," *The Dance Magazine*, July-October, 1929.

Elberfeld, mutilated and decapitated him and set his head on a spearhead. The spear was set on top of a wall, whence it still stares down at the descendants of its own time.

A more benevolent government exists today: the whole of the Dutch East Indies archipelago is under a system of direct government, focussing on the Dutch crown as executive power and on the States General of Holland as legislative body. But in many localities, native rule is left intact, thus affording an efficient form of independence. The highest executive of the archipelago is the Governor General, who receives a salary of fifty-five thousand dollars a year and resides in a palace at Weltevreden five times as large as the White House in Washington. He also spends a great deal of time at Buitenzorg.

He is assisted by the Council of India, consisting of five members, and the Secretary, a vital post of executive powers, the holder of which is stationed at Buitenzorg. Under this central power the Dutch East Indies are divided into Residencies ruled by white Residents assisted by Assistant Residents and Contrôleurs, white, and a hierarchy of native officials led by the Regent.

The origin of the Javanese race is not easy to trace, though I have tried in my research work to do so at first hand. A solution has been attempted by devoting attentive study to present day Javans, but this is ridiculous. Sir Stamford Raffles, in his otherwise commendable work on Java, declared that the stock of the Javan is Tatar, but it is clear that he referred to the Javans of his day, who are practically the same as today. Vestiges of an ancient stone civilization have been found: hatchets, spears, et cetera, in the Preanger district, south of Batavia. A great find, a fossil man (*pithecanthropus erectus*, five feet, six inches high with brain content greater than that of any anthropoid ape) took the study back to the Pleistocene period, and gave rise to the opinion that a considerably more primitive race of man had originally had the run of the Dutch East Indies. There may be something in this since the first Hindu invaders of Java referred, in their local demonology, to Raksha and to this day the inhabitants of certain mountain districts live in fear of Raksha, demons of particularly unholy aspect, to believe their descriptions. Later discoveries in Manchuria may prove older than this *pithecanthropus erectus.*

One must conclude, on the face of all obtainable evidence, that the modern Javan is descended from the same stock as the people of Borneo, Sumatra and the other nearby islands. This stock is—according to Raffles, Wallace, Horsfield, Crawford and Junghuhn—probably Tatar, though hardly wholly so. Other elements, such as Hindu, Chinese and Arab have been mixed in, resulting in an Indonesian race with a strong Tatar, or even Mongolian strain.

Going on to why the island is called Java, and not something else, presents a curious problem. The word might, it develops, have come from any one of many languages and roots. For example, a history relates that the Hindus gave the name *Yawa, Dwipa* or *Dvipa* (Land of Barley) to both Java and Sumatra. The ancient Sanskrit word for barley is *Yava,* but unfortunately for the legend, barley did not exist then either in Java or Sumatra. Alas for an easy answer to the problem!

At another time the name Javana, or Yavana, was given to Borneo, Sumatra and Indo-China, while Claudius Ptolemaeus (151 A.D.) had occasion to refer to an island called *Iabadion* which corresponds to the Sanskrit *Yava Dwipa.*

The matter is thrown into further confusion by ancient legends of the island which limit the name Java to the central and eastern provinces, while the name *Tanah Sunda* (Sunda country) is given to the West.

The Bible contains frequent references to Javans, Javan,

sons of Japheth, Isles of the Gentiles. So no final answer has been found. I shall have to quote from a certain German textbook I once had in school. In the preface the authors discussed their inability to discover any hard and fast rules concerning a certain set of conjunctions. They said: "We must, after all, welter in the prevailing chaos." I have joined them.

Neither has it been learned when the first Hindus, of those who had such a profound influence on Java, first came there. I have read certain old records at Surakerta which place the arrival of the first Hindus at 1000 B.C. and the end of Hindu power at 1570 A.D. More about the Hindus later.

The Java people physically resemble all other races between Siam and Manchuria. That is, they are short and robust, but sometimes and contradictorily running to extraordinary thinness; their faces are lozenge-shaped, with sharp foreheads and chins, broad cheeks, slightly narrow eyes, and small noses, though not flattened like those of Negroid races. Their hair is thick, wiry and a shiny black, while their skin is a beautiful bronze tone, slightly more yellowish than copper. They are good-natured people endowed with great innate charm and profound courtesy. This sometimes becomes timidity before strangers, but emphasizes their excellent birth and stock. They do not, as a rule, speak impulsively, but ponder carefully over their answers and observations. The natural courtesy and refinement come to their highest pitch in and around Djocja and Solo, where the two Sultans rule. My boy was a high Javanese of aristocratic Hindu blood, and was the concentration of cultured refinement at ease with itself.

Etiquette is a powerful factor in Javanese life; much more so than among any Western people. The proper conduct for every conceivable situation of a man's life is prescribed by the *adat*, the unwritten laws of behaviour. The words, the gestures and the attitude are set by tradition, and adherence to *adat* is strict.

The people speak the Javanese, Sundanese and Madurese tongues and also Malay. The Javanese language itself is extremely pleasant to the ear, abounding in soft nasal tones and vowel sounds. It is divided into dialects. First old Javanese, or Kawi, language of the poets. Then of the new Javanese the Ngoko is for superiors to subordinates; the Kromo for subordinates to superiors, and a third idiom exists for intercourse between equals. It is highly essential for a foreigner wishing to win the esteem of the natives to have command of the Ngoko, for the use of the Kromo would only lower him in the estimation of everyone.

As a result of these complicated matters, difficulty arose when the Bible was being translated into Javanese. Should Christ address Pilate in Ngoko, Kromo or the third dialect? Thousands of precedents were studied before a decision was reached.

The alphabet of Java derives from the Devanag'ari, which was used by the Hindu scholars in Sanskrit books. The beginning of the Javanese era dates from the visit of Aji Saka, prime minister of a great Maharajah. The visit was made to ascertain the sources of the wealth of the Phoenecians, and happened in 75 A.D. From this may well have resulted the subsequent Hindu colonial expeditions.

The predominant religion is Mahometan, with an admixture of a certain superstitious air left over from ancient idolatry. Mosques are plentiful on the island, the most beautiful one being the Astani, or palace, of the Susuhunan Gunung Djati (Monarch of the mountain teak trees), which is in Cheribon on the coast. I shall speak of it later.

In general, it is safe to say that the people, by and large, are very happy and contented. They appreciate the educational plans being carried out by the Dutch Colonial Government, as well as the many commercial and industrial plans by which the Javanese population will soon have an ever-greater share in the growing prosperity of the island. But they live well in their clean huts of plaited bamboo, thatch- or grass-roofed, or covered with *sirap* leaves. They dress in garments of brilliant batik—red, orange, yellow, blue, indigo, violet, purple, green—comprising the *slendang,* a garment, a sort of shawl which is frequently covered with allegorical designs, and worn either draped over the shoulders or bound about the waist. It is from five to seven feet long and a yard wide, while the *sarong* is the lower garment.

The lowest class of men wear short rough trousers and a *sarong.* Practically every Javan wears a jacket, called *kilambi,* and a handkerchief, of Tatar or Malay design, on the head, turban-effect. The ever-present kris is worn slantwise in the back of the waist-band, half above and half below. Women wear the *sarong* with a light body cloth, called *kemban,* worn above the breast.

A legend tells why the Javanese wear *sarongs* and *kabaja* like women and why the people of Minangkabau in Sumatra do not:

The people of Java and the Minangkabaus of Sumatra were tired of constant fighting and agreed to choose a champion to fight to a finish in their stead. Sons of Java selected a tiger while the Minangkabaus chose a buffalo. They agreed that the defeated nation should go dressed as women. The buffalo won, and that explains why the Javan wears a *sarong* and the hill people of Sumatra wear trousers and walk about with an air of victory.

Fʀᴏᴍ Batavia and Weltevreden, the way lies into the Residency of Bantam, coming first to the city of Tangerang, very near the northern coast. This community is the centre of the Javanese bamboo and Pandana hat industry

85

—of which United States buyers buy some eight million each year. This western section of the island was once the centre and headquarters of a powerful Hindu empire. In the north, near Banten, where once was the palace of the Sultan, stands Fort Speelwyck, built by the Dutch conquerors in 1684. It was near here, as a matter of fact, that de Houtman, the intrepid voyager, stopped for a while ahead of his more decisive visit to the mouth of the Tji Liwung. In the earlier years of that same century the courts of the Hindu empire had flourished, but the decadence of the Hindus in that section set in soon after.

Bearing back on the Daendels post road toward Buitenzorg, the residence of the Governor General of Dutch East India, one comes to Kampong Batu Tulis, once known as Pakuan, when it was the chief city of Padjadaran, the last Hindu empire in the Sunda country. In 1527 it was overrun and conquered by the onrushing force of Islam and the Mahometans, and little remains but many old Hindu graves.

The Sunda country hereabouts abounds in rubber, coffee and tea plantations, interspersed with rice *sawahs* (there are two thousand plantations of all kinds on the island!), which impressed me, as they do everyone, with the natural riches of the island. Withal, it retains its tropical, unfettered, natural aspect, and the forests, fields, valleys, abound in weird fruit and flowers, while myriad animals scurry or tread softly among the thick tree boles. Inhuman, and again sometimes weirdly haunting, cries float out from the topmost branches of the trees. A flash of red wing reminds one that the forest is thickly populated with fantastic birds.

It was in the village of Leuwiliang, not far west of Buitenzorg, that I first saw some of the dancing in which, according to Eastern ideas, the Javanese are nearly supreme. In Surakerta I later saw the dancing of the *serimpi,* or court

dancing girls of the Sultan, but this dancing of the common
people is almost as interesting, and certainly as typical.

A native official I met in Leuwiliang invited me to go
with him to the dancing festival. When we started out together the sun was vanishing behind the high green slopes
of Salak, a volcano to the southeast. Evening dew fell gently
on the thick vegetation that surrounded the village. Night
birds cried out conversationally, and small bunches of clouds
very white in the sudden moonlight clustered round the tops
of distant mountains.

We made our way to a wide compound, to which from
every side came groups of villagers, called by the deep reverberating boom of a gong which penetrated every house,
rustled down every ravine, for miles around. Torches bobbed
down the roads, revealing whole families coming to the
festival: dignified men striding ahead, women shepherding
numbers of small, scantily clad children. Thousands of
crickets chirped in a high-pitched unending treble in the
thick woods surrounding the compound on three sides. As
darkness grew, the violet-silver gleam of stars pricked the
profound blue of the sky. More and more villagers arrived,
subduing their chatter, as they drew near, to a more dignified,
watchful waiting. A large oil-lamp at one side threw a
peculiar glow on the dancing space and on the orchestra of
stringed viola, flute, tom-tom, and the curious instruments
on the xylophone principle that are a fundamental part of
the Javanese *gamelan*, orchestra. The flicker of the torches
played over the scarlet, brown and green *sarongs* of the
spectators, high gleams darting out now and then from the
personal jewelery of the more affluent of those present.

At a signal the dancing girl or *ronggeng* appeared. She
took up her position, back to the audience, the oil-lamp fanci-
fully illuminating her vivid green and gold dress and crown-
shaped head-gear. The wandering cool evening breeze

flicked at the skirt of the *sarong* revealing momentarily the smooth curve of well-shaped golden-skinned legs. I learned later that the livelihood of these dancing girls is made more profitable by the exercise of an exceedingly easy virtue. They will dance, in consideration of a fee, for white, Chinese or Javan.

The gong struck another short note and the dance began. The orchestra lilted a soft melody with a beat accentuated by the drums. The girl rose to her tiptoes slowly, picking up her *sarong* with the very tips of her long slim fingers. A few steps to one side in a gliding motion and with a sudden gesture she threw the *sarong* over her shoulder. Then she turned around, sank to her knees and made the *sembah*, sign of greeting to the spectators. Then she started dancing in earnest. Her hips swayed lithely, her arms and fingers wove themselves into multiple curved designs and patterns; her bare feet slid backward and forward in short steps.

The music grew more lively, her movements grew wider in scope, her arms flew more fantastically in the mixed light of the slightly dismal oil-lamp and the warmly flaring torches. The cool evening breeze played on our backs. The bells and drums of the orchestra marked out a stronger, more voluptuous beat; the stringed instruments almost wailed in ecstacy. At the end the girl sank again on her knees, this time directly in front of and close to myself and my friend. Again she made a salute, but it differed from the first. This was more revérent. She rose easily, turned and glided away.

This girl was followed by another, who did a dance more of a character type than the first, which was strictly conventionalized. Others followed: all uniformly good-looking girls, all, to my eye, equally good dancers, though one or another might succeed in drawing muttered comments of approval from single men in the assemblage. None made any attempt, in the undulations and swaying litheness of her body, to conceal the charms that made the other half of their profession profitable. At the end of the festival, I noticed a few men sliding unostentatiously toward the far end of the compound. There is no essential difference between the *ronggeng* and the European houris. As Kipling so effectively observed: "Semarang Siti and night club sweetie are sisters under the skin."

When all was over, lamps were lit, torches renewed, and the families and groups began following their bobbing lights down the paths, roads and winding ways that led in all directions from the compound. No loud talk or laughter; but the crickets kept up their interminable nocturnal uproar. My friend and I followed the main road back toward the village. Here and there groups stopped to take refreshments. The moon hung low, large and silvery, above us; the tiny bunches of very white clouds hung immovable about the caps of nearby mountains, and palm fronds swung softly and lazily in the light gusts of the night wind.

It is not far, in an easterly direction, from the village of Leuwiliang to Buitenzorg, which is a place of the greatest importance in Dutch East Indian affairs. In the first place, it is delightful in that a typically Dutch place exists in the heart of dead and ancient empires. White buildings gleam in the sun, gardens literally packed with riotous flowers of the most brilliant colours line the residential streets, and near the very centre of the town is the residence of the Governor General of all the Dutch East Indies. The present incumbent is His Excellency Jonkheer A.C.B. de Graeff L.L.D., and I had the good fortune to meet him there and also on the occasion of a formal reception at Weltevreden. The diplomatic business of Dutch East India is conducted here, so that there are many buildings devoted to it. Naturally the population is largely Dutch.

Literally translated, Buitenzorg, a Dutch name, means "Away from Sorrow" *(Sans Souci)*. Buitenzorg was originally taken in hand in 1745 by the Dutch as a relief from the then fever-ridden life of Batavia and Weltevreden before the stagnant canal was cleaned up. Buitenzorg enjoys a cleaner, more healthful climate, being more elevated. Its scenery is therefore more picturesque, and a dignity is lent to it by its official significance and importance.

Here in Buitenzorg are the Botanical gardens which, since their inception many years ago, have become famous for their completeness and beauty. Differing from most flower gardens in other and cooler parts of the world, these do not cultivate blossoms under hot-house conditions, for the climate of Java is such that the most glorious flowers of every known and bizarre description flourish without help. Palms, orchids that would make a débutante weep, vast rhododendrons, strange trees of huge size, either spreading or shooting up to the sky to extraordinary heights, other weird flowers measuring thirty-six inches from petal to petal, such as the Rafflesia Arnoldi, the largest flower known, all leading up to the enormous water lilies *(Victoria Regia)* which extend several feet across and which grace the lake, facing the Governor's palace.

The voluptuous colouring of all these flowers and fruit trees in a glorious unsystematic mixture is typical of all Java, where the strange eventually becomes the everyday. The botanical gardens here in Buitenzorg have been developed to afford scientists—and perhaps tourists in a hurry—a view of all of Java's trimmings almost at a glance. Men of botany, whenever they visit the East, are drawn irresistibly to Buitenzorg, to witness ample evidence of Java's fecundity.

From Buitenzorg I went directly across country still

heading East, via the Puntjak Pas, near Sindanglaja where the road crosses the boundary between the Residencies of Batavia and Preanger.

The boundary between the Residencies of Batavia and Preanger is indicated, at the highest point, by a wooden gate and a small wooden kiosk. From this superbly situated little house, I had a wide, strangely beautiful view of the surrounding territory. To the north, the plains of Batavia and beyond, the Java Sea; and to the south-west a vast irregular series of hills, leading to the distant climax of the high mountains around Guntur.

From this point on I equipped myself with a guide to take me to the crater lake of Telaga Warna. We had climbed through unbroken forest; but now we passed new plantations. At the far end of these the path plunged again into the forest and we climbed steadily until we reached the edge of the lake.

The lake itself is an extinct crater and the natives in its neighbourhood regard it with superstitious veneration. They bring plentiful offerings of fruit, flowers, rice and incense to the borders of the lake to appease the mountain spirit. No Sundanese will either fish from its surface nor will, much less, enter its waters for a cool swim. Legend has it that swimmers are sucked to its bottom by a sudden and irresistible force, which chooses that way of punishing them for disturbing the peace of the spirits.

The bottom of the lake has never been reached by sounding, and since it is never used for practical purposes, its waters are crowded with a host of fish. Its waters are very calm and reflect without blemish the thick luxuriant growth of ferns and trees around its circumference. On the side directly opposite us, the wall of the ancient crater rose to a height of some five hundred feet, its frontal surface covered with vegetation in the wildest colours, sharply contrasting with the deep green of the forest surrounding us. This too is reflected in the blue water, and a great silence prevailed, broken only by the gentle whisper of the breeze through the tops of the lofty trees. It was awe-inspiring, so that when I turned to my guide with the command to be led back, I instinctively lowered my voice, as if in a vast and dim church.

Keeping on, later, from the kiosk on the road, I went southward toward Sukabumi in the Preanger district. This town pursues its active career within a very few miles of the Gedeh volcano, which is one of the nine still active volcanoes in Java. The town is some eighteen hundred feet above sea level, and is cooler and clearer, in consequence, than the plains to the north-west. The country hereabouts is covered with rubber, cinchona, coffee plantations and rice *sawahs*. Rice, of course, plays a tremendously important part in the life of every Javan, with very few exceptions.

There the sun gleams from extended silver surfaces that furnish the necessary water for rice growing. Here one sees the bright greens of the young *padi*, there again are young shoots and beyond that newly grown rice, yellow. These *sawahs* are terraced also, and must, from an aeroplane, present the aspect of gigantic flights of silver steps in the garden of a Gargantuan king.

As I went along the road, I saw here and there in the fields single men driving caribou, ploughing up the soil beneath the water; there on the other side a long row of women, their vari-coloured *sarongs* and tucked-up *slendangs* putting a lively note of passionate colour into the silver and green background. Beyond there was suddenly a great bellowing and shouting and splashing; I ran to look. Five men, or perhaps more, were driving a small herd of cumbersome caribou across a large *sawah*. The men shouted and laughed and splashed through the knee-deep water. The caribou reared, pranced in ungainly fashion and darted off in an unexpected direction. One man fell down and was almost run over. There was a terrific uproar, so I asked my driver what it was all about.

He shrugged his shoulders and answered: "The owner of the *sawah* and his helpers are lazy. They do not care to plough with system. So they drive the caribou through without system, thus causing a great churning and confusion of the soil and the water. It is not good."

Not good, perhaps, but funny to see.

Down the road at that moment came a little man, bearing over his shoulder his *pikolan*, or bamboo contraption of woven trays and baskets. In these he carried food delicacies, going up and down the road, selling to those who toiled. He stopped, and the labourers, men and women, flocked around him rapidly from the nearest *sawahs*, fingering over and buying and eating his entire stock of baked and fried fish, *gourami, mangustans, durians*, red *macassers*, fishes, bananas, soup, cakes, and so forth. It is quite certain that the Javan can always find time and money to eat. Why not? They have many things worth eating and time besides.

Back in Sukabumi, I witnessed something that I actually saw only a few times during many years in the Far East spent chiefly in Java and Sumatra. This was a man run *amok*. The word implies a wild career of dagger-slashing, either of a specially sought-out victim, or of anyone else irrespective of responsibility.

This needs explanation, for the term has long since been adopted by English and American fiction writers, and twisted as a result. Most people picture Easterners suddenly, and for inscrutable reasons, flying into ecstatic rages and beginning to carve the nearest and most innocent bystander. It is not so simple.

It is a racial trait with the Sundanese and Javans that they are quiet, unspeakably courteous and restrained and innately averse to violent quarrelling. This is evidenced too

by their refusal to haggle in market-places. However, the
natural pride of their racial upbringing has at the same time
made them deeply sensitive to and resentful of slights, in-
sults and injustices done them. They will accept, in good
nature varying with their individual dispositions, a trouncing
from an equal. But from one of lesser standing or from a
white, an affront is not to be tolerated. The offended one
may reach for his kris at once. Or again he may wait—and
brood.

I knew this before, and was always careful, in dealings
with the people of that country, or any other country I was
ever in, to treat them with the same courtesy they meted out
to me. One night, then, in Sukabumi, two nights after I
arrived, I believe, I was roused from an early doze by the
sound of the easily recognizable *amok* signal sounding from
guardpost to guardpost. The signal is sufficiently creepy,
Heaven knows. It is given by beating rapidly, almost
hysterically, on a gong or long wooden pole with a very
penetrating tone. I was in sleeping clothes, but I rushed to
the door in time to see, not far from me, a tallish man charging down upon another. Shouts sounded from the head of
the street, heralding the arrival of the police. The tall man
brandished a kris, and the man upon whom he charged stood
his ground, with the evident intent of stopping his assailant.
The kris flourished in a wide hissing circle, and the tall man
let out a hoarse, low grunt of triumph. The smaller man
fell woodenly to one side, his shoulder cut almost under his
neck. The tall man turned then, and I saw his face. I retreated more within the door. No duty of mine to interfere
in his quarrels. But I knew he had started out to avenge some
past insult and the luckless small man had seen fit, for God
alone knows what reasons, to try to impede him.

The tall man's eyes rolled loosely in his sockets, and the

bloody kris swished down ferociously, finding nothing more, just then, to bite into. A squad of native police rushed up. They had with them a long pole pronged at the end. Inside the prong were barbs. They pinioned the *amok*-maker against the wall. They disarmed and fell upon him in a heap. When they arose one man limped away. The captive was very unruly and tumultuous. He shouted and raved and struggled, but the cluster of police held grimly on to him. No more *mata glap*, running wild, for him.

It is thus with those who go *amok*. They start for the object of their vengeance, but have no compunctions in wreaking harm on those who get in their way from whatever motives. When the *amok* gong sounds, most villagers are experienced enough to shut themselves up behind their barred doors while the braver spirits arm themselves and go forth to stop the marauder. Many such began arriving now, but the police took away the captive, later to be executed. A silent group of men carried away the body of the man with the slashed shoulder. He was dead.

At length the village quieted down. The Dutch authorities do not interfere in an affair of this sort unless a white is mixed up in it. Just as I was about to turn in, a figure in a long white gown-like affair seemed to float across the street toward me.

"Hello," it said pleasantly. "See it all?"

I replied that I had. Odd, I added, that no one else in the hotel had come out. My room was on the ground floor.

. "They're probably all peeking," said the ghostly figure in a nightgown indulgently, and he cast an eye over the front of the building. "Well, I can go back to bed now, I suppose," he observed in a tone of relief. "Nothing for me here. Good-night." He was an assistant from the local government office, airily attired in an old-fashioned sleeping robe of virgin white. He must have witnessed the whole affair from the shadow of a building across the street. I went in, but unfortunately slept little. I was thinking of the man who had, for reasons impossible to guess, stepped into the path of the tall *amok*-maker. And unarmed, too. What mysterious drama lay behind that?

Fʀᴏᴍ Sukabumi, where there is a cocaine factory, it is
north-easterly to Tangkubanprahu, which is a great
health resort for those who find the Batavian plains too
warm. It was here that Junghuhn laid out his first cinchona

(quinine) cultivation in 1864. This Preanger region is a tremendous tea-growing centre, its hills in many localities being covered with tea shrubs.

From Garut, another health resort, further on, I made several really wonderful trips to the Kawa Kamodjan, the Kawa Manuk and Papandajan. On one trip to the Papandajan (or the Forge) a party of us started on small mountain ponies, past coffee plantations and villages. The road started climbing steeply, and our carriers stopped frequently to scoop up handfuls of clear cool water from the many little brooks we crossed. When the coffee plantations were left behind, the road entered the jungle, where the heat broke off sharply and we could enjoy the violet shade of the thickly grown trees and vegetation. Monkeys travelled in the trees behind us, staring down in offended haughtiness, now and then pitching a bit of bark or branch at us. When the road began to creep out of the forest again, and the light grew brighter, they vanished in the thick foliage of the assam trees.

Out again in the sun, the heat became almost unbearable and a steady breeze blew hot white dust into our eyes. We rested. The carriers stood quite still, breathing heavily, the perspiration sliding down their backs. We alighted to give the ponies a breather. Our guide was the only one who did not suffer.

"Not tired?" I asked him frequently.

He was a tall fellow, a Sundanese, with a well-modelled, intelligent face. He wore a red *kabaja* and a head-dress of dark brown cloth wound around his head.

"I am not tired, *tuan*," he answered me several times, quietly. When we rode on he strode evenly with the ponies and seemed never to suffer from fatigue.

Beside the road I saw a large beautiful tree, covered with white flowers like lilies. The heart was red and the petals were long.

"*Djonges, minta ini Kamban,*" I said to the guide. "Boy, bring me one of those flowers."

He stopped at my voice and waited till my pony was beside him. Then he answered:

"*Tida ah tuan, ada radjun.*" "No, sir, it is poison." He went on to tell me that one leaf would make me drunk, two leaves unconscious; and many leaves meant sure death. I did not insist.

As we progressed he, sure now of my interest in such matters, pointed out many trees en route, describing their powers: some to heal, some to poison, some bad for the stomach, some good to cure headaches, some which would cause slow lingering death.

The road, after considerable time, grew much steeper. The ponies climbed like goats, and we all sweated mightily. The carriers with the bamboo panniers stayed behind. We went on a little further, and suddenly, coming round a turn in the road, found a vast rolling panorama opened up before us. Far below I could see a little silver brook cascading down over grey rocks. We left the ponies here at the turn and clambered on a short distance on foot. Here was no vegetation; we trod on lava slabs and sulphur-rocks. We passed a series of warm geysers, emitting evil smells. On their way down came many natives, bearing bamboo baskets filled with sulphur to sell.

We climbed on, until the guide told me we had reached a height of about fifty-six hundred feet above sea level. Then we came to the lip of the crater and peered down upon a fearfully impressive sight. Below us the crater bottom boiled and hissed, sudden bursts of sulphur and steam shooting into the air almost at every second. The sun beat down on us, and reflected painfully on our eyes from the white and yellow caked sulphur under our feet and everywhere around us.

We waited for the rest of the party and when they had caught up with us, we received a warning from the tireless guide to be careful. Then he led us down, in zig-zag fashion, to the crater crust, and then over it, winding our way with infinite caution, between the spouting, steaming fumaroles.

Near the very centre was a bigger and steadier cloud of dark steam. This, said the guide, was the large crater. It hissed and belched up clouds of foul steam that made us start back. I looked about the weird place. Some of the hardened sulphur resembled human figures with the outlines blurred, as if by an unspeakable heat. I poked my cane through the crust, to see what would happen, and came within an ace of having my face burned completely away. A jet of steam and sulphur shot up toward my face. I leaped back, and heard the guide shout: *"Hati, hati, tuan!"* "Take care, sir, take care!"

As we filed back toward the lip I asked the guide if he had ever been there at night, thinking that it must present an even more terrible aspect at night than in the frightful sun and heat. Bats would come out of the rock crevices at night.

The guide shot a frightened glance around. He said, in a low tone, that he had never dared to visit the crater at night, because miserable and vengeful ghosts came out to wander there. I dropped the subject at once, and became absorbed in watching how the crust trembled now and again under our very feet. Underneath was poisonous mud striving to break through, to overwhelm the puny beings who dared trample on the face of the crater.

Speaking for myself alone, I can say that the panorama of the country, viewed from the turn in the road where we had left the ponies, was far superior, artistically speaking, to the infernal crater. Before us was an unbroken stretch of green hill and valley. Villages with buff-coloured structures, *sawahs* with silver surfaces, sprinkled the view. Behind us was a cauldron of dire portent any way you looked at it.

The return to the cool of the forest was an immense boon after the heat and toil in the sun and the walk on the hot crust of the crater. I am still intrigued by the idea of a visit to the crater by night, though, and will make one soon.

Returning to Bandung, and thence indirectly to Purwakerta, I found myself at length in this smaller town, where few European buildings mar the completeness of the native atmosphere. Native law precedes all else here—as I learnt through the crowing of a cock.

In all Java cocks crow earlier than anywhere else in the world that I have ever been. One starts, and a multitude all over the surrounding countryside chime in. It is sometimes positively intimidating. The uproar makes it impossible for a light sleeper to get much rest after five in the morning, or even earlier.

One morning my boy awakened me even before the first cock had thought to crow. He told me that the sound of a bugle, which I heard just then distantly, announced the execution of a Chinaman, an "Orang Tjina," Tjiong hiang, who had murdered a Javanese woman.

This was not to be missed. I hurriedly dressed and the two of us ran toward the centre of town. Villagers, too, filled the streets, intent on witnessing the spectacle. There were also Chinamen, Arabs and stately hadjis, dressed in their usual scarlet robes.

The place of execution was ringed by a dense mob, silent. The Chinaman I saw standing coolly by the gallows, smoking a large cigar, blowing out great whorls of smoke, and surveying calmly those who stood near him. His fatalism kept him thus, I suppose.

But it was not a pleasant morning to die, if any morning can be that. It was still damp from the night dew; the sun had barely begun to suffuse the world with a dim grey depressing light. Just then the first cocks began crowing in the *kampongs* behind us. The Chinaman smoked with seeming unconcern.

Guards appeared on either side of him and led him before the official of justice, who read out to him, in a cold voice discouraged by this necessity for early rising, the nature of his crime and the reasons why the death penalty had been bestowed upon him. The Chinaman listened with unperturbed face. It was impossible to guess what he was thinking. The multitude of spectators was perfectly attentive.

The executioner and his helper now came forward and took the Chinaman up on the scaffold. From the gibbet dangled the noose. His hands were bound behind him, and he obligingly bent his head to one side to permit the noose being placed about his thin yellow neck. The executioner's helper came down and crept under the scaffold. A drum began beating a slow dirge-like rhythm, and at a signal the wooden prop under the doomed man was jerked away; the helper underneath grabbed his dangling legs and gave them a mighty pull.

Tjiong Liang had suddenly joined his ancestors in expiation of his having murdered a woman. Perfect silence greeted the sight of the limp body that swung and turned at the end of the slim rope. Suddenly a woman's voice screamed out; I saw a figure fall. Too much for one.

Beside me, for contrast, was a young Javanese mother with a child, at least five years old, at her breast. The child refreshed itself with gusto in the shadow of the gallows. Then it demanded, in a tiny treble, to be put down. Once down, it lit a cigarette, puffed it tranquilly for a few moments, threw the butt after a nearby chicken, climbed up

into the side folds of its young mother's *slendang* and again
partook of nourishment.

I walked back to my room, unable to forget so swiftly
the vision of the thin dangling body. It is a marvel that
I was not run over by the bullock carts that, now that the sun
had risen, thronged the road and streets. These carts are
very ornate, with elaborate carvings, loud painted colours
and steep roofs. They are the island's native means of transport, and are usually full of sugar-cane bound for a distant
refinery. The drivers never seem awake, but doze steadily,
uninterruptedly, on their seats, leaving to their lumbering
doleful bullocks the task of guiding the carts from village to
village. They keep to the centre of the road with great
obstinacy, since the drivers sleep, and are as great an annoy-
ance on some of the wonderful roads of Java as Sunday
drivers in the United States.

I left Purwakerta soon after, went to Banjumas, and
thence to Djocjakarta, where resides the Sultan, one of the
two Sultans in Java. This one is called Amangku Buwono
(He Who Has the World's Axis on His Knees), Sadjidin
Panotogomo, and Kalipatullah (cf. Caliphat) (The Representative of Allah).

The two sultanates of Java are called *Vorstenlanden*,
The Lands of the Sovereigns. The rest of Java, as is mentioned above, is divided into Regencies. The two Sultanates,
Djocja and nearby Surakarta, or Solo, comprise one-fifteenth
of the total superficies of Java and together measure one
hundred and sixty-five square miles. Their territories are a
little remnant of the once powerful empire of Mataram, and
are now divided between the Susuhunan of Solo, the Sultan
of Djocja and the princes Mangkunegoro and Paku Alam.
From one cause and another, the power of these four gentle-

men had become so limited that little remains of it. Succession to the thrones is now regulated with the assistance of the Dutch Government, since it would never do to have rebellious rulers. These territories are also the outgrowth of the ancient Madjapahit Empire, which centred around Madjakerta, where there are today the ruins of a gigantic city, which must have been like Babel. It was a great Javanese-Hindu empire, with the resultant mixture of tongues, customs and bloods.

The way in which the Dutch gradually came to control these territories, now comprising for the most part the two large Sultanates, is interesting. In 1749 Paku Buwono, the then Sultan of Solo, ceded his empire to the *Kompenie*, the Dutch East India Company. There may have been conniving here. Since that date his successors have reigned as lease-holders. The present sultans signed agreements which run something as follows:

"I declare and recognize the dignity given me as a lease-holder of the lands of Solo (or Djocja); that these lands were not obtained by reason of force, nor by inheritance, but merely through the affection and favour which the Governor General, Her Majesty's representative, has for me. So I declare to have received in lease these said lands and the Government always has the right to the possession of same."

There is a tale told of this same Paku Buwono who ceded his lands to the *Kompenie*. He was, in order of his family, the fourth. One of his courtiers had been so indiscreet as to be caught in incest with his own sister, Radan Aiu Sanah. The Sultan was annoyed and caused the man's sexual organ to be cut off and up and placed in his mouth to be eaten. The unhappy man was then quartered with great care and precision. The sister was given the poison of the great upas tree.

But the son of this cruel Sultan was more subtle. He was called Paku Buwono the Fifth. He found that Lesbianism was growing among his wives and concubines, to the extent that they were no longer attracted by him, despite his sternest commands. He fixed matters by causing all his numerous women to sleep on mats on the floor of his own bedroom, where he could keep an eye on them!

Court marriages today are planned on a higher scale. A hard and fast rule says that the Sultan of Solo (the older of the two Sultanates, the one at Djocja having been slyly set up by the Dutch) may have four lawful wives at once, and as many concubines besides as he may desire. It is the business of a certain official of the court to keep the ranks of the concubines constantly replenished with young and beautiful virgins. It is to be regretted that the children of these multitudinous concubines have no standing of any sort at the court, nor particularly in the considerations of their father. But their technical illegitimacy, on the other hand, does not hinder them in later life.

Should the Sultan, through accident or oversight, have less than four wives, and if at the same time one of the concubines is pregnant, he must marry that concubine, which is eminently just. Regular custom decrees that at night the Sultan shall sleep with the Ratu, or head wife. During the day the concubines must be at his beck and call. If he wishes to be accompanied on his bed by one of the lesser of his four wives, he notifies the Ratu, who helps the fortunate woman. She anoints her with salves and ointments, puts flowers in her hair and makes her promise that she will behave with obedience and sweetness toward their lord and superior.

Concubines of the first class are called *Selleer*, and when taken into the palace are usually not more than twelve years old. They are drawn from among the daughters of princes and regents, as are also the regular wives.

Then there are the *Serimpies*, unlimited in number, who are almost always related in some way to the ruler. The chief employment of these girls is dancing, and they range in age from ten to fourteen. These are followed by the *Mang-goong*, forty in number, who are the daughters of officers and officials. They are used as maids and personal servants in the *kraton*, palace. The chief carriers are called *porro njai kaparak* and number forty-eight in all.

The *kraton* of the Sultan of Solo is peopled by a host of relatives, wives, concubines, et cetera, numbering the staggering total of fifteen thousand, all of whom reside within the wide walls of the palace and its buildings.

First there is an administrator paid and appointed by the Dutch Government. Then there is the *Pangeran Adipati*, or Crown Prince, chosen at an early age with the consent of the Dutch Government. After him come the children of the concubines and the brothers of the Sultan, who are superior in standing to any "unreal" children the Sultan may produce. Soldiers, priests, village heads, local officials, civil employees, bring the number up to fifteen thousand, which includes a vast horde of servants as well.

The same arrangements as to wives and order of the palace obtains at Djocja likewise, but on a lesser scale.

The city of Djocja is large, with an active community life outside the walls of the *kraton*, just as any seat of government, when located at a cross-road, attracts commerce and life. This country, extended for a considerable distance to all four cardinal points of the compass, is the core of real Javan life. The people are more grave in thought and manner than the Sundanese of the West, who are frequently referred to as "the French of the Far East," since they run more to wit and liveliness in their speech and ways of thinking. But here at Djocja is seen Javan life at its best, influenced but not extensively altered, by foreign ways.

I put up at the homey Grand Hotel, and the next day started on a ride about town in an *andung*, a typical Djocja vehicle drawn by two little ponies, in preference to the many automobiles to be hired very reasonably. The day was a day of festival, being a celebration on the first day of the tenth month of the Mahometan year. It is called the *garabeg puasa*, and is also observed in the Sunda country, where it is called *lebaran*.

The crowd near the old water castle, Tamansarai, was so dense that my driver had difficulty getting his little ponies through, but we soon got close enough to see what was happening.

A procession was passing, led by the Sultan's body-guard, whose uniforms made them look like so many guests at a masquerade who had had the misfortune all to come in the very same costume. Dark jackets, fez-like hats, light-coloured baggy trousers and gaiters and tall muskets gave them an altogether fantastic and not entirely bellicose appearance. They tramped by solemnly.

Then came the Sultan, a small man with a dark-skinned, intelligent face. I later had the good fortune to come in closer contact with him. He was, on this occasion, dressed opulently. A purple velvet jacket and a draped batik *dodot*, court dress, made him seem like a figure transplanted from a stage play. On his small head rested a beautifully gold-embroidered *kuluk*, a sort of headgear which is something like a fez in shape. It was of a fine cotton or grass linen, and glistened in the bright sun from rice starch. The Sultan was followed by a group of courtiers or *pangerans*, all dressed, according to *adat*, in their special court dresses. These *pangerans* preceded a troupe of girls, all heavily smeared with an ointment of *boré* or coco-nut oil. These in turn were followed by a lot of bizarre clowns, leaping and grimacing, who wore feathers in their hair, but otherwise no traditional head-dress. Among these was an albino, which astonished me. I somehow had not thought that so dark a race could produce these unfortunate phenomena. This one was almost pure white in complexion and the poor fellow kept squinting his weak, pink-rimmed eyes in the glare of the sun that must have been a ceaseless and unbearable torture to him.

Very soon after the day of the procession, through friends at the Government office I received an invitation to a reception given by the Sultan, at which time there would also be a dance by the *Serimpies,* his dancing girls.

I left my hotel at eight o'clock in the morning. The sun was already up and casting down its burning rays. I was attired, as custom demanded, in full evening dress and silk hat. Thus I marched, in solitary, all too solitary, impressiveness, down the street. I cursed the necessity that made me put off the whites that everyone wore all the rest of the time. This was grotesque.

Ill luck would have it, of course, that I had come out too early in my eagerness. The reception was to begin at nine. I had more than half an hour to consume before presenting myself. So I strolled down and around the market-place. This institution, as with all peoples who have not highly developed the retail sale system of merchandising, plays an important and indispensable part in Javan life. A real *pasar* happens once every five days, and is as great a temptation to the girl or housewife as the bazaars of Paris, London and New York. Gilt-lettered sign boards announced the specialties for sale in each booth. Fish, game, fruit, *kains,* articles of dress, *sarongs, kabajas,* jewelry, and what not. Here and there were the booths of native *pienter* (wise) women, who sold medicine. These affable ladies will, besides selling you medicinal decoctions, also interpret dreams, select grains for seeding, advise how to recover stolen goods; in short, fulfil all the possible obligations of a clairvoyant. Besides incantation and exorcism, they will assist in the application of salves and poultices, and will administer pills and charms.

On the general subject of native remedies, it is interesting that the Javans widely distrust the white man's methods of healing the sick. This is true practically everywhere in the world, despite the sometimes spectacular work done by the white doctors in the way of plague and epidemic prevention, sanitation, et cetera. But this does not mean that some native remedies are not highly efficacious. The natives believe in the supernatural curative powers of certain animals and plants. A widespread belief in Java has it that hanging the genital organ of a tiger or crocodile over the bed will achieve rejuvenation; much as we whites believe in monkey glands. A spray of a certain flower under the pillow will induce sounder sleep. This flower is the *daun tidur tiduran,* *tidur* meaning sleep. Leprosy may be halted by the application of a solution derived from the tails of the *tjitak,* or small lizard.

I later went into the subject quite deeply, for it interested me. The natives, in their daily work, come in contact with dangerous animals, reptiles and insects, they work often and for long periods in constant danger of their lives.

In all the Dutch East Indies the Bataks of Sumatra are the most far-advanced in ready-made, native remedies. The Javans depend greatly on certain precious stones and the saliva, urine and feces of humans and certain animals for their curative powers. In general, they fear the knives of white doctors, but once this fear has been overcome, they will place themselves on the operating tables with the greatest calm, even appearing to fall into sleep by autosuggestion before chloroform is administered.

It is natural that a people exposed to constant danger to health and bodily well-being should have developed many simple means of protection. Some of these methods are far wrong, simply because they have no accurate knowledge of human physiology, but in numerous cases in which their knowledge is commensurate with their reasoning the results are for the most satisfactory. The toasting of an open wound over a fire, to dry the wound, may sometimes work—and sometimes not. The warming of a mother and her new-born child on a bench over a slow fire may be helpful. Warmth is necessary, and the great normal health and bodily strength of Javan mothers enables them to avoid much of the great pain and exquisite agony undergone by Western mothers. It is difficult for many to believe that childbirth is a more casual event among more primitive peoples than among the Western peoples who have centuries of body-torturing clothes and habits to thank for the weakness of their bodies. The Javan mother gives little thought to childbirth. Within a few days she is up and about and at work. The deliveries are easier because of strong, constantly exercised muscles. The ease of childbirth, in combination with the warm climate, is responsible for the failure of the Javanese to enshroud the great god of sex in a cage—of glass. The result of sexual intercourse, says the Javan, is a child.

The result is a race that is deteriorating neither in quality nor in number. They have not yet hit upon the moral maxim that has converted the western world into a moralist's heaven: over-indulgence in a virtue makes it a vice!

Coming back to the medicine women of the market place in Djocja, I saw that they sold openly and without fear large varieties of poisons, such as arsenic, pounded glass, shredded bamboo, tiger's whiskers, et cetera. These women are said to be able to calculate to a nicety the effect of various lethal means of inducing an apparently innocent death. I shall have occasion to speak of this at greater length when telling what I learned about *guna-guna*, the love and other philtres, used by the natives and the Eurasians.

I now went on up to the Dutch Residency, and joined the
rest of the party there, in my full formal attire. Presently a squad of envoys of the Sultan arrived, indicating that
the Sultan would receive us. We followed them to the
kraton in carriages.

The imperial body-guard, the same I had seen parading
several days before, was drawn up in the *aloon-aloon,* the
large open space before the main palace building Pendoppo.
On our appearance a terrific din was set up suddenly by the
band of drummers, pipers and trumpeters. We were welcomed by the court master of ceremonies. Three young
princes then came out of the building to welcome in person
the Resident, who was dressed in an official uniform of black
with gold lacing. These three handsome young men led
him a little way, and then his arm was taken by the Crown
Prince. The whole lot of us entered the reception hall.

We were surrounded by throngs of those who made their
home within the walls of the *kraton.* Bright *sarongs* and
jewelery glittered on both men and women. In the large
yard were huge *waringin* trees, in the shade of which clustered groups of respectfully watchful court attendants.

We crossed the reception hall, where a *gamelan* orchestra
was playing gravely, and at the entrance to the throne-room
the Sultan himself came out and shook hands in European
fashion with the Resident. The Resident was led to a chair
on the sovereign's left. The Ratu came forth then to greet
the visitors, and after a few moments of solemn talk we all
moved out to the edge of the large *aloon-aloon* on the other
side of the *kraton.* We were to review the palace troops.

Several hundreds of men went by, rather than marched.
The imperial body-guard led the way, attired in their short
jackets and bunched-up *sarongs.* Long lances rested on their
shoulders. The rest were mainly quite ordinary warriors
with lances, krises, and oversized daggers and scimitars. Not

very formidable as modern troops go, but nevertheless extremely gratifying as a spectacle. We perspired mightily in our dress clothes and my collar wilted almost at once.

Back we went to the large hall. The Sultan and the Resident whom he called his Big Brother walked arm-in-arm in most friendly fashion. And the Sultan was an imposing sight with rings on every finger (the fingers long-nailed to indicate his noble birth!) and jewelled strings about his neck. He wore a short black jacket, with a small kris stuck in the waitsband. A white head-dress surmounted his keen dark face. For the rest, he had on a waist-band of violet and mauve, a narrow brown *sarong* over his shoulder and trousers of voluminous blue silk. He surely looked the Eastern Potentate!

Back in the hall speeches were made. Those who spoke to the Sultan addressed him in high Javanese, while he replied in low Javanese. Wine was served, the Sultan and his Big Brother drinking red, the rest of us, including the court, drinking white, as prescribed by *adat* or tradition. Another procession now got under way, headed for a large hall on the other side of the great courtyard in front.

The Sultan and the Resident again marched arm in arm, under the large golden umbrella, chatting now gravely, then again with gentle smiles on their lips. We toiled along behind them. Directly behind us came a vast number of women of the court, holding in their hands the various emblems of dignity: golden figures of elephants, snakes, bulls, deer and fighting cocks. Some carried golden spittoons, pots of betel tobacco. Others carried bamboo baskets of fruit, flowers and scents. Behind them came many fully armed warriors.

Ahead swayed the golden umbrella, or *payong*. Rank is indicated in Java by such umbrellas. The Sultan uses a golden one, his first wife and her family have a white one, province governors use green with a gold border, the Sultan's sons, yellow, and so on from the lesser nobles on up. Rank is also shown by the manner of inserting the kris in the waistband, and by the details of dress and headgear.

Thus we came to the hall where the *serimpi* would dance. (These latter are taken in when about ten years old and are usually discarded at the age of fourteen.)

We entered the hall, grouped ourselves about, sat down on chairs, and the girls appeared.

They were dressed according to the dictates of ancient custom in silk woven petticoats, chiefly of green stamped with golden flowers. The waistband worn by these girls was of the Chindi pattern, and this day they wore a cistus composed of golden plates, thickly ornamented with jewels at the front. The bodices were like corsets and called *pemakaks*. They passed above the breast and under the arm, confining the waist into the smallest possible space. The ends of their robes fell in long graceful lines down the back to the floor. Threefold necklaces, arm-bands, bracelets, tiaras, comprised the jewelery, and the hair of the girls was studded with white and perfumed flowers.

Two old women, their preceptresses, had opened a double door to let them in and they came gliding smoothly across the floor toward us. They sat down in a row facing the Sultan. The *gamelan*, composed of metallophone, Arabian violins, *rehabs*, gongs, drums and violas, began a slow measure, and the *serimpi*, in the most perfect unison, brought their hands together and slowly raised them to their foreheads, in a *sembah*, or salute of reverence. They rose, their eyes fixed in their heads, and glided to and fro to the music. Their heels were lifted off the ground with each step, imparting a curious smoothness to their movements.

Their flexible young bodies flowed from one posture to another with strange compelling majesty. Through it all their eyes remained on the ground in modesty. The *gamelan* flowed, whispered, hurried and sank to a grave and measured rhythm. At the end of many minutes the girls again fell into their seated attitudes before their lord and again they made the respectful salute. Thus they sat until the Sultan gave a signal. They arose in unison and glided away across the floor. Another and still a third troupe of girls came, each leaving behind it an intangible essence of an old civilization that is able to produce so fine and perfect a technique. And during it all, crickets, flies and mosquitos harried us in our dress suits.

Such events, as we had witnessed back in the throne room, take place on the first day of the tenth month of the Mahometan year, and the twelfth day of the second month when the Sultan holds levee, and at these times the people come to do honour to the head of Javan Islamism. They approach him with the greatest respect and awe, giving the *sembah*, and addressing him in the high Javanese vernacular. It is on these festivals that the inferior will kiss the sovereign's knee, instep or sole.

A friendship grew up between myself and the brother of the Sultan, Pangeran Hidisooryo, as a result of which I had a permit to the *kraton* and was even permitted to drive my car within its walls. This became known, and one day at the Grand Hotel the representative of an American film company, a Dutchman, there to obtain news reels, spoke to me:

"You are the very man I want. You are the only one who can get into the palace. I can't." A festival was coming off in the *kraton* next day, at which many resplendent costumes would be visible.

"Well?"

His manner became stealthy and he drew nearer. "Will you take my camera with you and shoot for me?"

I began to form protesting phrases in my mind, but he

continued: "Now, I'm sure it will be all right. They know you. The Sultan's brother is your friend. Why not?"

The idea grew upon me, so that the next day, when I went to the festival, I had with me the camera of the apostle of the film art. When the festival began, I set the thing up and started cranking. I explained matters to my friend, the royal brother, and he smiled indulgently. I carried away with me a goodly amount of footage, which pleased the cameraman immensely.

Besides the dances of the village girls and the Sultan's *serimpi* the greatest national source of entertainment is the shadow plays, generically called *wayang*. They originally developed as a means of calling up the spirits of the dead, and the chief performer, the *dalang*, was a priest.

But since that time they have grown into out-and-out theatrical performances and there are numerous *wayang* troupes throughout the island.

Actual *wayang* shows are divided into seven well-known classes, including: the *wayang purwa* (but with a varying repertoire of plays); the *wayang kelitik* or *karucil*, using flat wooden puppets; the *wayang topeng*, given by masked human actors and dancers; the *wayang wong*, with unmasked actors and dancers; lastly the *wayang beber*, using scrolls.

Of all these, with their material for plots and stories dating back to the period of Hindu-Buddhistic colonization, the *wayang wong* is the most apt to be appreciated by outside audiences. But the *wayang purwa*, an actual forerunner of our movies, in which the shadows of leather puppets are thrown on the screen, is the oldest. Manipulation of the puppets lies in the hands of the *dalang*, whose voice, spirit and imagination lend colour to the performances. In achieving his effects he is assisted by a *gamelan* ranged round him, while the audience is on the opposite side of the screen from him.

When, little by little, the shows in which masked actors took part grew into public favour, the *dalang* fell away somewhat from his pristine glory, an additional body-blow being dealt to his prestige with the growth of the *wayang wong* of unmasked actors and dancers.

In this connection it was customary, once every ten years in the Sultan of Djocja's court, for a great *wayang wong* lasting four days to be given, in which the members of the royal household participated. In these, traditional plays were enacted, and the leading parts were taken by princes. Rehearsals of the principals and ensembles occupied more than a year previous, so that perfection was produced during the four-day performance. The company of such a royally patronized production might number as high as three hundred, with gorgeous costumes and drapes. But in general the scenic effects of the ordinary stationary or transient troupe are sober, poor, relying upon suggestion more than realism, as do the Chinese. A flower-pot containing a meagre cluster of flowers will signify a garden, for example.

The *wayang wong* is understandable to a degree by the outsider, but a complete and colloquial knowledge of the language is indispensable to the comprehension, let alone the enjoyment, of the puppet-shadow plays. For here the plots were originally barely outlined by the author, perhaps hundreds of years ago, so that the embellishment of the skeleton is left to the wit of the *dalang*. He suggests his Western counterpart, the master of ceremonies, in finding himself constantly in need of new and diverting remarks. Thus he employs quotations from old books, statements of religious creed, and caps matters by directing facetious quips at familiar faces in the audience. The cabaret *conférencier* and the *dalang* are blood brothers; the Colonel's lady and Judy O'Grady are not the only ones whose innards display a mutual likeness.

Almost directly north of Djocja is the Barabudur, one of the greatest Buddhistic monuments known to the modern world. It is on the Dieng plateau not far from the Merapi volcano, which I later visited. Buddhism once played a tremendously important part in Java, though now its practice is limited to a few villages in the Tengger mountains in the east, whither the remnants of the Hindus were driven when Mahometans came in droves many years ago, and to the islands of Bali and Lombok, east of Java.

Nothing definite is known yet about the date of the erection of the Barabudur in Hindu-Javanese times, but it may have been built in the time of the Caliendras between 750 and 850 A.D. Many other Hindu ruins are found around Djocja, Modjokerto and Malang, and the others, beside the Barabudur are: the Chandi Pawon, near the Barabudur, on the plains of Prambanan, considered the highest examples of Buddhistic art; Chandi Sari, supposed to have been a monastery; and Chandi Kalasan, built probably about 779 A.D.

The Barabudur is, however, the greatest of them all. To my mind there are not many examples of architectural virtuosity in the world to equal it. It must have been, in its first condition, more costly and imposing than the Pyramids, and I personally consider it superior to the Angkor in Cambodia.

I actually started for it by going from Djocja up to Magelang, in the Residency of Kedu, which is an important military station. From Magelang the Barabudur, in the middle of the plains of the Kedu district, is about an hour's journey, while towering in the distance is the volcano Sendara, and nearer the smoke plume of the Merapi. The entire effect of the scenery that day was soft brown, grey and green.

The first sight of the Barabudur does not, because of its size, give a full impression, beyond its rounded pyramidal shape. Then one begins to take in details. It is built in the shape of a giant stupa around a hill which forms a cone. Four great sculptured tiers enclose the hill, rising in a great sweeping slope. Atop these two are three terraces, culminating in a bell-shaped stupa. These stupas originally contained ashes of Buddhistic disciples.

The tone of the vast pile is the grey of volcanic stone but it is brightened by an infinity of carving and sculpture. The sustaining walls of the first gallery, on upward, are covered with bas-relief depicting episodes in the life of the Buddha. The corners and angles are decorated with gargoyles and finely sculptured birds, flowers, animals, and a similar scheme of decoration and embellishment was applied to the cornices.

The summit is a central dagoba containing an unfinished statue of Buddha. To give an idea of size, difficult to convey in description, statistics become valuable. The temple measures five hundred and thirty-one feet on each of the four bases; stairways connect the galleries inside.

I later looked back at it against the evening sky, and saw its great architectural precision, worked out so many hundreds of years ago, shown in its perfectly rounded contour. The whole work is so harmonious that, though it must have taken several generations to construct, one would almost believe that it was the work of one man. In any event, there can be no doubt that the original architectural plan was scrupulously followed. Originally, it is evident that there were seventy-two dagobas surmounting the temple, each containing a full-size statue of Buddha, the face turned up toward the core of the shrine. On top was the fifty-foot spired dagoba containing a very large image of Buddha.

The bas-reliefs of Buddha's life attracted my interest. The faces are distinctly Hindu in cast, while certain ships I noticed were of ancient Egyptian design. There must be over two thousand individual pictures and episodes! Some represented the pre-birth life of Buddha, others his descent to earth to teach, and others the five disciples who wandered with him during the early years.

Another single one depicted his enlightenment, when he

arose and went forth to teach the world what he had learned. In another panel, the Buddha was seated under the sacred fig tree; in still another he was shown hurling back armies of demons who attacked him. The last series showed the death and funeral preparations of the great teacher.

The decay of the Barabudur from its early glory must have begun when the last middle Java kingdom, the kingdom of Mataram, fell and when the hordes of Islam began to arrive. This was probably during the Ninth Century. The vast temple was then deserted, under pressure, by its last monks and priests, and for years it lay a waste, overgrown jungle. No word of it appears in history until a certain Mas Dana rebelled against the Sultan of Solo. He retreated to the Mountain Barabudur, and soon after excavations and exploration trips were begun.

The first white man visited the ruins in 1814, but the work of recovery and reconstruction was placed on a scientific basis by Sir Stamford Raffles. From that time until recently the work has gone on steadily, gradually bringing back into the light of day one of the greatest works that mankind has ever erected in adoration. Earth and vegetation had injured it; time and lack of care had nicked it badly. Much credit is due the Dutch East Indies Government for its work there between 1905 and 1911, under the leadership of Mr. T. van Erp and others.

The greatest architectural works of mankind have always stood forth because of their judicious combination of size and symmetry. So does the Barabudur. It is a spectacle of exciting quality as a whole, and in the contemplation of its component parts becomes a procession of ecstatic moments. I am not the first to marvel that men did so much without mechanical assistance. The Maya ruins of Yucatan present the same problem of how men that we are prone to regard as primitive so well understood the principles of every art and science necessary to the construction of stupendously beautiful edifices. The answer may lie simply in that they were not concerned with two of the curses laid upon us by modernity: lack of time and space. Of both they had plenty. Land was cheap and in most cases needed only the taking; of time there was an infinity, for faith led them on. I doubt if a railroad station could ever achieve permanent grandeur for that very reason.

FROM Magelang I went back to Djocja, unable to forget what I had seen: a sight that had wiped out previous memories of the marvels that man has worked, at long intervals, with the stone of the earth. A few miles southeast of

Djocja is found Kotah Gedeh, which means Large City. For the hundred years of the Sixteenth Century this was the residential seat of the old empire of Mataram. Here rest the remains of one of the old rulers, Astana Senapati. Astana is an ancient word for Sultan. The ancestors of this worthy surround him. Ruins encircle the present modern and exceedingly active community.

Kotah Gedeh today is the centre of the ancient Java art industries of silver and copper work, leather and tortoise shell. Here, in large sheds, hundreds of skilled artisans labour to turn out exquisitely worked ornaments and practical articles: jewelry to be sold to the women of Java; headgears to be worn by the priests and officials of the country; trinkets to be sold to tourists and the wives of resident foreigners.

Directly south of Kotah Gedeh is Imagiri, sacred as the burial place of the Sultans of Djocja and Solo.

From Djocja I journeyed on over the excellent motor roads built by the Dutch administrations over the spine of the island, through Klaten to Surakarta, more colloquially known as Solo. Here, in a *kraton* greater by far than that of the Sultan of Djocjakarta, reigns the Pinnacle of All Possible Perfections—the man whose titles with a lack of reticence really admirable in this day of press-agentry, proclaim him to be the very essence of all things, the concentrate of virtues both here and hereafter, and mayhap before, the figure because of whom the very winds veer out of the way. This is the Susuhunan of Solo, the Sultan. His predecessors ruled the greater part of Java; it was his forebear who, for reasons unknown, willed his empire to the Dutch. By definition of his followers, if by nothing else, he is the greatest man on earth; and the badge of his personal service represents the earth transfixed by a spike.

He lives within the walls of a *kraton* which shelters fif-

teen thousand people besides himself, much as enumerated
in the case of the Sultan of Djocja, between whom and this
chap the greatest rivalry exists. But since both are forbidden
by custom and the kindly eye of the Dutch East Indies Government, to leave their own peculiar territories, they go on
disliking one another, probably because of their jealousy.

It will be noticed that I have referred to both Djocjakarta and Surakarta by shortened forms. This is the custom
there, for Javans, as well as tabloid newspapers, sometimes
find brevity serviceable.

The Sultan of Solo has a multitude of titles, to wit:

Hingkang, Sinuhun, Kankpaku, Bumono, Senapati, In-
jaloge, Rachman, Sajidin (Head of the Religion), Panotogomo (Regulator of Religion), Paku Buwono (Axis of the
Universe), Senapati Ingalaga (Commander-in-Chief), Ngab
Durrahman (Servant of the Merciful Allah).

His wife, no less imposing, is called:

Ratu, Kantjana, Wungu (Purple-gold), Mas (Gold),
Bendara (Mistress), Sepuh (The Old), Anem (The Young),
Ageng (The Great), and Maduretna, which is the Sanskrit
name for "honey and jewel."

The salary of this potentate is not negligible. He receives
from his own treasury four million guilders a year, roughly
a million and a half dollars; besides which he is subsidized
by the Dutch East Indies administration at the rate of
seventy thousand guilders a year. In addition to holding all
the titles listed above, he is also a Knight Commander of the
Lion of the Netherlands, Chief Officer of the Order of Orange Nassau, Grand Knight of the Cross of the French Colonial Order of Cambodia, Knight of the Grand Order of the
Crown of Siam, Grand Officer of the Order of Leopold of
Belgium, a Major-General in the Dutch Army and an Ad-
miral in the Navy.

As a matter of fact, he is a very pleasant fellow, who is

greatly beloved by his subjects, even after they have come in contact with him. Neither too much nor too little dignity sits upon his bronze shoulders.

I went the first day to the *kraton* to locate a man who expected me. This was Raden Mas Ng'Sudjonopuro, an adviser to the Sultan. We met in his suite of rooms in the palace.

We exchanged the usual greetings, and I found him genial and at the same time thoughtful, a habit grown upon him from giving advice to royal people for a living. He was a high-caste, of course, and a man, I realized, of very considerable intelligence. His stature was not great; his hair was dark, almost shiny black; and his keen dark eyes looked out watchfully from a somewhat flat Hindu face, smooth and unwrinkled for a man of the forty-odd years I judged him to possess. He smiled at the opportunity to be of service to me, for I was bent on visiting some of the Sultanic sugar plantations in the neighbourhood. Through this gentleman I later met two of the agreeable nephews of the Sultan of Solo: Raden Mas Hario Atmodjo and Raden Mas Ngabehi Atmosapootro.

At a later time I was the guest of Raden Mas Ng'Sudjonopuro for two days within the *kraton* on the second evening of which I ate a meal that in itself was distinctly an event. You must know that throughout Java one of the Javanese culinary institutions has become standard in all hotels, so that I was familiar beforehand with the *rys tafel*, or rice table, served in all Javanese homes. But this one stands out in my mind because of its elaborateness.

We sat down to it on mats, and servants waited upon us with a great noiseless scurrying. We sat on the floor, and helped ourselves from a dish of well-cooked rice offered me by the head boy. Behind him paraded no less than twenty-two more boys, each of whom offered us a different edible.

From these I stacked upon my plates the following ingredients:

Fricadels, vegetable curry, boiled and fried chicken, desiccated and fried eggs, old duck eggs, stewed beef, fried banana, shredded cocoanut, flaked cocoanut, cucumber, desiccated beef, gurami fish, codfish, little red fish, macassars, with an evil smell, pickled bamboo, chopped livers and chillies, and last a sort of fish hash called *trassi,* which gave forth an unspeakable odour.

Having heaped these up in a great bowl, I mixed them up as custom dictates, and began eating. We ate valiantly, bothering not to maintain the amenities of polite table conversation. Our host, Raden Mas Ng'Sudjonopuro, gobbled his up at once, or almost at once at any rate, so that he might have more, since *adat* forbids a host to eat when his guests have finished. He need not have concerned himself on that score. We ate with great caution and slowness. A meal of that sort is something that should be gone through, like drunkenness or a game of bridge with three old-lady card fiends, just once for the right to say that one has done it. It is astonishing how different things can taste. Codfish is a familiar taste, but it will surprise the codfish devotee when eaten simultaneously with fried banana. Vegetable curry is a respectable dish, but its respectability vanishes completely when it is overwhelmed by the indefinable savour of duck eggs of unguessable antiquity. Eating away at the bowl of mixed foods is like nothing else on earth. The most amazing things are unearthed: a dried egg nestles under a slab of stewed beef; the tip of a cucumber peeps out from beneath a layer of fish hash with a penetrating effluvium. This fish hash was beyond my powers of assimilation. So I ate away, turning over the sod, as it were, in search of things I could eat. Like the sediment in cloudy water, the fish hash sank to the bottom of the bowl. Beside me was an Englishman, a gentleman of enthusiasm. I heard him, but could not look. He did not, as I once shot a sidelong glance at his bowl, forego anything. Fish hash and all were sacrificed to his enthusiasm. Which shows what the bulldog determination of the English race can bring a man to.

What it actually did bring him to was the hospital, where I went to see him two days later. He lay upon his cot a pale wraith. He had indigestion in the most acute form, complicated by the consequence of a general assault upon his digestive faculties. He said with a ghastly smile that he thought the climate did not agree with him.

To those who doubt the hopeless veracity of this instructive incident, I recommend a *rys tafel*. It convinces, if nothing else. ·

AMONG his multifarious activities, the Sultan of Solo operates many sugar mills. These are managed by members of the well-known Dézéntjés family, who are connected by marriage with the royal Surakarta family. On frequent occasions I was the guest of one or another of the hospitable Dézéntjés at the sugar mills. Through the Dr. Dézéntjés branch in and near Solo I was able, more than once, to be introduced into the immediate family circles of prominent Javanese of the neighbourhood, even attaining a footing of friendship with the royal family itself rarely accorded a foreigner.

In the same town of Solo lives a fat man who is also a ruler of some influence and wealth, being owner of sugar estates and mills, fibre and coffee estates and a hotel—the Karang Pandan on the slopes of Mt. Lawu. He is the Prang-Wudono and his sovereignty came about in the following manner:

The Sultan of Solo is, by himself and all Surakartans worthy of the name, considered the only monarch by heredity and legitimacy over the ancient Hindu kingdom of Mataram and its descendants. I have mentioned this old nation several times before; it occupied central Java about two hundred years ago. About that time a rebellious prince precipitated a civil war which resulted in the division of the Mataram empire into the two principalities of Djocja and Solo. The Dutch East India Company supported the rebel leader who had installed himself in power of Djocja, since it was the astute motto of the company to "divide and rule." Thus both principalities were maintained, the new Dutch-supported Sultan of Djocja adopting the name of Mataram, the Sultans of which were called Paku Buwona. Thus he became heir by force to the mystic atmosphere which surrounded the Hindu rulers of former times. To this day, though the Sultan of Djocja and his subjects are Mahometans, the royal crest retains a Buddhistic ornament.

But Allah in his wisdom, and possible alliance with the Dutch East India Company, ordained a further division. Only one hundred years ago a member of the Solo ruling house rebelled against his chief. This man was named Mas-Said, and his revolution was successful. The Dutch assisted the division in order to facilitate their own domination of the island, so that a new kingdom, composed of a slice of Sura-karta, found a place on the map. This kingdom is called Mangkunegoro, which means: "He Who Carries the World in His Lap." It includes a third of the territory and popu-lation of the Solo which existed before the secession. But the prince did not move away from Solo; he resides there now. The tradition of his house demands that until the prince is forty he shall be known as the Prang-Wudono, and after forty as Mangkunegoro. He and the Sultan of Solo are independent monarchs and are theoretically equals, but the Sultan of Solo addresses his rival in low Javanese; which the Prang-Wudono does not resent, for he replies in high Javanese, as from inferior to superior. Matters are further complicated by the fact that the Prang-Wudono is married to the younger sister of the Sultana of Solo. Thus they live in harmony, and everybody is more or less satisfied. The grandiloquence of the titles of all three monarchs is not ham-pered by their individual claims to be the pivots, axes, or what not, of the universe. It may be that the universe has not been informed.

Another curious matter in Solo is the tribe of Kalangs, who serve as foresters to the Sultan. They are a people who until recent years wore their hair long, contrary to island custom, and their skin is a darker brown by several shades than the general run of Malays in Java.[1] I asked about them and was told the following legend of their origin:

[1] In Raffles' book *History of Java*, he tells that a certain Baka, min-ister of Kuda Lulean, the sovereign of Mendang Kauwelan, and his son-in-law Bandung Pracusa (descendant of Karang Kalang, the last ruler of Brambanan) were the tribe-fathers of the Kalangs, which latter were said to be the true autochthones of Java. While the Javanese chroniclers, in their curious methods of recording, made no mention of any empire of

An ancient prince, Ratu Baka, attempted to attack the virginity of his beautiful young daughter, Dewi Retna Tjendila. She repulsed him; he banished her to the forest, where she occupied herself in weaving. A certain young prince chanced to see her, and was at once captivated. He asked her father for her hand, and the old gentleman agreed, provided the young prince could build a temple (Tjandi Sewu) overnight. The young lover laboured with diligence, and had but ten statues to place on the temple when the sound of girls hulling rice warned him that dawn was breaking. He had, alas, failed. He went to his mother, an *endang* (I have been unable to learn the translation of this word, though it seems to mean "queen" or "queen mother") and told her that he would now take the girl by force, temple or no temple. The *endang* retaliated by changing her son into a brown dog. This was taking an advantage. But she could not have foreseen that the metamorphosis, so astonishing to the young prince, did not change his feelings a single bit. In the shape of a dog, accordingly, he went to the mid-forest hut of the lonely princess and circled it round and round. It so happened that the princess had lost a spool, and in her anxiety to recover it she vowed to marry the person who returned it to her. The chivalrous dog found it and brought it to her in his mouth. The princess kept her vow and shortly after, ashamed of her intercourse with an animal, she retired even deeper into the forest, where she bore her canine husband a son: the tribe father of the present-day Kalangs. In corroboration of this venerable legend, a Javanese showed me a grave purporting to be the burial place of that very son of woman and dog in the *dessah* Praguman in

Kalang, it is to Chinese sources that the history of the existence of Kalangs is owed. It is the author's belief, however, that the Kalangs could not have been the autochthones of Java because of their appearance; particularly their absence of curly hair.

Semarang, when I was there.   Nevertheless, the amazing
legend of the Kalangs and dogs cannot be dismissed, though
in all probability modern skepticism will cause the legend
just told to be rejected on the grounds of incompatibility with
scientific knowledge!

Leaving Solo, with its pivots of the universe and pleasant
typically Javanese life, I went direct to Surabaja by train.   I
should say that there are many hundreds of miles of railroad
in Java, all electrified.   Surabaja is the second largest city of
Java, and is cut in two by the Kali Mas, the Golden river.
The name of the city itself is derived from two words: *Sura*
meaning "danger" and "brave" and *baja* being an old Malay
word signifying crocodile, while crocodile tails decorate the
official crest of the city.

Surabaja is a great port, included on the ocean itineraries
of the sea lanes to Australia, Batavia, Singapore, Borneo and
Sumatra, among other places.   Sugar pours in here for trans-
shipment, as does batik, coffee, tobacco, rice, rubber and other
produce.

An event which befell me here was a Chinese dinner.   It
is not my fault if food plays such an important part in this
chronicle: to many food is the focal point of interest in a
strange land.   This dinner did not compare either in prodi-
gality or complexity, with the *rys tafel*, but its composition
was typical and unusual, from our angle.   It was given by
the Captain Chinaman, the head man, so to speak, in the
Surabaja *kamp*.   There is such a man in every Chinese *kamp*
in Java.   He was a wealthy man, with much of his riches derived from profitable gambling in sugar and coffee.   There
were four of us as guests: a Dutchman, myself and two ladies.
The meal began with shark fin soup, which was followed by
hors d'oevres, some *kwie hoa tjie*, an indefinable and un-

translatable conglomeration of small spices and oddments. The entrée was a small portion of *oe mo thung,* which is a dream of a stew, if there be such a thing as dreaming of stew. Its foundation was pork, and the Chinese excel all other peoples of the earth in the variegated and loving preparation of this meat. We are carpenters in the matter compared with them. This outstanding culinary triumph was succeeded, for the ladies, by some *ang sio hie* and *kepiting tja,* which is crabs *à la Chinoise.* This was all merely leading up to the *pièce de résistance,* which was a combination of *Bahmi* and *souw bah.* The first is in aspect like spaghetti, and is similarly made; the second is chopped pork generously surrounded by a multitude of delicate spices: another example of Chinese superiority in the field of pork. The dessert, besides Canton ginger *au jus,* was an egg one hundred years old. Of this we will not speak. Throughout the meal our host scratched his stomach and belched repeatedly to demonstrate his enjoyment.

The consequences of a Chinese meal are by no means as serious as that of the *rys tafel;* in the course of years of *rys tafel* eating I became experienced, and know how to conduct myself, but the Chinese dinner demands no such training. It is a more delicate and subtle affair, since the Chinese backed up by thousands of years of profound philosophy have almost turned eating into a purely intellectual pleasure. They eat heartily, but they have a way of doing it. Chop Suey, and its companions, do not enter into it, since they are inventions of the West.

Not only in food are the Chinese a significant factor in Javanese, and Dutch East Indian, life. There is not a branch of the industrial, commercial and agricultural activities in which they are not heavily and energetically engaged. Every large community has its Chinese *kamp*—with all appurtenances, such as cemeteries and so forth. A considerable bit of the volatile capital of Java and the rest of the islands passes through their hands: They are bankers, speculators in all products, ship-owners, land-owners, farmers, storekeepers, owners of sugar mills, plantations of every description, and lastly a tremendous force in the very life of the people of Java.

They are Confucians, of course, which is in itself, in my private opinion and in that of many Oriental students, the finest of all Eastern beliefs.

In the light of the general Confucius doctrine emphasizing knowledge and government of self, education and supreme virtue, we may see why the Chinese have turned out as they are: impenetrable, secret, ancestor-worshipping people. Dangerous in the sense that they are not easy to understand; fatalistic in the assurance the sometimes unsuccessful pursuit of virtue gives them. The importance of the Chinese element, dominated by the oldest philosophy in the "modern" world, in the Dutch East Indies, or anywhere in the East, must not be underestimated. The situation bears there an aspect altogether different from the "Yellow Peril" of America. It would be too much to say that eventual supremacy in the East lies with the Chinese: the revivification of Chinese nationality is in too embryonic a state to venture so daring a pronouncement. It must, in fine, always be remembered that the presence of multitudes of Chinese complicates a far from simple task.

In all forms of activity productive of financial profit the Chinese is a worthy rival of the Westerner. For his mind is attuned with greater delicacy to the mechanism of other Eastern minds. The history of Western influence in the east shows a picture of domination by force. For this reason the Dutch East Indies administration deserves the highest commendation: it has governed with some attempt at understanding those under its domination set up by the sword. It has been not only a task of governing wisely, but governing wisely from the viewpoint of him who is governed. Whether or not the native mind is entirely satisfied with the state of affairs is a question that I may not touch upon. Peace has come to them, if they really want it in preference to the constant precariousness of warfare. An increased measure of prosperity likewise is theirs, visible in greater and steadier markets for agricultural and industrial products. Their religions have not to any extent been tampered with by the Government, which does not, as I pointed out before, encourage mission work, though it places no obstacles in its path. Education is a Government task, executed through administration schools.

The most familiar argument against missionaries in such places the world over is: Why butt in? why can't we leave them alone? But critics of that attitude say this: If we give them the benefits of our modern civilization (medicine, science, labour-saving devices, improved business methods, et cetera) why withhold the benefits of Christianity? Likewise, if the advent of the white man brings with it intoxicating liquors (as if they did not exist before, though not in such large quantities), venereal diseases, the degradation of native women, do we not owe it to them to make it up by conferring on them the wisdom of a higher spiritual existence?

This may well be a sound argument, especially in those parts of the world where the grade of civilization is much lower than our own. But in Java, Bali and many other densely populated regions of the East, it is not the best argument. The level of civilization there is not, in a broad way, much lower than our own. The minds of these people are as subtle, their modes of reasoning as refined, as our own; and in many things their tone is higher. Their religions are for the most part satisfactory to them, and on practically the same plane as Christianity. Confucianism, Buddhism, Mahometanism and Christianity have the same roots. This alone is a tremendous obstacle to missionarying by Christians. But another and more formidable one lies in the path of those who would convert more primitive peoples: Dyaks of Borneo, Bataks of Sumatra, Toradjas of Celebes, and so on. The beliefs of these people are founded on animism, and all other religions are fundamentally spiritual. There is a great gulf between these beliefs, not easily spanned by learning formulæ by heart.

There are many additional moral aspects to the eternal question as to what right one race has to dominate another. Probably no race has such a right. The fact remains, however, that such things frequently come to pass. So let us consider rather the facts of the matter; the moral questions will, anyway, have to be settled by later historians.

The consideration of hard facts brings to mind one that the Dutch cannot avoid taking seriously. This is the place and eventual destiny, in the Far East, of the Eurasian. Brusquely speaking, Eurasians are half-castes: a mixture of white and Asiatic blood.

The law of the Dutch East Indies declares that the son or daughter of a mixed marriage shall be considered white. The result of this is the rapid growth of a large class of people who are looked down on by the whites and by natives, and who in turn act like whites and despise the natives.

The reason the Eurasian is a more acute problem in Dutch East Indian possessions than in the territories dominated by the British, for example, lies in that very law cited above. Officially the Dutch Government recognizes the half-blood, and gives them the political status of Europeans. He may, if he wishes, move in white society, and often does.

But the British in Malacca and British India, et cetera, make no such concessions. A half-caste is a half-caste and is therefore grouped with the natives. British soldiers have not been permitted to have native women in their barracks. Dutch soldiers have.

It is a generally established fact that Eurasians do not make good citizens. There are of course a great many exceptions, but we are speaking here sociologically. Their breasts are filled with resentment against both white and native; it is a biological fact that mixed marriages do not produce children of ultimate worth. Though often extremely handsome, their temperaments are volatile and vengeful. The women are beautiful, fascinating—and dangerous. But the class is growing, and might in a few years, be a problem of first gravity for the Dutch Government.

I have spoken before of native poisons, and in that connection, of *guna guna*—magic. This is a sinister side of native and Eurasian superstition, and its horror is thinly veiled. This sounds like novelistic spell-binding, but the threat of *guna guna* is active and alive today. Poisons are sold openly in village markets, and the entire practice of *guna guna* is, as I see it, the power of suggestion combined with a profound knowledge of drug and herb properties.

Guna guna has many uses, chief among which is that of love philtres. Eurasian women resort to these means to capture or regain lovers. They visit a *dukon*, magician, and magic spells are woven over a lock of the beloved's hair. Debilitating drugs are concocted for use on the beloved, making him weak, physically and morally, and thus open to mental and imaginative suggestion.

These actually do work, and produce of course not love, but simple animal passion. But *guna guna* goes much further than this. Ground glass, tiger's whiskers, shredded bamboo fibre, and similar devices are used to cause slow agonizing

death, puncturing the internal organs. Such is the skill in
the use of these delightful weapons that they can be administered unnoticed, and may be timed to take just so long to
produce the desired effect.

One of the poisons used is that coming from a sort of sea
cow found off the island of Billiton. This animal, hunted
with a harpoon, makes a noise like a human wail, and in
former times was taken by seamen to be the mermaid. This
animal is said to be desirable because of the contents of its
glands—called by the natives *ajer mata dujong*—to which
wonderful magic powers are attributed. On the native markets this fluid sells for two-and-a-half guilders a drop.
Dukons will tell you that that one lone drop is sufficient to
win the love of the most obstinate maiden or hard-hearted
man.

Superstition? Perhaps, but personal observation made
me think differently. For example, in Batavia I lived in the
Hotel des Indes right next door to a young German-Ameri-
can in the employ of a large American film company. We
were good friends and he introduced me, one evening, to a
beautiful Eurasian woman. He was living with her and she
had his devotion. I once took the liberty of warning him,
but I do not entirely blame him for ignoring my words. The
veranda walls in Javanese hotels are very thin, and since his
rooms were right next to mine, I could not avoid overhear-
ing one afternoon what the girl said:

"I tell you, S—— if you ever marry that girl in your
country you will not see the end of it."

I did not catch his murmur in reply.

Her voice continued, excited, smoothly high-pitched: "I
ask you not to bring her here to marry her. Do you hear?"
The voice climbed to a crescendo. I heard then his soothing
tones, without being able to distinguish words.

But he paid no heed to that warning either. He cabled

his fiancée in Germany to meet him in Medan in Sumatra, where they would marry. But in the two months that next elapsed, he changed from a vital, if high-strung young man into a worried, haggard shadow. The Eurasian had him undoubtedly in her power.

I had meanwhile gone to Malacca, but since I had promised to be his best man at the wedding in Medan, I took ship and met him there with his pretty fiancée from a small city in northern Germany. She was happy to be with him after a long separation—supremely glad. They were married in the American consulate and I saw them off on a steamer for Singapore. Their honeymoon was to be a tour of the Orient.

The next I knew was a cable in Batavia, advising that the young couple were both dead. She had taken poison and he had committed suicide likewise. It is impossible to be sure, but I am reasonably convinced that the Eurasian girl had had recourse to *guna guna,* and had given him something before his departure that would take that much time to work. This may sound fantastic, but let me cite another example: that of the English doctor who employed a Eurasian housekeeper with whom he had been on the most intimate terms. When he decided to return to England she wished to go with him, but he refused, promising to come back. But she was not to be fooled and warned him that if he left without her he would not live beyond the Suez Canal. We later learned that he died while his ship was passing through the Suez. Possibly a tiger hair or ground glass.

FROM Surabaja I made a side trip south to Tosari, which is not far, an hour-and-a-half in a car. The place is situated at an elevation of 5,400 feet above sea level, and is a cool health resort for Surabajans. This village, like many

others in the neighbourhood, is inhabited by the Wong Tengger—people of the Highlands, or Tengger Mountains.
Most of the villages are situated between 5,100 and 6,300
feet above sea level, and the people are Hindu-Javanese.
They retreated here during the Fifteenth Century upon the
onslaught of Mahometanism, and now they keep apart from
other Malay peoples, marry among themselves and maintain
the religion of Brahma, Vishnu and Siva—very similar to
the Balinese in this respect.

In the books of the Hindu Philosophy, particularly in
this case of Mahabharata, marriage and ancestor worship are
urgently recommended. Thus among the Tengger people,
service to the ancestors is divided into three parts: honour of
Dewas, the heaven gods; of *Kalas*, bad spirits, and *Pitaras*,
ancestors pure and simple. Here becomes noticeable the
close relationship in religious matters between the Tenggerese and the Balinese. The Tengger family houses and
the walled family compounds of Bali greatly resemble one
another, while the Balinese also have their house temples.
To correspond with these the Tenggerese have attic-like
places in their houses for offerings.

While it is true of all Java, it is especially true in this
part of the island, that no man may take an important step in
his life without a celebration, called *slamatan*. These *slamatans* are the inevitable accompaniment to marriage, birth,
moon eclipse, a girl's first haircut, the seventh month of
pregnancy, and so on. A new business proposition causes a
buffalo head to be buried in front of the house. I may mention here that throughout all the islands, among Mahometans and Hindus, pregnancy is accorded the highest respect
and attention, since children are of the first value. The most
important *slamatans* of this type take place during the seventh month of pregancy, considered a critical period. After-
ward, the father must always attend the actual delivery, after

which confinement lasts fourteen days. The woman lies face down and the mid-wife walks on her back, to ease the flow of blood. Then the mother is led to the bath for cleansing, and is given the diluted juice of the tamarind fruit to drink.

In Ngadiwono I attended one of these *slamatans*, a *slamat rambut*, the festival for the first haircut of small girls. There was a great deal of eating, offerings to the gods, and a celebration for the girls who were reaching maturity.

Also in the Tengger it was my fortune—or misfortune—to be present at the longest wedding I ever attended in my life, purely in the capacity of spectator. There is probably nothing in the world so complicated and serious as a wedding of a young man and woman of the Tengger people. This ceremony, precisely typical of all its kind, lasted something like four hours and included every conceivable form of symbolism known to this people. But four hours is a little long, even to get married.

Another time, in the earlier days of my East Indies career, coming by car from Surabaja to Tosari, I had an experience which may well serve as a warning to other travellers in this land. I sat alone in the back of the touring-car, which was driven by my own chauffeur. I had been warned not to continue the journey through the noon and hottest period, from twelve to two. We stopped at a *dessah* for luncheon, and I forgot the warning sufficiently to order the trip to continue at once. It is the custom throughout the entire island for a siesta to follow the noon meal. The fact he was driving did not deter my driver.

We were following a winding road into the Tengger mountains. On one side of us was the mountain side, on the other, steep slopes down to a creek bed filled with sharp rocks. As we proceeded I noticed that the car crept close to the edge.

Then it swerved away—and then back again. I shouted; no answer. He's asleep! it dawned on me. I jumped forward, the car swerved again even closer to the edge. This time we are over! I exclaimed to myself just as I grabbed the wheel in time. With one free hand, I belaboured my slumbering monitor. He awoke with a start to feel my clenched fist falling on his shoulders. He stopped the car in order to listen meekly to the tirade I launched against him. I threatened him with all kinds of blood-curdling disasters should he doze again. But I never tempted the sleeping proclivities of Javan drivers again. From twelve to two I rested, thereafter.

From Tosari I went on to the Bromo volcano, which is one of the highest peaks of the Tengger and also a very active fellow on its own account. With a group we left Tosari at four in the morning. At that elevation above sea level the air was sharply cool. We mounted small mountain ponies and filed off in the darkness on a steep path, unaware of the steep cliffs on our off sides, but able to see, in clusters, the lights of awakening villages below. For three hours, by the end of which time it was quite light, we rode without stopping, over a terrain increasingly steep, winding through the thick forest which gave forth a sharp, moist smell. At length quite suddenly, the forest ended.

We came upon a strange, stirring sight: a sea of greyish-black sand, stretching away from us without a break. This point is the Mungga pas, a cleft, as it were. The sinister sand was as if an ocean had been frozen at night. Far out on this dark sea there projected, like an island of the dead, the Batok crater, now inactive. Batok means "top of coco-nut," and the crater resembles one closely. Behind that is another and larger island, the Bromo, derived from Brahma and revered as a holy mountain. The colour of this was in various tones of grey from the lava, and from its mouth belched yellow vicious fumes.

Even farther away, high in the distance, reared the Smeru crater and to one side was the grey mass of Wido-daren. We descended to the grey sand sea, and traversed it gingerly to the smoking cone. Steps had been cut on the side of the cone to facilitate ascent; we left the ponies at the bottom and climbed labouriously up. Once there, we threw ourselves face down on the edge to peer down upon the awful sight of the boiling pit. Great rocks rose slowly and with horrible majesty into the air, whirling, only to fall back and disappear in the churning lava below. Yellow fumes billowed up and filled the air with a reek of sulphur. On our way we had passed the bleached skeletons of wild horses, on which wild dogs prey. Above the sand sea wheeled carrion birds with their beady eyes.

Sitting on the cone lip of the volcano, the guide told me the legend of the Bromo, which accounts also for the origin of the Tengger people—to their satisfaction.

A certain man and his wife had set up on the lower slopes of the mountains, but were unhappy because they had no children. They moved up on the outer slope of the Bromo, and one day when the father had fallen asleep, the spirit of the Bromo appeared to him and told him that he might have children, if he would consent to sacrifice them to the crater afterwards. The father agreed, and forthwith his wife delivered unto him twenty-five children. When the time came for the sacrifice, the youngest son bravely volunteered to throw himself into the crater to save the rest, provided that the day be commemorated every year by the commencement of ploughing and the making of offerings. So the youngest son hurled himself into the boiling pit, and the Bromo sent up a thunderous burst of flame and lava in acceptance of the compromise.

So it is that on the first day of the month *Kesodo*, anniversary of the boy's self-sacrifice, a pilgrimage to Bromo takes place. Thousands throw offerings into the crater in thankfulness for the volcano's affability in permitting the first Orang Tengger to live in peace and prosperity.

The sand sea is a weird depressing spectacle, with the two islands rising abruptly from it to pour forth lava and fumes. The sand trembles with the suppressed force of the underworld boiling, while above, in contrasting serenity, shimmers the light blue sky. Its perfection marred at times only by tiny white clouds that scurry across its vast surface and the black silhouetted shapes of alert carrion birds.

Fʀᴏᴍ Surabaja it is really worth while to make the trip
along the coast up to Grissee, the name of which derives
from *gressik*, the Malay word for dry land. It is reached,
however, by passing through a horribly swampy region full

of rhizophores, giant ferns. At the very outskirts of Grissee, the landscape changes and becomes dry. Here is a large cemetery, Gapura-Wekatan, in the ancient Hindu style dating from the Fourteenth Century, wherein is the grave of the Islam apostle, Maulana Malik Ibrahim, dated 1490 A.D. Southeast of the town is a hill with a large mosque containing the grave of the holy *raden* Paku Susuhunan Giri, and even having his sacred kris. This man was a pioneer of the Islamic faith and taught his beliefs around the year 1519. Ruins of his *kraton* may still be seen on the Giri hill here. Also among the ruins of former times are some old buildings of the V.O.C. East India Company.

Grissee itself is now a port, it's people specializing in fishing, but also industrially active in copper and brass work, coffee growing and batik.

Batik is probably one of the most intriguing industries that any Eastern land has to offer. It is less known than other industrial products, or artistic works, for it is both. It has been imitated by every Western country in designs and materials, and even methods, yet little is actually known about it.

Batik is a Malay word for the hand-decorated textiles made by a resistance process using wax as the mainstay. The term first appears historically in various writings by East Indian officials as early as 1656. When the English occupied Java, imitations of batiks were sent there. This caused a European rivalry between the English and the Dutch, which eventually moved the Javanese manufacturers to inaugurate the Tjappen system in 1850, a system which remains in force to this time.

The word batik itself (it is also called *ambatik*) is not pure Javanese, but is related to almost all the other Malay-Polynesian tongues. The word, in various forms, is found in Borneo, Celebes, Philippines and the Fijis. Its basic meaning is related to tattooing, but in Java it has come to mean the dyeing of white cotton in several colours. Hence, wax painting or drawing. The art came to Java in the Thirteenth Century with Hindu colonists. But the advent of Mahometans later gave the industry a strong boost because of their demand for brighter colours. The chief batik-making centres are now in and around Tulung-Agung, Kedong, Bangil, Grissee, Pekalongan, Djocja and Solo.

There are three processes in batik-making: preparing the cloth; designing the pattern; and dyeing and finishing the decorated cloth. The cloth is first thoroughly rinsed in water, boiled in a solution of rice, starch and water, after which it is dried and pounded with a mallet. Then it is starched, and the design is applied with a small copper instrument on both sides. All of the cloth not to be dyed blue is covered with wax, and the cloth is immersed in blue dye. When this has dried, the blue parts are covered with wax and a similar procedure is followed for other colours, until at last the design is completed. Pure bees-wax is used because of its resistance to cracking and high temperatures.

When the design is completed, the cloth is dipped in a mixture of sugar-whiting and alum to give it a high finish. The wax comes off, floats to the top and is collected for repeated use.

The dyes used are all native cultures, such as indigo, the *kasumba* giving red-rose dye, the *tjangkudu* red and brown, the *tjempedak-nangka* yellow, the *manggusta* or *manggistan* producing black, the *soga* giving an ochre-yellow and red-brown, and the *sari-kuning* a strong yellow colour. But artificial dyes have of late been coming into use, cutting in on the native dye cultures to a considerable extent.

There are many traditional designs, showing in the main Javanese and Chinese influences. Designs were handed down from generation to generation, and through many different classes of designs easily distinguishable motives run clearly. Naturally different designs have different uses and purposes: a special black and white (the Parang Rusak) for the Sultan of Solo, some for the priesthood, others again for the common man and woman.

Batik serves as the principal clothing material in Java and as a matter of fact in the entire archipelago. There are many different garments of batik used, including the *sarong, slendang*, head-pieces and loin-cloths.

It is batik, perhaps more than any one thing, that gives such brilliant notes of visual colour to Javanese life. Any large gathering becomes at once more dazzling than a flower-bed of a hundred species. Any appearance of sombreness is automatically avoided, and the combination of unrestrained colour and the bright sun make life a more cheerful matter. The high artistic standard of the designs and patterns is esthetically satisfying; it turns the humblest dress into a garment of state. A relief, certainly, from the drabness of Western attire, particularly that of men. In Java it is a disgrace not to be gaily dressed; not that I recommend batik for men's wear in the West!

From Surabaja there is still another excursion that is historically interesting. This is to Modjokerto. The ancient name of this locality was Madjapahit, and it was one of the greatest of the old Hindu empires which flourished all over the island. Refugees from here had an important effect upon Bali. A museum is maintained here for the preservation of the relics of antiquity. One such is a statue of Erlanga, a ruler of Java of the Eleventh Century. He is represented as Vishnu on the mythical bird, Garuda. Though the section around Modjokerto is predominantly Mahometan, many Hindu women leave offerings before this statue of Erlanga in the museum. Just before closing time, the native curator cunningly takes away the offerings! The region abounds in madjapahit trees, which on account of their bitter slime apples gave their name to the old empire.

From Semarang on the coast I started toward Salatiga, stopping on the way to visit a native friend of mine in a very small *dessah*. I came upon him at a crucial time, for his daughter, a girl of six years, was being circumcised.

In Java all men are circumcised, and women likewise. The progeny of the wealthy have it done during the sixth year, the poor during the eighth. My friend here was a considerable land-owner, with rice and sugar fields.

He permitted me to witness the operation. We entered a room of his large house. An old woman was in charge, and the small child lay, stark naked, on a white mat. The father watched gravely. The old woman drew the forepart of the organ forward with her finger and inserted under it a small piece of wood, called *korkuma*. Then, she cut out an infinitesimal piece of skin with a knife, while the child emitted not one sound, nor so much as moved a muscle of her face.

This bit of skin was then placed in a small, elaborately carved box and buried near the house. Obviously this operation has not the hygienic effect achieved by circumcision of men, but it has come to have a more symbolical meaning.

Before reaching Salatiga I passed through Ambarawa where are many coffee and tapioca plantations. But in Ambarawa I also saw a Javanese wedding. It was not nearly

so long as the four-hour ceremony I had attended in the
Tengger mountains for it contented itself with suitable prayers and offerings, and pronouncements by the priest.

But about eleven o'clock at night, the groom awaited his
bride in his house, in the bridal chamber. The bride was in
another room with a woman, called *pangarih*, whose especial
duty it was to cheer the bride at this important time. When
she had succeeded, she led the bride to the groom and left
them together. But precisely one hour after this, a group of
the wedding guests went bursting into the bridal chamber to
dispel the evil spirits jealous of the couple's pleasure, with
flaring torches. I was told that this is a regular custom.

From Ambarawa to Salatiga is a short distance, bringing
one up to an altitude of 5,700 feet. Salatiga is a mountain
resort for the people of Semarang, attractive with its cool
climate and pleasant Hotel Kaliman. A natural pool, the
Kali Tama, is used for swimming. Directly south of Salatiga are many rubber plantations, and beyond is the Merbabu
volcano, from which can be seen the smoking peak of the distant Merapi volcano.

Here in Salatiga I learned something about the national
sport of cricket-fights. In Java the cricket is a considerably
larger animal than his American relative, some of them there
growing two to three inches in length. It has been discovered
that crickets congregate thickly under big shady trees, or near
ancient Moslem graves; therefore the cricket "manager"
goes forth at dusk equipped with a small bamboo cake containing a decoy cricket. He tiptoes away to return in the
early grey morning, where he is sure to find a host of crickets
surrounding the decoy cage. By the exercise of combined
agility and speed he captures at least one, and carries him tri-
umphantly back to begin training.

The education is conducted along perhaps brutal lines.
But they are effective. First of all the cricket, a beast inor-

dinately and naturally fond of personal freedom, is placed in a thickly woven bamboo cage. He tries to batter or gnaw his way out. At the moment the collapse seems imminent, he is withdrawn from the cage and dropped into a basin of water. Crickets cannot swim, so that after a very few moments of heroic struggle, he must again be saved on the brink of oblivion. The owner massages him very gently and then, by means of a coarse hair attached to one of the cricket's hind legs, suspends him in mid-air. This revives the little animal, and lo, he behaves in a subdued manner.

Then in order to kindle the fires of ferocity, he is fed on rice and red pepper, and is tickled with a brush until he flies at it in a rage. When he does this at the mere sight of the brush, he is considered ready for battle. The manager carries him to the market-place in a little cage, which is placed door to door with another. He who flees first is loser; the victor lives to flee another day.

LEAVING Salatiga, I went directly to Cheribon, an important place of some twenty-five thousand inhabitants with a large Chinese *kamp* as usual, and sugar mills. But it is also important as a place of religious pilgrimage. Near

it, just at its outskirts, is the ancient palace (Astana)
of the Sunan of Gunung Djati (Djati=teak-wood). It is
revered by almost all Javans because it is the burial place of
the Sultan, or Susuhunan (also Sunan) of Gunung Djati,
the very first Javanese ruler to preach the doctrines of Mahomet.

The Astana is a vast space in the shape of an amphithea-
tre, cut out of rock and divided into five courts, each one rising above the other and communicating with the next by
flights of steps. The front is guarded by a row of palisades,
behind which is a five-foot wall, in the centre of which is a
flight of seven steps leading to the first court. This first courtyard is the largest of the five, one hundred feet wide at the
front. Against its walls are arranged nine huge Chinese
vases filled with flowers, while in the open space grow two
large teak trees. Ascent to the second court is made by a
flight of five steps. In here are eight teak trees and only
four vases, for most of the space is taken up by the ruins of
handsome old houses once used to receive visiting royalty.
The third court is smaller and reached by passing up another
short flight of steps through a five-foot wall. On trying to
enter the fourth court, guards stopped me: no unbeliever,
they told me, may go further than the third court. They
looked very determined, so I turned and went away.

But I knew that the fourth court enclosed a magnificent
Moorish temple, or mosque, containing the very body of the
ancient prince of Islamite convictions. What lies behind the
entrance to the fifth court—only Moslems know.

IT was on a subsequent sojourn in Batavia that I found that I had to go to Surabaja. Not wishing to go by train, I started, all by myself, by motor. My way lay through Bandung and Sumedang to Cheribon, where I intended to pass the first night at the Hotel Hollandia. I went along smoothly enough until late in the afternoon, when I was in the mountains around Kadipaten between Sumedang and Cheribon. The car stopped.

My first thought was that something was amiss with the carbureter. I had come to a halt directly before a *kampong* and the villagers, to the number of close to two hundred, men and women, poured out to observe my troubles. The *Kapala* or head of the village asked me if he could help.

I investigated, and found of course that there was no more benzine in the tank. I turned then to the friendly fellow, a short man, thin and complacent. It was getting dark, and I had yet to go on to Cheribon. So I gave the chief five guilders, whereat he got into his antique wagon, drawn by a somnolent horse, and trotted, to be euphemistic about it, off into the growing dusk.

I was growing very hungry; the mosquitoes came and attacked me. A woman brought me a bunch of bananas, and in the interim I must have eaten at least twelve, one after the other. The same woman offered me, by way of variety, a dish of something she was cooking. But the smell of copra oil, which all Javans use to cook in, dissuaded me from accepting. I peeled and ate another banana.

Three hours later, my friend emerged from the darkness, smoking a cigar bought with my money, and carrying in his wagon two bottles of benzine. I thought that this was strange, since benzine came usually in tins. He assured me that the benzine was good. It was now pitch black, there was not even a moon.

We filled the tank, I stepped jubilantly on the starter, but nothing happened. I fumed, and the chief fumed in sympathy, but kept on smoking his big cigar. The matter clearly became hopeless: I stayed in front of that confounded *kampong* all night. I put up the curtains, first asking the chief to stay nearby for a while to drive away some of the mosquitoes with his cigar smoke. This might have done, but he sneaked away, returning about ten-thirty with his two daughters. He thought, he said, that I might want company.

I said no in a loud and determined tone, and tried to sleep. Dawn broke, as dismal as any dawn I have ever seen. At five o'clock I climbed stiffly out of the car, and washed myself in a stream. Then I ate more bananas. I felt as if I had been raised on bananas. It seemed to me that I had eaten nothing but bananas ever since I had been old enough to use a knife and fork; yet I could not bring myself to accept the other food from the copra-smelling village. So I took another banana and smoked a cigarette.

At seven o'clock I made the chief transport me to the assistant-*Wedana* of the district a half-mile away. When I appeared in this worthy's doorway, I told him, in so many words, that I represented the United States of America, and that I wanted to go away from there at once. The man retreated without a sound into the rear room, emerging in a moment in a black coat, as befitting a representative of the Nonja Besar (Queen Wilhelmina). He himself went off to another village to telephone to Sumedang for a service car, which arrived about noon. Ignominiously I was hauled away to the Sumedang garage, where I left my ill-fated vehicle to be looked into. I went for a shave and a good meal at the *pasangrahan*, or rest-house.

At this point I write, with pathos, that they offered me fried bananas, and bananas for dessert.

And with greater pathos I write: I have never eaten another banana from that day to this. I shudder to think that there are three hundred varieties grown in the East Indies.

On returning to the garage, I was further humiliated by being heartily laughed at: the villainous chief had brought me, they discovered, one bottle of benzine and one of water. At that moment I gave up the idea of the motor trip and went to Surabaja by train.

A month later I was back in Batavia relating the incident to a group of friends in the *Societeit Harmonie* in Weltevreden. The villainy of the chief so captivated and enraged them that a few days later we went there again. A short distance from that fatal *kampong* we came upon my friend complacently smoking a cigar—he was everlastingly smoking, that man. He was gazing pridefully on his rice fields. He seemed glad to see me when I hailed him, and accepted my invitation for a ride. So we rode, while my friends, including an oversize specimen of a Dutchman, some six-foot-three, sat in back. We rode well past the man's village, some three miles, I suppose, and I stopped the car beside some particularly muddy ditches which serve as drains for the rice fields.

I asked him to step to the rear of the car. Pointing to the tank, I asked him if it was water or benzine. He had the grace to begin trembling. He explained volubly. He explained everything but having given me water, and making me eat so many bananas.

So we picked him up, the big Dutchman and I, and hurled him, with a singular lack of ceremony, into that muddiest of all possible ditches. We thoroughly enjoyed the spectacle of his slow labourious climb back to solid earth; swearing very reprehensibly all the while. Once out he fled down the hill toward his village three miles away at a terrific rate, like a hare.

But on later trips through that section I stocked up well on benzine, for had I ever stopped in that village again, I should not have lived. That I almost did not the first time may be due to bananas. Daggers would have been the answer the next time.

These pages are not enough to give a complete picture of Java. Rather than limit myself to describing scenery, or ruins, or agriculture, or the life and people, I have tried to combine something of them all, since any picture, even if partial, is always composite. Java is incomparably the most difficult place in all the archipelago to write about, for it is more complicated than any of the others, its history more involved and interrelated with many outside things. Three religions have played a part in its development; a host of agricultural products form its articles of commerce; a minutely developed tradition determines the behaviour of its many million people.

I do not think it is enough, as I have said already, to say that a man behaves in such a way in such a set of circumstances. It is interesting to know why. Psychology I have not touched, of course; that is for other and abler hands than mine. Were I so minded, I could dwell upon many faults, failings and blemishes with which, by virtue of my stay not of a few months, but of a number of years, I am intimately familiar. I must refrain however, from recording what derogatory criticisms I may have formulated for two main reasons: First, because I do not believe it is right to decry a country and a people whose hospitality I have so fully enjoyed, and whose civilization far antedates our own. Second, because it is the task of their own Government to dispense constructive—or even destructive comment. But background I have tried to depict, so that the reader shall visualize an island, a jewel in the crown of the archipelago, which bristles with colourful life, exciting discoveries and the possibilities of a brilliant future.

III
CELEBES

MACASSAR is the Hong Kong of the Dutch East Indies. Flanked on the right by the eight-hundred-thousand-year-old limestone hills of Maros, in the rear and on the left by low and swampy terrain, and its background formed by the mist-hidden bulk of Bonthain mountain, ten thousand feet high, the chief city of Celebes is a nest of nationalities. In its busy and noisy streets floats a babel of twenty-seven languages and more dialects almost as many and various as in the streets of the real Hong Kong. Here swarm the omnipresent Buginese-traders, rovers and sometimes unconventional marauders; Arabs in their robes; hadjis moving in holy dress on unholy errands; Chinese with their own restaurants, temples and graveyards; Malays from all of Dutch East India, looking faintly sad at being temporarily absent from their home *kampongs;* and last, men of Holland in whites, sitting in the cool of the Harmonie Club, or Oranje Hotel with spreads of drinks before them.

Macassar—once famous in England for a Macassar hairoil—and the Antimacassar, a shawl to protect furniture from oiled heads—does not look as non-European as Bulelang, say, but its chief charm lies in its variety—the variety it possesses by virtue of having become the cross roads—the meeting place for those who trade, as a part of world commerce, on the Java seas.

I got my first glimpse of Macassar from the sea, by boat from Surabaja. The route over, short enough, is marked by buoys, and as the *Barentz* neared the Macassar roads, the water became pale green and milky in spots. We worked in to a pier, while roundabout, in the morning light, went on the native activity of shipping, little *prahus* filled with shouting or silently paddling men darting among the score or more twenty-to-thirty-ton sailing boats used by the Buginese traders. On scattered ones among them I saw slow-moving men laboriously making their craft ready for the day's work, whatever it might be.

Macassar, besides being the largest and most flourishing town on Celebes, is the seat of government. Behind Fort Orange the palace of the governor is conspicuous, partially hidden by clumps of palms and small flower bushes. Close to the palace is the always reappearing Harmonie Club, as ever the centre of Dutch life in a town of the East Indies. Not far from the palace is the wide avenue of tamarind trees, their slim boles supporting the thick growths that throw wide, deep and grateful shade on the walks and road.

Celebes is off the beaten track of the archipelago, but has won its way to prominence because of the as yet incompletely explored riches of this strangely shaped island. As a result of its comparatively hidden location it remained perfectly free of European influence of any kind for a much longer period than any of the other important islands of Dutch East India. Even the nomadic peoples of much earlier times seem to have left it severely alone—no one knows why—preferring to concentrate on the nearby Moluccas or Spice Islands.

At length the Portuguese, in the course of their bold adventuring in these parts, were the first Europeans to land on Celebes in 1512. But it wasn't for many years, until 1540, that they established themselves there in anything like security. This came about because the newly developed trading routes to the Moluccas demanded a stopping place. Macassar was that place.

The people, one gathers from history, were a pagan lot exclusively, Moslems and their spreading Mahometanism not having reached there. Portuguese historians of the middle of the Sixteenth Century mention no religion other than the local paganism and animism.

Celebes consists of a central main continent and four distinct peninsulas, enclosing three large fine bays, Tomini, Tomori and Boni. It stretches its fruitful length some eight hundred miles across the sea at its greatest width and has an area of some seventy thousand square miles. Despite this not over-large area, but because of its wandering coastline, it boasts over two thousand miles of contact with the sea.

Though the first accurate mention of Celebes occurs with the Portuguese in the Sixteenth Century, the Portuguese sailors having brought home news of the place right after their first landing in 1512, our old friend Claudius Ptolemeus, map-maker of old, shows three islands referred to as the *Suide Insule Tres Anthropophagorum*. These, though situated too much to the west, are judged to have been intended to indicate Celebes, Halmahera and Ambon. Subsequently, Celebes is to be found on all sorts of maps, wandering from spot to spot and turning up with many and different names.

As with every island of doubtful origin—doubtful, that is, as to its earliest inhabitants—there is much disagreement over the derivation of the name Celebes. Let it be enough to say here that the northermost tip seems to have been called the "Cape des Scelebres," which later became the name of the whole island. In its four-peninsula shape it resembles almost perfectly the octopus-like contour of the island of Halmahera nearby; the four peninsulas of each point in identical directions. Industrious map-consultation will show that the only parallel of this on the face of the earth is a like resemblance between the islands of Peloponnessus and Chalcidice.

Unlike Java, Sumatra and Borneo, the shores of Celebes rise sheer from the milky-blue sea. The coast does not present to the eyes of the coastwise traveller the low-lying, dense green and sinister-looking jungles of Borneo and Sumatra, but shows steep glistening rocks, often drenched by white and feathery spray in times of storm, and revealing above, as if silhouetted against the blazing blue sky, the plumed tops of palms and the luxuriance of tropical vegetation of every sort.

But, at varying distances from the sheer and gleaming

coastal rocks, the unwearied polyps have built an almost impregnable ring of coral reefs. At widely separated spots, such as at the west and southwest coasts of the island, the coral reefs cease to lurk just under the surface of the milky-blue water, but rear themselves up above the level of the sea. For the most part, however, the coral reefs encircling Celebes content themselves with remaining just under water or awash. Naturally, then, the actual shore line is almost impossible to reach except by small boat.

It is possible, from a small boat, to peer down through several feet of water, and perceive the tops of the coral formations: the movement of the water giving to one's view a sort of wavering, dreamy aspect, as if the pink and white rock, its cavities being slowly filled with broken coral in the form of sand, were not real. Here and there may be discerned the olive-brown colourations of live coral colonies, with their growing points of emerald green or violet.

And here and there I noticed the imperceptibly moving starfish, seeming jewelled in the crystalline sea-water; in some places the entire surface of coral formations, built up solidly from the strong foundation beneath, seemed alive and flowering like a garden with the myriad shapes and forms of anemones, fantastic little animals coloured like the coral they inhabited, pale worms, snails, sea-lilies, with waving plumes of weeds and moss at the edges.

And beyond the coral reefs, inside which large ships may certainly not pass, are the rocky coastal lines of the main island, its shores fringed with copra plantations; for here palms grow almost without attention. This self-nourished growth, fostered by men, necessitates a steady round of steamers of the K.P.M., which, as I mentioned previously, has a virtual monopoly on the sea lanes in and among the Dutch East Indian islands.

I have journeyed partly and wholly around Celebes on

different K.P.M. steamers, watching interestedly as, perhaps
near some lonely jetty, boats loaded with copra put out to
unload into the ship for Macassar, and later for all parts of
the world. A white man would appear, perhaps come off in
a dinghy for a chat and a dash of gin with the captain—later
returning, after a last regretful look at the white women on
the decks, to his jetty. The steamers come once every few
weeks, and between those stops the one white, or perhaps a
few, are left alone in a fragile house to boss a lot of native
labourers.

To some that means romance, especially to readers of
adventure stories. The idea of facing long, hot and monotonous days of labour is attractive, in the abstract. To those
who have done it, as I have, it is not so much fun. It is work,
and work has a discouraging tendency to be work no matter
what the climate is. The consolation to many of those who
put in years on lonely copra centres on the Celebes coast is
the financial reward; copra is profitable most of the time.
And not one of those men, unless it be that the natural gre-
garious instincts of mankind have been squeezed out of him
by a different life, stays there any longer than he can help.
Besides, not all take their wives out from the main towns;
the climate is warm and assistance of any kind, for any conceivable emergency, is far away and frequently impossible to
obtain. Thus I was always glad to be on the deck, when such
a figure waved an arm from a jetty. For the life on a
K.P.M. steamer is pleasant; awnings stretched over the decks
give cooling shade; the *djonges* (boys) are swift in dis-
tributing refreshments, and the captain, presides over his
temporary families impartially. He has a good berth and he
knows it.

THE island of Celebes is not nearly so Europeanized as
is Java, or even Bali, from certain points of view. Its
mountainous construction, together with the strange geological shape of the whole, did make travelling in Celebes a mat-

169

ter of riding—not the automobile touring that can be done so much of the time in Java and Sumatra.

Central Celebes is the land of the Toradjas, a peculiar people who were once head-hunters. They are heathens, disconnected from every religion known in the East; very little, actually, was known about them until only a few years ago. Their land has not become a cross-road; no wide smooth post roads have been plunged through their territory, for the simple reason that any one wanting to go from Macassar to the northern capes and the regions of the Minahasians, Menado or Gorontalo, finds it much easier to go by steamer.

One morning, accompanied by my boy, brought from Java, and a native guide, forth I went, heading first for Paré-Paré, then through Naros, Pankadjene, Tanette and Barru, all coastal or near-coast towns. Macassar was soon left behind, and the mountain slopes began almost at once. Our mountain ponies found the going to their liking as we trotted through endless ravines, around the shoulders of rocky, bush-covered hills, other times skirting towering rock-masses along narrow paths. Below us then stretched the uneven surfaces of green valleys choked with trees and smaller vegetation, bursts of varied colour attracting the eye where wild fruit trees in blossom grew unheeded. Bamboos flourish through here, where live scattered Buginese, Alfurs and Duriers.

Having passed Rapeng, I came to the Sadan River. On a bend in its long and meandering course is the town and government military post of Enrekan; its native houses seem to float, on their piles, above the course of the stream. After resting at the *pasangrahan*, we went on the next morning toward Kalosi, first climbing the steep grade to Sosok— thus we clambered some fourteen hundred feet, so sharp a declivity that we had to stop frequently to rest our sturdy ponies. Behind us stretched an ever-growing panorama of roundly broken country, through which winds the silver thread of the Mataalo River, the White River, which had shortly before overrun its bed. Not far ahead of us stood the Leta mountains, a whole range in themselves; southeast of us was Buntu Batu mountain, rising to a height of thirty-two hundred feet, while to the distant south shimmered the bay of Paré-Paré and the straits of Macassar.

On another side I could see, again, the Sadan whose banks we had just left, and a narrow ribbon of the real road, leading from Enrekan, by which we had come. The climb continued, but not so steeply now, and the panorama, further on, of the juncture of the Mataalo and Malua rivers, was a welcome and refreshing sight. Here they join, spreading out noisily over the rocks, and plunge on together through a still wild country—almost jungle-like in growth—that the average white man as yet knows little about.

From that point it is not so very far to Kalosi—my immediate objective—a smallish native village, but boasting a rest-house where it is possible to obtain the conveniences necessary to a European's idea of a night well spent.

Well spent, while it lasted, for to get on the next and last lap of the run to the land of the Toradjas, I started at five in the morning, aiming at the village of Makalé. It was terribly cold, not only because it was 5:00 A.M. but also because we were several thousand feet above sea level. My poor Javanese boy shivered miserably, but when I looked at him he managed to flash me a genial, but always respectful, smile. My guide led the way stolidly, and without concern for us who shivered and wished for the sun. So bad did it become that more than once we stopped, dismounted and threshed our arms and ran around in little circles to restore circulation. Not bad if I had been dressed for it, but no one had thought to tell me that here, in Celebes, it could get so infernally chilly. This went on for something more than an hour, when in a field I spotted a tall, dark-skinned man, half-naked, working busily. He used a couple of pointed wooden sticks to turn the soil, and did not seem to mind the weather, partially clothed though he was.

It must have taken him a long time to make progress with his pointed sticks in ploughing, but I found later that the Toradjas get better results and a bigger yield on their crops using this method than the Western machinery that has been brought, in isolated spots, for them to use. Doubtless they have little confidence in the wheezing machinery.

From here on we worked our way deeper and deeper into Toradja land, passing through Baroko, where there is a small and struggling mission school, Garotin and at last to Makalé—beyond which is Toradja land in earnest. On the roads hereabout we passed many of the Toradjas—big, stalwart, very undressed fellows, walking seriously along intent on their own business. They wore nothing, absolutely nothing, in this cool country, except tight little waistbands drawn securely between the legs; the waistbands couldn't have been more than two or three inches wide. Secured in this abbreviated *slendang* each one had a large knife in a wooden sheath, which was decorated on the outside. Several of them carried, slung over their shoulders, cotton bags—the usual suitcase of the Toradja—in which he carries his necessities of life, including the omnipresent betel, or chewing kit.

Nearly every one of these men—and quite a few men I saw later—had their heads shaved in front. This, together with their filed-off teeth, makes them all look like animated mummies. In addition, each man wears a piece of heavy string wound about his forehead. This strange custom originated when the Luwurese, Mahometan coastal tribes, dominated the Toradjas and indicates the slavery of the Toradjas, and it was said, "They could be led about by the strings."

In Makalé I stayed several days, living at a rest house.

This first contact with the Toradjas impressed me greatly with their qualities, which are those of clean living, industry and temperance carried to the verge of almost perfect sobriety. This high and carefully observed moral standard has turned them out a healthy race, inured to the hard ways of keeping themselves prosperous in what is not the most hospitable terrain, and able to withstand hardships. Now I knew how that man, certainly not an exception, could stand the cold of early morning.

You would think that if the men were such a hardy crew the women would be likewise. The men wear as little clothing as any I have ever seen anywhere. They might almost be said to err in the extreme, but the curious thing is that the women do not follow the same principle; they, on the other hand, wear so much clothing that they make themselves look ridiculous. The garments of Toradja women, some of whom, I found, were not bad-looking, are made of *fuija*, a kind of soft bark, which they rarely change or clean. I asked a woman one day when they did change, if ever. "Six months," she replied, implying by her air that my question was out of order and idiotic. She was probably right, but it would help me to a good opinion of the cleanliness of Toradja women if they renovated their clothing more often than twice a year.

They are a democratic people, as I learned by association with them, and by observation of their customs toward one another. Unlike the Balinese and Javanese, they care almost nothing for caste and grade, and do not go in for pomp in any form. Yet they have three divisions of society, corresponding somewhat to caste gradations: the *Puang*, the highest and ruling class, the *Tomakaka*, the middle class, and the *Kaunan*, the lowest and hardest working class. Despite this arbitrary and loose classification, they are tolerant in behaviour toward each other.

Makalé differs from most Toradja villages in that it is larger and more spread out, for most communities in this luxuriantly wild land are very small, of only a few houses located on segregated rocky plateaus and surrounded by walls of loosely piled up stones. The Toradjas have always had to defend themselves against marauding and tyrannizing Buginese and Luwurese, and for centuries more or less consistently and successfully fought off invaders, from their strongholds at the end of practically impassable rocky mountain paths and roads. In fact, to this day they much prefer not to have good roads. For while a smooth path may be a good and easy way out, it makes it too easy to get in.

This same mental attitude has made it difficult for any foreign influence to enter, for in every case they have savagely resisted intruders of every kind. With great persistence they have kept to their own *adat*, their own habits and traditions; with the result that they are not as advanced as other peoples. I do not mean to say that they should have welcomed the foreigner—that is, the white man. What I do mean is that contact with other tribes would have made them see the world, or their own part of it, in larger perspective. As was the custom originally, they build their homes shaped much like *praus*, and in many cases houses and their various parts have the same names as their craft.

Many years ago, when they first left the river and entrenched themselves among the ravines, they did not prosper. But they had to grow things in order to live. So they planted rice, extending their area almost unhindered, for few other tribes have wanted to make a permanent residence in central Celebes. Then they did prosper, for some natural adaptability enabled them to cultivate rice with enormous success, so that they grew well-to-do. To this day their own *sawahs* exceed those of the Javans and Balinese in proportionate yield and efficiency of labour. One feature is an ingenious irrigation system, evolved from the necessities of the country they chose as a home. Long pipe-lines of bamboo bring the needed water to the *sawahs* from the watercourse higher up in the hills. Rock-hewn pathways for the pipe-lines are to be found, still in everyday use, plentifully in the rocky hills.

Despite this ability to make much out of practically nothing, the Toradja has little or no commercial sense; he is not acquisitive. In this connection, there is the story told by Albert Kruyt, the famous Dutch missionary. It was 1893 when coastal dwellers first learned that a people unknown to them inhabited the interior. On the surface of rivers Kruyt and others saw pounded sago and bamboo fibre floating. Some Buginese went up the river and found no one; for the villages, then, were on hilltops, hidden. But still certain that where civilized things like sago and bamboo fibres came from there must be people, the astute Buginese left some salt, in return for the palm wine they found left behind, and went away. The Toradjas came cautiously out of their retreats, tasted the salt when they found the wine gone, and liked it. When the Buginese came back, the Toradjas, albeit somewhat suspiciously, began to trade and barter with them. This continued steadily, but failed to develop the commercial instinct in the Toradjas.

Money, as coin, is a comparatively new thing with them, and they care very little for financial gain or loss. They have what Westerners surely consider a strange notion of purchase, for they pay according to their want or need. In other words, they think not so much in terms of how much actual minted money they possess as against what they want, as they do purely of what they want. This is a fine point, for peculiarly enough some modern Western thinkers have advocated this very principle as a help toward calmer living in the hectic world of today. The principle has been stated as follows:

that the value of an object to someone else is not what counts; it is what it means to you that is the determining factor.

For instance, you might want to sell a washing machine to your Toradja friend for two guilders. Cheap, but if he didn't want it he wouldn't give you one guilder for it. But if you possess a knife he ardently desires, he will give you fifty times its value—because he wants or needs it—and depart in elevated spirits. Needless to say, the Buginese are clever enough to exploit them shamefully as a result, but the Toradjas do manage to get what they want.

I REFERRED before to the absence of outside religions in
Celebes, baring of course the few coastal tribes influenced,
as were the Luwurese, by Mahometanism overflowing from
the islands to the west and south-west. The Toradjas in par-

ticular have kept to their animism with dogged persistence, suspicious of any attempt, by no matter whom, to intrude on the domains of their spirits. They live in a community made up of the living and the dead. They honour their deceased in a way which leaves methods of other peoples I have seen much in the rear, particularly in the materialistic sense. That is, the Chinese revere the memories of their ancestors, but chiefly in a mental and spiritual sense. The Toradjas, not so sensitized to existences in the mind, honour their dead by a thousand and one minute observances of custom, and by treating the departed precisely as if the old ones had not left the earth at all, but had merely changed from visible to invisible structure. Thus to the Toradja the world is full of invisible things, since ordinary logic tells him that the dead must perforce, and by great numbers, exceed the living. He lives in a universe controlled by unpredictable and magic powers, communicable but not necessarily amenable to command.

One of the Toradja's chief calls upon the spirits, either of the dead or of nature, is in rain-making, a highly important matter to any crop-raising community. The practice of attracting rain is the prerogative of every Toradja: he takes a young sago leaf and binds it together with an aren palm leaf, pronouncing over the operation the following words: "If there is no rain tomorrow, we shall bind you two much more firmly together." The binding more tightly together can go on until rain actually does come. They are convinced, besides, that the croak of the bullfrog and the call of the Koloko bird are rain-producers.

But when rain is really overwhelming, they call upon the *Sando* to exercise his art—art, mind you—of rain-chasing. This is more serious and cannot be entered upon lightly. The *Sando* is a man of priestly standing who, before, during and immediately after the process of driving away rain after a severe plenty, must not allow himself to touch, or be touched by, water in any way. He may not bathe, does not wash, must not wet his feet in crossing any body of water, eats with unwashed hands, but drinks large quantities of palm wine. Most of the time he sits solemnly before the *kampong*, tending a little fire which may not go out until the rain ceases. He burns special wood in the fire as a medicine, and has a little package of *pangawa* and *waru* leaves and *pakanang* bark, which he takes in his hands and blows upon, holding it in the direction from which the superfluous rain arrived.

Besides rain-making and chasing, there is *Mobolobiangi*, or divination, common enough in all East India, but with the Toradjas brought to a point of extremity in daily life.

Every Toradja carries in his bag, besides his *sirih*, a number of maize kernels wrapped in *fuija* bark; the greener the kernels with age, the more precious. Suppose, now, our friend wishes to know if the next day will be auspicious for a journey. He takes out his maize kernels, shakes them in his hand as we shake dice and drops a quantity at random. Those left in his hand he replaces in the bag; those which have fallen he counts in pairs. Now, if there are so many pairs and no kernels left over, the morrow is-no day for him to travel. If, on the contrary, he has a kernel left over, he will travel.

This test of the maize kernels is applied to almost every important act of the Toradja's life. He applies the test-to questions of good and bad luck; he applies it to find an answer to a "yes or no" question; did So-and-so cheat him the day before? will the stream rise or will his child get well?

In almost everything the Toradjas apply the test of numbers. In planting, for example, the householder will first sow seven rice seeds. If all seven sprout, it will be a good crop. If any lack, so much the worse for the growth, in proportion as so many more or less seeds out of the seven fail to grow.

This is all, to the Toradja mind, a call upon the invisible spirits which abound in the atmosphere. These he never ignores.

When sitting at a table, the Toradja family counts among the heads present those visible together with those there in the spirit; small offerings are put aside. Certain property rights are reserved for those who have left, and each rice *sawah* has one corner especially cultivated for the benefit— of what kind?—of the dead. Every celebration of no matter what description is marked by offerings to the deceased members of the community; this custom achieves its highest and most intense pitch at the Feast of the Dead.

When some one dies, the body is at once mummified, and then laid out in a special house—House of the Dead—to be viewed by relatives and friends left behind. During its temporary rest, before entering the land of souls, the body is elaborately dressed, having, previously and at last, been thoroughly washed. Before the soul may actually be speeded on its way, the family must have a feast. This has no specified length, as I judged by watching them eat, rest and eat again, but lasts until plenty of new rice, pigs, chicken and what not has been consumed in an effort to fortify the living souls against their sorrowful task.

I learned that shortly before I had arrived here an incredibly old lady had died, and that the feast had just ended. Following directions from my guide, I came upon a large compound filled with a press of people. All the women were dressed in white cotton, while off to one side stood a not very high wooden platform on which lay the little old woman. From this platform, said my guide, her soul would presently depart.

At the far end of the compound, where the forest began

again, I could hear a lot of men excitedly shouting. But my attention was distracted back again by the entrance, through the crowd to a central cleared space, of a troupe of young dancing girls, uniform in their cotton dresses. They danced for a long time, solemnly and not very interestingly. Across the heads of the crowd, which, I began to notice, consisted chiefly of women, floated bursts of savage shouting. That sounded more interesting, so we left the dancing, edged quickly around the compound and found it necessary to enter the forest a little way to find the scene of the yelling. My first intimation that we were nearing it came with a terrific smell of freshly killed meat.

Several men, wild-eyed, shouting unintelligently to my ears, whisked back and forth, flourishing in their hands large raw chunks of red caribou meat, dripping blood, on themselves and on the ground. I came nearer to the centre of the yelling and saw at last what was its cause.

In the middle of an excited mob of men was a wooden stand on which was the carcass of a huge caribou. On its far side towered a huge Toradja delivering accurate blows with a sharp ax-like weapon on the bloody mess before him. Now and again he paused, wiping sweat from his forehead, while those around him plunged clawlike hands on the torn flesh, pulling away fragmentary, dripping chunks. A chief stood close by, watching closely, frequently picking out select portions and throwing them to certain men. I gathered that the flesh of the caribou was distributed in this odorous and ruddy way according to the rank of the men; several times I saw the chief irately snatch a morsel from one man, throw it to another and give the first something else. The smell of hot steaming flesh was almost overwhelming.

It was growing darker. Near the low rude platform on which lay the caribou a large bonfire leapt and crackled, throwing its dancing light on the grotesquely gesticulating forms pressed around the bloody mass of the dead animal. Unexpected figures, mouthing shouts of greedy joy, jumped back and forth between my vision and the fire, appearing, for those split-second intervals, like devils in silhouette. Each one held in his right hand a shapeless and dankly soft chunk of red meat torn and hacked from the diminishing carcass of the caribou, and as the men dashed by me blood spattered and flew; blood, warm and heavy in the strangely cold flesh.

As I watched, the stalwart chief now and again dealing out buffets to those of his followers who were too forward, the caribou disappeared almost to nothing. Its stripped bones were tossed carelessly and fiercely away, while a fresh carcass appeared in its place. And after that one, another. Between their sorties on the meat, the men refreshed themselves by innumerable trips to a corner of the compound where palm wine was given them by girls. Then they dashed back, howling, laughing insanely, and watched with weird drunken attention as the axe-blows bit deeply, soggily, into the brown hide of the newly dead animal.

Between the bursts of yelling and the roar of the bonfire flames as fresh logs were thrown on, I could hear the terrified squeals as still more caribou were being killed. Triumphant shouts came in gusts, and above us the tall trees stood, silent and scornful.

Some of the men, I saw, tasted their meat, swallowed mouthfuls of it; others merely brandished it about, splattering everyone about them with thick, dark-red gore. Their shouts grew wilder, fiercer, and now and again a man would suddenly stumble, sprawl across a tree-root, and then lie still, as he had fallen, snoring raucously. And as they slept troubledly, their mates clawed at one another in the bizarre frenzy to get at the dripping meat, though, as far as I could observe, comparatively few of them actually ate it.

Through it all the chief stood guard, while those who

chopped at the carcasses changed on and off, delivering their sweeping, thudding blows with inspired enthusiasm—while no one paid any attention to the increasing number who lay in sudden sleep.

I left the forest celebration and went back around the crowd into the compound proper. The girls were not dancing any longer, but the little body, in its pitiful cotton dress and plentiful ornaments, still lay on the wooden platform. It looked calm, and content, not a bit impatient for its soul to join its companion souls in the invisible world beyond. The little old woman had probably led a difficult life.

EDUCATION, or schooling of any kind, except of the missions, is totally unknown. There is no writing, yet the Toradjas have a vast spoken literature of folk legend. Almost everyone knows them, yet chiefs and prominent men are considered to be the best raconteurs. Similarly, there is no codified law in the strict sense, but there are more than seven thousand *pemalis*—prohibitions which the Toradjas must observe:

There must not be maize at any offering festival; the hair must not be touched during a thunderstorm; the meat of white caribou must not be eaten except at certain times; mice and rice birds must not be killed; *sirih* must not be begged of an undertaker; and so on to the number of seven thousand and to the regulation of life's most minute maneuvers.

For further examples, among the Posso Toradjas, a little beyond Makalé, a woman must "purchase" milk if she cannot herself nurse her child. Either she or the child's aunt place a copper bracelet—the ring being the symbol of the universe and insurmountable by evil spirits—in a basket, and the basket is placed in the centre of the road on the outskirts of the village. This is the price of milk-filled breasts from the spirits.

Adoption, regulated likewise by a multitude of *pemalis*, has strange uses among the Toradjas. I learned of it by happening to notice that a certain child referred to two different men as its father, and two different women as its mother; both married couples. This was too complicated. I discovered that frequently an aunt or an uncle will ask of their relatives that a child be given them to raise. But the true parents are perfectly free to refuse the request, without hard feelings on either side, if they consider that the child will not be brought up as a true Toradja. There is no ceremony of adoption, and the child does not give up the real authors of its existence, though it goes to live with the new ones. Why they do this I could not find out, though it may be through some obscure, incompletely understood notion that thus a child will avoid suffering for the sins of its fathers.

Despite this multitude of custom dictates, requirements, prohibitions and superstitions, the ordinary Toradjas are not the least concerned over their lots in life. They are, as a whole, among the happiest and jolliest people I have seen, though they can become ferocious and unfriendly enough when occasion demands, as witness the long defense of their native land. They celebrate as frequently as possible, often going in for their crop feast, which becomes almost as sanguinary an affair as the sword dances of Bali. Here, too, the girls danced until they became unconscious, upon which all sorts of drastic methods were used by the Balians or Basirs to revive them, including the steady beating of a resounding quivering drum to exorcize the evil spirits that had taken possession of the fallen persons.

The participants inflict ragged wounds on themselves with sharp pointed bamboo sticks—and later are quietly proud of their scars. All this to commemorate the successful conclusion of a harvest.

In all I spent several weeks among the Toradjas the first time, though later, on journeys through Celebes, I came past the same points and saw the same chiefs several times. The rugged country makes it easy enough to believe that not many years ago, until discouraged from expeditions by the Dutch, these people were ardent head-hunters. I have seen heads, in all stages of preservation and decay, proudly preserved in the houses of able-bodied warriors. They have given it up now in the face of superior force, but it will be, I think, a long time before they unbend sufficiently to become much more impregnated with foreign influences than they are now.

Unlike the Javanese and Balinese, they have not a finely and sensitively organized civilization; their is more the product of a hard and bloody life, where simplicity and an emphasis on fundamentals, like food, warmth, and self-protection, are the foundation. They are barely polite, and not always that, to the hopeful and sometimes enthusiastic missionaries who come out to them. A small missionary school exists—not flourishes—in Enrekan on the edge of the real Toradja stronghold. The natives have their animistic religion; their heaven which exists invisibly about them, and their daily life is amply regulated. Here again, as I have commented previously, is the difficulty Christianity meets in attempting conversion of an animistically minded people. The gap between a material set of beliefs and one essentially spiritual is too great for uncivilized minds to grasp.

The principal point is that here, by some quirk of fate, a people leads as tranquil a life as is possible under these circumstances of pioneering. They are not an old, super-sensitized race, like the Balinese, but they possess one ironic advantage: they have not yet benefited much by white man's advantages.

Thus, their spoken literature contents them, and their houses on small rocky plateaus and on high piles over glistening river surfaces furnish them with homes and happy meeting places.

I was due to leave Makalé, having come back to it from the Toradja country north, at five in the morning. The evening before, therefore, I accepted the invitation of one chief, my particular friend, to attend a meeting in the village communion house. Its purpose was to hear stories told by the real, professional *raconteurs* who retail the racial legends with feeling for their meanings, like the bards of ancient Ireland and Scotland.

Unfortunately, I spoke little of the tongue, and could catch only phrases, though I did grasp the general meaning —the drift, so to speak, remained within my power. As we gathered, some thirty of us, all men, friendly phrases were exchanged, smiles translated themselves from face to face, dishes of rice and gourds of palm wine travelled from hand to hand. Two men, seemingly in their middle fifties, sat at the head of the gathering, not unnoticed by the guests, but accorded courteous greetings and then left respectfully alone. I must have been there nearly an hour before the telling actually began, modestly enough.

The signal for it was a clearing of the throat by one of the *raconteurs*. Silence fell at once, almost eager in its intensity, though obviously all these men must have heard the same tales dozens of times. But they have the same attitude toward their stories, never varied in detail, that the Chinese and Japanese have toward their historical plays, and that we have, in our Western way, toward the Passion Play, say. Reverence, respect and a search for ever-new meanings are the roots of the attitude, I suspect. Be that as it may, the story-telling began about ten-thirty, and went on indefinitely.

I didn't grow tired, though I had a long day's journey ahead of me, for the facial expressions, flickering in and out of clear vision with the unsteadiness of the dry palm-leaf torches, fascinated me. Some kept smiling recurrently, as at familiar passages. Others listened with absorption, rarely removing their keen attentive eyes from the countenance of him who related the tale. The legends were long, the shortest being perhaps only ten minutes in length, told with great simplicity of language, for I understood more of that one than any other. Most continued for well over half-an-hour, yet no two were alike, even to my uninitiated ears, for the *raconteurs* varied their repertoires of expression, gesture and voice infinitely, so that there might have been a dozen bards, instead of the dignified two, who refreshed themselves at intervals with copious swallows of palm wine.

It seems incredible now, as I write this, that I sat there

and was amazed when my boy touched me on the shoulder and pointed to the entrance. He had crept quietly in, and now I looked where he pointed. For the first time the oblong of the entrance, facing the house on piles out across the narrow river, showed a faint pearly grey. Dawn. As I stared I could make out the bending fronds of shore palms on the other side of the river. A chill gust of wind swept down the river valley, and mist, almost invisible in quality but for its greyness, swirled and changed the texture of the morning. I rose, and bade my hosts good-bye. They were courteous, and the chief, my friend, saw me out. But the rest, after nodding in my direction, centred their attention on the old man who was talking.

As we rode south on the river bank I looked back. The same doorway from which I had issued now glowed a dull, vague red, but I could not hear a sound. It was chilly and we rode on swiftly. I grew very sleepy.

Back to Macassar, much the same way we had come, out of the rocky, broken country, into the slopes of the mountains, shouldering our way past the edges of deep ravines and valleys, past the rich coffee-lands around Bonthain, coming across the swampy lowlands that brought us by the Governor's palace, back to the hotel.

And then on a K.P.M. steamer, the *Barentz*, which we caught on its regular run. On its way around the island we stopped at Dongala, Amurang and Menado, where I debarked, and the ship steamed on to Gorontalo, the Moluccas or Spice Islands. On its stops it had picked up copra and rattan, hides, buffalo heads, horn and coffee, among a multitude of things. The towns here in the northern part of the island are more spacious, cleaner, for they have not, due to their comparative isolation, attracted the crosscut wanderers that congregate in most busy seaports.

Menado, more or less important as a seaport for the north of the island, is chiefly interesting because of the Minahasians, who are Christians. The town itself, containing a bad hotel, a Harmonie Club for the local Dutch, a Dutch and commercial quarter, and widely spaced bunches of native houses with thatched roofs, lies on the Menado river, which is very small and consequently dangerous to ships in any sort of real weather. A mile out from its breakwater is a tiny island consisting entirely of the volcano Menado Tua, while back of the town is the famous volcano Klabat (Celabat), from which some scholars say Celebes, by a series of orthographic adventures, received its name. But the difficulty of the landing in squally weather such as we had offers little real obstacle to the efficient officers of the K.P.M. steamers; those gentlemen who, attired in pajamas when not on duty, are ardent bridge players, interspersing their comments and remarks during the game with shop talk on copra tonnage, the chief topic of conversation, or a bottle of *koentjies* beer.

Business kept me in Menado many weeks this time, though this was far from my last lap on the three-week steamer voyage around Celebes. I was glad enough to be able to stay, for though the Minahasians are not as likeable and congenial a people as one might prefer, they are one of the most fantastic I have ever seen. Fantastic because they illustrate, more nearly than a true lover of humanity may contemplate with pleasure, what a Christianized Malay native is like.

For though the Minahasians adopted Christianity, many years ago, the spiritual value of it has made little impression. They have somehow arrived at the belief that to be a Christian you must wear white man's clothes, and stoop to his deceptions. So they adopt jackets and long trousers of European style, copy European mannerisms, and profit, among each other, by imitating European methods of life, including laziness.

There is some reason to believe that they, like the Toradja, used once to hunt heads for a pastime. Not only that, but that also they were cannibals, and lived in remote, dismal villages protected from raid by palisades of thorny bamboo. That they needed such protection must indicate that they fought constantly with other villages, even with those to which they were tribally related.

But somehow, by dint of the extraordinary missionary zeal of the Jesuit St. Francis Xavier in 1547, and of Magellan, who also converted 1,500 Minahasians, combined with a quirk in the Minahasian nature which made them, more than any other Malay people, amenable to Christianity, they profess beliefs of the Christian Church. "Profess" is therefore the word. For though they wear European clothes—that is, those who inhabit Menado and several nearby towns —carry canes and gloves, own sewing machines (Heaven knows what they do with so many) and have orderly little schools and churches, and well-kept villages, there is, underneath all this, very little real departure from the customs of old, excepting cannibalism and head-hunting.

Compared with the people of southern Celebes, and with

the Toradjas, Buginese and Macarese, they are surprising. Though they are of the same Malay-Polynesian racial and language stock as all the rest, their hair is curly in Negro fashion, the skin is lighter, tending sometimes to pure yellow, and they are stocky in stature, though not burly. Some of their legends refer unmistakably to a dim period when ancient Minahasians immigrated from some place supposed to have linked the lands north of Celebes with the Philippines and Sangi, and later to have been destroyed by a volcanic upheaval. The date of this immigration is vague, but it suggests, and their looks appear to confirm, a racial relationship between the Minahasians and the Japanese. Probably some people from somewhere north of them did come to northern Celebes, conquer the local tribes, and later intermarry with them. This would account for their really astonishing difference from the tribes in the south and other parts of the island.

Our first knowledge of them came when they called on the Dutch East India Company in the middle of the Seventeenth Century for help and protection against the Spaniards. The protection of the *Kompenie*, as was so frequently the case, became conquest, ending in the construction of Fort Amsterdam in Menado. This, as usual, was not diplomatically called conquest, but permission for the fort was obtained in a treaty of alliance in 1679, eventually extending the domain to the four divisions of Minahasa; each of which has its own dialect: the Tombulus, around Menado, Tonseas, on the Klabat peninsula and nearby Ajermididi and Kema, Tondanos, at Tondano Lake, and the Tompakewas, around Sonder, Langowan and Amurang. Of these, the Tombulus are the most Christianized, at least visibly speaking, for they have copied to the greatest extent the mannerisms of the West. The curious thing is, however, that beneath this veneer the old Minahasian customs still exist, though modified, to be sure, by the new superimposed beliefs.

For example, Genesis has made little real impression, since they cling obstinately to their own legend of the origin of mankind and the earth. It tells that Lummimuut, a young girl whose existence is not clearly explained, left her parents as soon as she was able to walk, going in a boat equipped only with a handful of earth. Having traversed some distance, she threw the small quantity of soil on the waters, at the same time calling upon the gods to create from it some land upon which she could live. At once there was land, but soft and slippery. Then immediately the boat struck a rock, splitting it in two, releasing Karenna, the priestess of the gods. This lady thereupon prayed to each of the winds in turn to fertilize Lummimuut. The west wind obliged and after a time the young girl, incredibly young, gave birth to a son named Toar. Karenna then gave each one a stick and sent them out into the world, instructing them to compare their sticks with whomever they met. If the sticks were equal in length, the two who met were mother and son. If the sticks differed, they should return.

Now after a certain period spent in wandering, Lummimuut and Toar met and compared sticks; Toar's had sprouted. So they returned at once to Karenna, who forthwith made them man and wife. A multitude of children resulted from this union, which served to populate the earth, some of the children being the forebears of the Minahasians.

It is easy enough to trace the mythological symbolism of the legend, marriage of heaven and earth, the growing of life, and so on. The point being that the Minahasians accept Genesis as a genial tale, and believe the legend of Lummimuut as an absolute fact.

In one district, for further example, I ran across the

pesendeen, the festival celebrating the sham marriage of children from five to nine years old.

This *pesendeen* must not be confused with the child marriage of India, for the Minahasian children are not considered bound by the oaths of this mock marriage, and they return to their parents immediately after the lengthy ceremony. The vows mean nothing, apparently, for when the children reach the age of puberty they may court and marry whom they please. It makes no difference whether the eventual choice falls on the participant in the *pesendeen* or not.

For this ceremony, the parents of both children meet in the house of the child bride, accompanied by the groom, who is dressed up in his *kabaja* and a pair of flaming red trousers for the occasion. At the one I saw, the little fellow, obviously not aware of what it meant, sat stoically, with that silent uncomplaining heroism which is a characteristic of children the world over, in one corner. Meanwhile the two sets of parents, verbally supported by hordes of relatives, conferred gravely on the dot. That was settled after an argument, not very bitter, lasting nearly an hour.

Then the group all gathered together in the middle of the large house, courteously oblivious of my presence, and in spoken prayer humbly invited the gods to attend their festivities. Then everybody ate cooked rice, pork and chicken, after which the groom, having downed a drink of *sagoweer* (a native sago brew as strong as rye whisky) grasped a sword, while the bride held in her tiny hands some pigs' food and a cluster of tree-leaves to symbolize her worthiness.

After more prayers, incantations and offerings, a real meal took place, the child couple keeping their trophies carefully beside them, all this ending in their being led for the night to separate bed chambers.

This long and seemingly meaningless ceremony was repeated for five days, to the exhaustion of everyone, including the married couple. At last, on the afternoon of the fifth day, drums were beaten as a signal that the ceremony was over. Then all dispersed to their various homes, the groom's parents taking their son home with them, and all was as it had been before.

What it all means baffles me, for no matter how I questioned, I could learn nothing, either from Dutchmen who had spent years there, from anyone in the missionary schools, or from the Minahasians themselves. These last, however, were more enlightening than any one else, for a young man said to me blandly in effect:

"It is very nice, everyone enjoys it. No harm is done, and we are all impressed by the munificence of the bride's home. Is not that enough?"

Well, isn't it?

More than among many other peoples of the same level of refinement, however, true love results in an astonishing number of marriages. Without wishing to be cynical, I mean that marriage among the Minahasians is almost invariably an affair of the heart. Of course it frequently happens that a pair united in a childhood *pesendeen* might later embark upon the same adventure for life, but I doubt if many young Minahasians would willingly forego the pleasures of a method of courtship that is unique.

Consent of the parents is not an imperative adjunct to marriage, but courtship remains as secret as possible, consisting of nocturnal visits of the youth to the side of his beloved. The girl, probably expecting the youth, places a mat beside her own on the floor, and after dusk the swain arrives to recline upon it. In some sections these visits are attended by moral lapses, temptation running rife even in Celebes. But in most districts the courting routine, of conversation and sleep side by side, is decorously and formally observed. But the young man must not, on the occasion of his visits for the first eight weeks, stay later than a few minutes before dawn, for he must not be seen leaving. This would provoke scandalized comment.

All the while this is going on the parents know all about it. In fact, their daughter's powers of attraction gratify them. Nevertheless, to fulfil the demands of social usage, they advise the young man to be cautious in his comings and his goings. At last, after eight weeks, assuming the youth to possess both the moral and physical stamina to endure so protracted and intensive a period of wooing, he remains one morning after daybreak, then walking out of his beloved's home in broad daylight. This indicates to everyone that the formal engagement will be announced presently.

So he sends a batch of prepared *sirih* to the girl, for here as everywhere else in Malaya, betel is the stock in trade of society. She, to indicate her grateful and delighted acceptance, replies by sending back a full grown betel nut, together with the necessary ingredients for the preparation of *sirih*. Then all is well, and the ceremony takes place.

The betel has grown sentimentally into the language among the Minahasians, incidentally, as witness the phrase, "to make love," which is *pahaleya leyan lemaan*, or "continually to ask betel of one another." And besides, doesn't this Minahasa courtship system bear an extraordinary resemblance, in some respects, to the good old American custom of bundling? now, alas, gone beyond recall!

This does not by any means, bring to an end the recital of the immensely entertaining customs of the Minahasians concerning domestic relationships. The true Minahasians are monogamists, though some outlying tribes, not really Minahasians, long ago adopted exogamy from the Mahometan influence. But this has not affected the real children of Lummimuut. Wives invariably leave their own homes and go over to those of their mates, though in some southern districts, I was told on extremely reliable authority, there were frequently marital households consisting of fathers and daughters, mothers and sons, brothers and sisters. In explanation it was advanced that these worthy natives experienced no horror or feeling of degradation at this incest, for the legend of their very origin recites, on the best possible authority, that a son was united to his mother in matrimony. The results of this union were fruitful, for a long and unspeakably complicated genealogy brings the sons and daughters of Lummimuut and Toar down to the present day.

These exuberant Minahasians, whose lives are replete with surprising and apparently reasonless customs (which enhances the air of affable idiocy which blankets the country) have one which is called "shunning the mother-in-law." There is little conscious humour attached to it, otherwise one would suspect that the universality of the poor, downtrodden, overworked but sure-fire mother-in-law joke was an assured matter. This custom grew out of the times when husbands in days long ago resided in the homes of their wives. Though the man lived there, he was nevertheless considered an interloper, and not a bona fide member of the family, the members of which, to demonstrate their independence, cut the husband regularly and ceremoniously, and in return he cut them in the same fashion.

Though today wives move to their husband's homes, the custom persists in modified form, for no husband may mention the names of his parents-in-law. Should he do so by error, he must at once spit on the ground and say: "I have done wrong!" This he does in expiation, for otherwise, by the order of an inscrutable fate, he is told his nose will immediately be covered with ulcers.

Today, in the land of the Minahasians, honours and titles and property descend from father to son; similarly, marriage laws are patriarchal, and genealogy is traced down the male side of the family. This despite the custom of parents renaming themselves after the first child. For example, the first may be a boy called Mangko. The father will then drop his own given name and call himself "the father of Mangko," while his wife becomes the mother of Mangko. This appears to be a vestige, indirectly, of the pre-patriarchal days, for the modern system was not always in force. It is on record that when Christian missionaries first came to northern Celebes, another system prevailed, which was a modification of a very ancient and quite respectable plan by which genealogy was traced through the female side of the family.

The subsequent switch from the old to the present patriarchal manner must have come about, as I see it, as a result of the growth of the capture method of marriage among the Minahasians, similar to the same institution among the Balinese. When, above, I have said patriarchal, it should be understood that there has not, as yet, been a perfect evolution, for though matriarchy has well nigh passed, traces of it remain.

For example, the wife in the Minahasian household is not the piece of property or voiceless chattel a wife is apt to be among a multitude of Eastern peoples. As a matter of fact, she is on equal footing with the husband in the household and in business. This certainly indicates that matriarchy has not entirely vanished. In addition, the modern Minahasian marriage ceremonies bear all this out. The first part of the marriage feast and the consummation take place, not in the husband's village, as they would have in the days of out-and-out capture-marriage, but in the home of the wife's parents. This, and the customs of shunning mothers-in-law and naming the father after the first-born, are indubitably evidences that there was never strict patriarchy and exogamy in northern Celebes.

Whether or not the long years of Christianity and the growing European influence, have been responsible for this, there is really no knowing. Probably things will go on as they are, for while direct Christian influence will undoubtedly tend to glorify the male at the expense of the independence of the female, it will be difficult for Minahasian men to extend their influence much beyond its present bounds without arousing the moral indignation of the European ruling class.

It may be that the schools and churches which have spent thousands in money and in years of the lives of devoted servants are well satisfied with the result of their long labours. But it must be discouraging to them to discover, as they must from time to time, that the veneer of Christianity is a thin one, manifesting itself too much, during these comparatively early years of conversion, in superficial aspects. A people which has hundreds of years of animistic beliefs behind it does not, I believe, forego them so easily for a subtle religion difficult to understand.

While the Minahasians believe not only in the spiritual life in certain trees, rocks, waterfalls and other objects in nature, but also that there exists a hierarchy of free and foot-loose spirits with powers for good and evil in varying degree, they are in turn called upon to accept doctrines not relying in any way upon physical phenomena. The fetichism found in every savage and near-savage race is an obstacle here, for despite the teachings of schools and churches, the Minahas-ians cling to their own legend of the origin of the universe.

This tells that a certain girl, denied entrance to her own house one night, was plucked up to the heavenly village of Kasendukan, where she was killed and cut apart like a pig. This redounded to her honour, for the various parts of her body became the different prominent stars, planets and con-stellations in the heavens.

And likewise, they have their own ideas on a version of Samson and Delilah. They believe that the hair of the head is the seat of human strength, courage and even life to a certain point. An ancient hero, it appears, married a girl who warned him not to touch her hair. Nevertheless he tore some out, a mist came and she vanished.

And these legends were confided to me by dapper young men who came and went in the streets of various seacoast Minahasa towns dressed in neat white suits, carrying canes and gloves—in very hot weather, too—and who regularly attended the social and religious gatherings fostered by the local Dutch colonies.

It is this double mental, or spiritual, life which lends to Minahasa land an air of unreality and absurdity, as if no one there did anything seriously. I have no wish to be accused

of heretical doubt when I say I am quite at a loss to understand how and why the doctrines of a Christian church have
been able to make such headway here, while all about in the
Dutch East Indies there are peoples far better equipped,
mentally and by heredity, to understand Christianity.

Not far from the Minahasian centres of Menado and its sister towns is the village of Kema. It is not very important now, but once it was, for here used to come the ships of American whalers, ships from Gloucester, Salem and Boston, to rest, revictual and fare out again. But sperm whales are no longer so plentiful north of Celebes, having probably been driven much farther north by their instinct of self-preservation. These sturdy whalers used also to frequent the Moluccas, but no more, for the same reason.

And right outside Kema live the Burghers, or Mardykers, called by the latter name when the *Kompenie* first came to the north of Celebes. Because of their small numbers, and isolated industriousness, they are treated somewhat better than the Minahasians by the Government.

The whole question of the exact origin of both the land and the people of northern Celebes is a doubtful one, for geology and orthography both seem to indicate some link between Japan, the Philippines and this island. Little islands, scattered on the surface of the sea, are populated by isolated peoples who speak highly developed Malayo-Polynesian dialects. Sangirese, for instance, the finest Malay spoken in the archipelago. Some day, I venture to say, many astonishing facts and discoveries will be worked out in this strip of the earth's surface, for while in Asia scientists labour to unearth the physical remains of men who lived in an almost unbelievable antiquity, other scientists may well labour to find where the peoples living today come from, and why.

There is, in reality, a vast amount to be learned in the Netherlands East Indies, just as in any other seat of an ancient civilization. But here in Celebes no archives have been kept; men have not thought to keep consistently the records of tribal wanderings. About the peoples of Java and Bali, for example, we know comparatively much, but the full extent of our ignorance is revealed in a place such as Celebes which has not yet, I believe, reached the peak of its glory. It is rich in population, though sparse compared with Java, and immensely wealthy in natural powers. It is not by any means the least of the jewels in Holland's East Indian crown.

In these latter pages I have not been able to cover all of Celebes, for there are many tribes, and subdivisions of peoples, inhabiting the island besides the Toradjas and Minahasians to which I have so far given my chief attention.

The south of Celebes abounds in the Buginese, that wandering people to whom I have referred previously. When I say that the south abounds, I mean that they have congregated more thickly there than anywhere else on Celebes, though hardly a coastal settlement is without its temporary quota of Buginese.

Around Macassar particularly, on the coast on both sides, they are plentiful, living in small *kampongs* of only a few houses, say from ten up to as many as forty, each. In one house, however, I found thirty-five men, women and children, living happily and comfortably.

In appearance the Buginese, and their companion people, the Macarese, are different from the other peoples indigenous to Celebes. They are more like the Javanese, but here too they differ in the matter of height, being taller, and often above medium height. This tendency to height, which gives an effect of muscularity in men, gives the women greater beauty than that of the Javanese; especially in Western eyes, since the Buginese complexion is lighter than almost any other Malay group. In character, however, they are in many ways not as admirable. Though they are honest and industrious, they are easily swayed by their own impulses, which leads them to wander off at the slightest notice. Naturally this makes them bad servants and employees, particularly since they are also inveterate gamblers and adventurers. This lust for adventure and excitement leads them sometimes into theft, and I even found some villages where the girls deviated enough from the standard morality of the Malay peoples, who abhor actual dishonesty, to prefer the men who were thieves and murderers to their more conventional fellows.

This occasional laxity may be occasioned by their Mahometanism; not that I mean to imply that the followers of the Prophet are all somewhat lacking in moral restraint, but that the credos of that young religion do admittedly allow more latitude to the individual in his dealings with the world, than would another faith. In telling about the Toradjas, I said that they were at one time practically subject to the Mahometan Buginese; but it is strange that the Buginese either made no effort—or failed—to impress the hill people with their religion. On the other hand, though the Buginese have come in contact with almost every Malay people, they show no signs of picking up the customs and *adats* of alien groups. They remain distinctly and independently themselves, vagabonding from island to island in the archipelago.

In the lives of these Vikings of the East, women play an important part. Not infrequently, when more or less permanent settlements build themselves up, they become rulers, or at least, very high counsellors. In the household woman holds no subservient place. She runs the home, eats with her husband and children, and is consulted on every act involving the welfare of the family. As for marriage, husband and wife must be of the same station in life, and the dot, paid in money and presents and often of a value up to eighty dollars, is divided so that a dollar goes to the wife and the rest goes to her family.

To a nomadic race children are very important; so with the Buginese. They have a custom, not found elsewhere, of "dividing" the children. That is, the mother owns the oldest child completely, the father the next one, and so on; if the number of the children is uneven, both parents share ownership in the odd one. Thus the responsibilities of upbringing are shared.

In a people such as this, and the very similar Macarese who centre more closely around Macassar, you don't look for much in the way of handiwork and art. Yet they are known for certain artistic kinds of *sarongs*, basket-work, and beautiful gold and silver work. But on the whole their no-madic, adventurous lives leave them little time for industry and the development of land resources. They would rather board their sailing boats and cruise off to another island, to fight a little, start a settlement, and then again board the little boats and sail away.

It is wonderful that this broken-up existence has per-mitted them to develop any sort of tradition, any *adat* pecul-iarly their own. But they have done so, nevertheless. They have their festivals, their customs, all built largely on Ma-hometan foundations. And everywhere you go in the archi-pelago of Dutch East India, you will see Buginese, restlessly wandering, vanishing from one locality, only to turn up calmly and unexpectedly a thousand miles away.

And this too is strange: that while the usual Malay fears separation from his own little plot of ground as he fears the visitations of the evil spirits, the Buginese care little. They are not homesick, because they have no place to be homesick for. Their supreme indifference makes them immune.

But somehow they are thickest in Macassar, the second Hong Kong. They are the first people I noticed, their sail-ing boats clustered together like alien birds on a home roost. And a closely grouped bunch of those gently rocking craft was the last thing I saw from the deck of a K.P.M. steamer bound for Surabaja. I looked back on a peculiar island, where live white-drill-dressed Christian Minahasians, semi-savage Toradjas of the hills, fringed by the impermanent *kampongs* of the Gypsy Buginese.

Different, differentiated peoples; landscape different from the rest of Malaya, and altogether distinct customs. Every inch of Celebes offers startling contrast to the coffee land of Java. It lives, in truth, a life apart, relatively un-known to the world except as a name.

IV
SUMATRA

Though many early travellers made reference in their writings to an island identifiable as Sumatra, the first man to speak of it under that particular name was Nicolas de Conti of Venice, who returned from a series of Oriental travels in 1444. Then in subsequent years it became famous, being mentioned by King Emanuel of Portugal in a letter to Pope Leo X in 1513 as a discovery by Portuguese subjects. Following these developments, Sumatra took its place on the main trade route between Asia and the Spice Islands, most of the trading being done on its east coast, while the west coast was considered wild, barren and uninhabitable.

By 1601 the Dutch were deeply interested in Sumatra, and soon after established a trading post on the east coast, where the factors spent more time in fighting off the ravages of the Portuguese than they did in trading. In 1616 this became such an unprofitable enterprise that the post was given up. But meanwhile Dutch influence had been growing in the rest of the archipelago, and when the Portuguese had been greatly weakened by the constant attacks of the Atchinese, a strong Netherlands force was sent to oust the Portuguese from the islands completely. This was accomplished in 1641. But meantime the British also had displayed a keen interest in the development of Sumatra, in common with all the other Java Sea islands. Their efforts were not very successful, until the end of the Eighteenth Century when, in 1795, as a result of a clash between Holland on one side and England and France on the other, Malacca and the west coast of Sumatra were ceded to England.

But by 1814, after Napoleon was shipped off to Elba and Holland again stood on her own feet, an Anglo-Dutch treaty was signed by which the English retained the Cape Colony, Ceylon and Guiana. In 1824 a further treaty was entered into, by which England promised not to establish factories south of Singapore, while the whole of Sumatra was given to the Dutch, with the sole proviso that Atchin remain independent. Thus the Dutch were left with a free hand in the entire island, excepting Atchin, where British influence was the only factor that kept the native state alive. In 1871, however, still another treaty was signed, removing English power from Atchin. But when the Dutch went in they encountered stern resistance from the Atchinese, lasting from 1873 until 1904, when Atchin became an integral part of the Dutch colonial state of Sumatra.

Thus was brought to an end the power of the British East India Company after two hundred years of struggling for supremacy. The enterprise was profitable for no one until recently, for the English trading company, so successful financially almost everywhere else, faced defeat here. But the unity of government and trading, in force under the Dutch since 1904, has worked wonders, and it is the opinion of Eastern experts today that Sumatra is headed for an elevated place among the wealthy islands in that part of the world.

Such is the history—briefly summarized—of an island that now bulks large in the destiny of Holland in the East. Lying just south of the British-controlled Malay Peninsula, a stone's throw from Singapore and northwest of Java, it is on the main trade routes, and is in a strong strategic position to dispose of its vast rubber, tobacco, spice, palm, oil and tin production. With an area of a hundred and seventy thousand square miles, Sumatra is second in size to Borneo in the Netherlands East Indies, and has the additional advantage over the second-named of a more pleasant and dry climate. It'has not been necessary to contend with such natural obstacles here as have faced the pioneers of industry and development in the larger island to the east.

The native population, despite the size of the island, is much inferior in numbers to that of Java; where, also, there is greater ethnographical unity. This in itself, coupled with the fanatical independence of the native Sumatran peoples, has served to make the development of this island an infinitely more difficult task here than in Java. The northernmost tip of the island is inhabited by the Atchinese—many of its chiefs claiming descendency from Alexander the Great —who formerly lived in a state approaching independence under British influence, as pointed out above. And Malays are mixed up with the indigenous population in the northern half of Sumatra, in consequence of the process of infiltration from the Malay Peninsula so little distance away. All over the islands, as is the case throughout the islands surrounding the Java Sea, there are to be found in great numbers, Chinese, Klings, Singhelese, Bengalis and Arabs.

The interior tribes live in a mental and physical state far below the level of the Javan and Balinese peoples. Through their intercourse with Hindu and Islamic customs, the influence of these two religions is strongly impregnated in their consciousness, though the strictly local imprint is much stronger in every case than any outside influence of any kind whatsoever. The tribes generally have a common Malayo-Polynesian origin and fall into several divisions— of which the Lampongs, Redjongs and Lebongs; the Mandailings, Gayos, Malays (Menangkabaus), Bataks and Atchinese are the most important. The most interesting and characteristic of these are the Menangkabaus, the Bataks and the Atchinese, and to these I will devote the most attention.

Starting one of my trips from Sabang, a free port on the small island of Pulu-Weh (its harbour having been built as a coaling station in 1887) where the palatial liners of the large Dutch fleet touch, I crossed over by ferry to Kota-Radja [1]—the capital of the government of Atchin—on the mainland. The town itself, very important because of its location as a receiving point for imports to the island, straddles the Atchin River. It was once the headquarters of a powerful

[1] Kota-Radja: Kota—town; Radja—chief; thus, chief town.

monarchy, the Sultanate of Acheen, and the remnants of its glory are visible today in the shape of various old buildings, including a large Mahometan mosque in the centre of the town, its dome standing out conspicuously from afar.

Despite this evidence of piety, I was one evening pained to discover that the western world has no corner on the rascality market. The particularly irritating thing was that the brand of charlatanry I encountered smacked strongly of the home grounds.

It happened in this fashion: I sat one evening on the piazza of my hotel when a native approached me. What precise feature of mine attracted him—what infallible sign of pudding-headedness on my countenance appealed irresistibly to him—I do not know. He came up and said he would tell my fortune by means of a small bamboo contrivance he brandished under my nose.

I should have known better—in fact, I cursed myself in a whisper—but I agreed to his suggestion. I had no excuse other than my ethnological curiosity. Anyway, he held out his bamboo container and, rattling its contents—a lot of little bone sticks—asked me to choose two. I did so. He placed them in my right hand and had me balance a silver coin on them. Then he handed me another thinner stick, asking for a larger coin. I gave it to him.

His face at once assumed a grave and weighty expression. He mumbled an unintelligible formula, and at length regarded me with a bright smile. The Tuan, he said, is born lucky, and will have large quantities of business luck. This was all, though he added that were I minded to give him a still larger coin he would then feel able to tell me some more intriguing news. But I had had my money's worth. I assumed a haughty look and dismissed him. He went off, casting a roving eye about for others with unmistakable signs of willingness to listen to him.   Then he vanished into the throngs of people moving constantly in the streets.

For the city is a busy one.   It is also the railhead for the line down the east coast of the island to Medan Deli, the biggest and probably the most important town in Sumatra. The trip from Kota-Radja to Medan Deli takes two days, including a stop-over at Lho Seumawe.   But before it is possible to reach Medan Deli, the whole of the Atchin territory must be traversed.

Fʀᴏᴍ an ethnological standpoint, Atchin (called Atjeh by the Dutch) is one of the most important units in the entire Dutch East Indies archipelago. Here there is to be found a melting pot of customs and institutions, so that we are led to infer that in the course of history many different influences made themselves felt in the northern sector of Sumatra.

When an outside government desires to impose its sovereignty on a people, the first task of that government should be to study and attempt to understand the habits and customs of that people. The importance of the *adat* in the lives of Malay peoples is a point I have done my best to emphasize in the other portions of this book. Here, with the Atchinese, it is similarly important. For the *adat* of the Atchins is perhaps more complicated, more heterogeneous, than that of other less mixed peoples scattered throughout the Netherlands East Indies.

The Dutch colonial government has, I believe, made every effort to understand the peoples it finds under its sway in Sumatra. Thus, though the domination of the Dutch was begun only some fifty years ago, with sword and bayonet, the island is now governed on a system based on careful comprehension of the people who inhabit the land. Safety to government and safety to the lives of foreigners are thus assured.

As I intimated at the outset of this chapter, the Atchinese are not a homogeneous people, but are a weird mixture of several Polynesian races. There are to be seen the traces of the people of Malacca, the Malays of the Padang highlands, the heathen Bataks, cannibalistic Niassians from the island of Nias off the western coast of Sumatra, Klingelese from British India, Arabs, Africans, Javanese and others. All these, blended over a period of time with the autochthonous people, form the present-day race of Atchinese.

Ever since the Sixteenth Century, Atchin was continually open to Arab influences, including that of Arab law and the reigns of Moslem sultans in the days of Acheen. In those years Atchin was visited by navigators from the Western

world, including Mendez Pinto and Beaulieu. But besides
these, the real force in moulding the early history of Atchin
was the invading Malay peoples—particularly the Mantras,
definite remnants of whom are today found in Atchin in the
region between the Ophir mountains and the Selangon River.
These peoples emigrated from their own land in India to
northern Sumatra, and undoubtedly forced out of that territory the original inhabitants. Undoubtedly some of these
original people were the Bataks, forced south by the arrival
of the Mantras. Later on, according to the hypothesis of
Jacobs, noted Atchin authority, these people were in turn overcome by Hindu encroachments. The Hindu influence was
very great, until in the Sixteenth Century they were over-
thrown by the Moslems. This resulted in the Islamization
of the local Hindus, so that at that time the Atchin region was
inhabited by a people of mixed Mantra, Hindu and Moslem
strains.

It is interesting to note that in 1723 a Buginese—one of
that ever-wandering people—ascended the throne. From
this and all other available evidence it is clear that there is
little, if any, residue of the original peoples—if there is any
such residue, they have been so overloaded with outside
forces that they are hardly recognizable as such today.

In writing of these people, or of any people, the real
interest lies, of course, not so much in the broad outlines of
their history, as in their customs prevailing today and for
years past. That is a matter I have tried to bear in mind
constantly throughout this work.

One of the most revealing points about any people is its
marriage customs, and among the Atchinese, it is not surprising to see that these customs are based on Islamic beliefs.

Marriage by purchase is the outstanding and most used
method here, a girl being purchased at the price of from
forty to fifty dollars. Such a dollar is worth two and a half

guilders. Marriages among the Atchinese are contracted when the men are about fourteen years old and the girls between seven and twelve. Their *adat* declares that the father is the outright owner of his daughters, and may do with them exactly as he pleases with no one to gainsay him, which tends to obviate from Atchinese life any kind of romantic procedure.

The marriageable time for men is always determined by their parents, who will choose their son a mate at a time when they begin to fear he will fall into a life of sexual debauchery. The young man who objects to this is rare, for he will gladly accept the mate chosen for him. This may seem strange, until one realizes that the ties of matrimony among the Atchinese are extremely loose.

Marriages between people related by blood are strictly forbidden, though I once came across a couple who had married in opposition to this ruling. He was the son of an older brother and she the daughter of a younger brother. Such a case is rare, however, for the prohibition is based on the Koran, Chapter IX, Verses 27-28, saying: Thou shalt not marry thy mother, daughter, sisters, aunts of mother or father, the daughters of brothers or sisters.

Another variation of marriage forbidden by *adat* is a union between two young people who had the same wet-nurse. A relationship between child and nurse is established when the child has been fed three times by the same person. From the same root springs the prohibition against marriages between a man and the relatives of his wife, or vice versa: which is directly opposite to customs among dozens of other racial divisions in the East.

Now, since the act of purchase completes the marriage in the eyes of Islamic judicial belief, the woman is the property of her father first and of her husband afterwards. As the chattel of her husband her primary duty is to propagate children—to further the race—a duty from which no serious-minded Atchinese will hold back. In consequence of this, there is no need for a Mussolini law taxing bachelors. There are no bachelors of marriageable age among the Atchinese.

Despite this very cold-blooded and cut and dried method of arranging marriages, the Atchins resort to very strange means to arouse the purest of passions, including the *pegaseh's* or secret means. These are all love philtres, concocted by magicians. These gentlemen also invent proverbs which are guaranteed to inspire love when correctly pronounced. The user must learn the proverb by heart and mumble it to himself when chewing a mouthful of *sirih,* the idea being to impregnate the *sirih* chew with the meaning and power of the *doa,* or proverb. Then it is necessary to hand the chew to the object of love, by means of an accomplice.

But there are times when this method fails and the love-inclined Atchin must resort to another way. This is terribly efficient, but is in consequence very expensive, and thus out of the financial reach of the ordinary native.

Jacob tells considerable about this concoction, by virtue of which the youngest man can be made to fall in love with the homeliest spinster. These last are the very ones, however, who find the severest need for this philtre, and employ it whenever possible. When I was in Kota-Radja one of the native officials told me about the specially appointed men whose task it is to prepare this philtre when called upon.

This official was called Hakum Hasjii Hamalu, and he said:

"The medicine man who is commissioned to prepare this *prupuk* (concoction) attempts to capture a young owl, which he then tames and feeds. When the little owl is fat, the medicine man awaits a pitch black night, when it is cloudy overhead and the spirits move about invisible in the air. Then he ties the little owl's feet together by means of five metal rings—of gold, silver, tin, copper and iron. Having done this, he plunges a knife ringed with gold into the owl's heart to kill it.

"Then he must steal a ripe coco-nut, for it is forbidden to buy one or take one from his own garden. This he shells and removes its contents and grinds it to a pulp which he boils, but not so long that the oil comes to the top. The juice of this he pours into an earthen bowl, and he buries the shell of the coco-nut with the greatest care so that no fibre is left above ground. The careful burial of the coco-nut is very important, and has a powerful effect on the working of the recipe.

"Having made certain that every detail has been taken care of, the magician takes the coco-nut preparation and the dead owl, and goes outside the village to a spot where, preferably, three roads meet. By this time it is midnight. He also takes with him, on this expedition, seven strips of aren palm. Then, in the middle of the road, the magician strips naked, removes the five metal rings from the feet of the owl, and places the dead bird in the coco-nut mixture. He sets the whole thing over a wood fire, holding the bowl in his left hand as much as possible, at the same time waving the aren palm strips in his right hand. This is done to drive away the devil, who is naturally anxious to destroy the handiwork of the magician.

"What with staring into the fire, waving the palm strips, the dark night and solitude, the magician eventually falls into a trance. He is convinced that the devil, the dread Tjuba, will appear, and soon he sees him. But every time the devil does appear, the magician touches him with the palm, and the spirit disappears again. When this has happened six times, the devil appears once again, at which time the magician asks politely if he will now be permitted to use the brew for its special purpose. The answer from the devil is always yes, upon which the medicine man touches him again with palm strips and the devil flies away.

"Then the magician dresses and hurries home, where he ladles off the skim and preserves it in a bottle. With this brew he now has, it is in his power to set aflame with passion any one he will. It is necessary to put a drop or two only on the clothes of a person, and the proper incantation will direct the consequent passion."

Besides this potent philtre, there are many others in everyday use among the Atchinese, all leading, one may freely suspect, not so much to love as to greater sexual freedom.

THE Atchinese as an entire people are divided into four
tribes called *sukees*, a division attributed to Alau 'din
al Kabar which still obtains today. First there is the Kaum
Lehee, consisting of the Mantras, the original Batak popula-

tion. Second is the Kaum Imanpeet, composed of Hindus converted to Islam. Third is the Kaum Tuk Batee, composed of the foreigners in the country at the time of the division. Fourth is the Kaum Dja Sandang.

Each of these four divisions is represented in each *kampong*, and the representatives have very special powers. Under them is the *selangkee*, comparable to the Hebrew *Schatchen*, with power over marriages, and acting as a kind of marriage broker.

It is this gentleman who goes to the home of a girl and asks parents if they are prepared to give her over to him. They in turn ask for whom he wishes the girl. It is his duty then to name the intended groom, upon which the men of both families are brought together to discuss the affair. Marriages, as in fact all social life, are entirely under male supervision, the women merely carrying out their orders. Only under special circumstances, as, for instance, in the case of a widow, is the intended bride consulted.

When all details have been arranged, the father of the groom gives the *selangkee* a suitable gift, and the purchase price of the girl is finally agreed upon. From this day to the date of the actual wedding ceremony, the meeting of the future couple is strictly forbidden, and even should they sight one another out in the fields, they must take separate roads in order not to pass closely by each other. Likewise both young people must avoid their future parents-in-law. I made a point of following one ceremony all the way through.

The wedding day arrived. The groom dressed in his wedding clothes and, accompanied by the *tengku*, or village priest, went in procession to the bride's house to call upon her formally. A feature of this procession is a huge pot for all *sirih* chewing ingredients.

A strange point in connection with Atchin weddings is that the bride is never present at the actual ceremony, but sits calmly at home with an old woman and her four bridesmaids. The girl in question remained here until her husband to be came and sat down on a mat, where he took her on his knees as a sign that he would assume all future responsibility for her welfare and for their children. He touched her face a few times, offered a few casual remarks, dropped a *ringit* [1] in her hand, and then departed.

This was followed by a deputation of male relatives of the groom visiting the male relatives of the bride in order to stage an oratorical contest, discussing many general topics, in order to establish friendly relationships in formal fashion. Then, at length, the groom was escorted by a procession back to the steps of the bride's house, where he was showered with rice.

Accompanied by his pages, he entered the room where the bride was and greeted her, she being still carefully watched by the old woman and the four bridesmaids. This was the sign for the commencement of a general party, everyone in any way related to either family sandwiching him or herself in the foregallery of the house. The only ones absent from this congenial gathering were the two fathers who, in company with a group of friends, were busy drinking and planning to spend the girl's dot.

At the end of the evening everyone departed, leaving gifts in the hands of the bride's mother who gave the feast. This evening was also the first occasion when the groom could address his mother-in-law, though he too, together with his pages left the house to go to his own for the night. The next night the groom and his companions again visited the girl's house with the dot, after which some ritual maneuvers were gone through in the bride's room, though at all times—both this night and the next seven consecutive nights, the bride

---

[1] A *ringit* is 2.5 guilder or valued at a dollar.

and groom were never left alone together, the groom's pages being constantly on hand.

This procedure is parted from only when the wife has been married before, or is already a mature woman, but is never varied in the slightest in the case of the ordinary marriages of the extraordinarily young brides and grooms.

At last, after nine days and nights of feasts, processions and nightly vigils in the bride's house, the two people were left alone in order to consummate their marriage. And I ended my watching in triumph.

But so frequently are the girls too young for sexual intercourse, that Atchinese men are widely addicted to masturbation. Some over-ardent young husbands have been known to hurt their child wives grievously, on which a midwife is called in, who reproaches the young husband sharply. In general, however, the Atchinese attach very little importance to virginity in women at the time of marriage. Husbands do not complain if too early masturbation in a woman has resulted in the loss of her maidenhood. In cases where intercourse is completed on the wedding night, the husband will present the wife in the morning with a special kind of belt, and a sum of money. The wife will wear this belt without shame, and everyone knows what has happened. In fact, the mother-in-law finds this cause for celebration and the village priest makes it the occasion for a sermon on the benefits of married life.

But, barring these various obstacles in the path of procreation, the time sooner or later arrives in the life of every Atchinese woman when she realizes she is to have a child. She is then placed in the care of a midwife, well versed in native obstetrics.

These methods were such as to cause me a feeling of horror, but the faith of the Atchinese in their guiding powers and in the genius of a frowzy old midwife is great.

During actual birth, the mother is held in a half-seated, half-reposing position. The midwife assists the actual delivery of the child, while an opening in the floor is made at the point of the *parturiens* to allow for the passing of blood and *partes* water. The pain and suffering caused the mother by the inept methods of ignorant old women are naturally tremendous, but their native strength enables them, almost without exception, to go through many births quite successfully.

IN childbirth, as in every phase of Atchin life, mysticism and superstition play a great part and often replace the simple teachings of Islam. Polydemonology is in many ways the foundation of Atchin beliefs. I believe I have space here to recount an illuminating legend in this connection. Many years ago near the Atchin river lived a great philosopher, whose daughter, though very beautiful, was still single owing to the poverty of her father. Nearby lived a young fellow who soon became a frequent visitor to the philosopher's home, so that he and the young girl fell in love. The father realized what was happening and locked the girl up in her room. He then left the house. But right by the house was a tall tree and the desperate lover used this to gain access to the girl's quarters. Then, the father unknowing, many months of violent passion ensued, so that after a time the girl was no longer a virgin. But the young man could not marry her because he was a pauper. They proposed then to elope one night when the philosopher was absent. The girl, despite her misgivings, fled with the young man, and at length they came to rest in a forest.

The girl trusted her lover, but he turned out a villain. She rested her head against his breast, and as she did so, he cut her throat with a bamboo knife, and threw her corpse in the bushes.

There it was found by friends of her father, who brought the body back to him. Quietly she was buried by the river's edge, and a gravestone was placed over her. The spot where this grave was supposed to exist is the spot for religious festivals today to propitiate her spirit. It is believed, because of her tragic experience, that she begrudges all women the happiness of motherhood and consequently flies about as a witch and enters the houses of pregnant women to frighten or harm them.

But, despite the great importance and enshrinement of motherhood in the abstract among the Atchinese, prostitution is widespread. In every *kampong* there are several girls devoted to this profession, who, when they wish a patron, send a small child to him with a message. Of course the child does not understand why it is sent with a small gift of *sirih*. If the man accepts, he returns a gift of money.

Atchin prostitutes live in groups in the different *kampongs*, usually under the watchful eye of one or two older women, called *pangulee tutup*. They also travel along the roads from one village to another, and may frequently be seen moving slowly along in pursuit of greater revenue. Should a man pass them, and wish to have one of them, he will address the old crone at their head in the following stereotyped statement: "Mother, I have thirst. Yet I do not desire water. I am hungry but I do not desire food. Are you able to satisfy my desires?"

The old woman answers that she can, and a meeting between the man and one of the girls is arranged in one of the *ladang* houses, little watch houses in rice fields which are scattered all over the Atchinese country.

This custom is the most flagrant of the sexual debaucheries current among the. Atchinese, for otherwise their lives are fairly respectable, in Western eyes. A woman may not show her breasts in the presence of a stranger, though in other localities throughout the Dutch East, no importance is attached to the state of dress or undress of women, particularly on the score of modesty. No man may speak to a woman when she walks alone and they are very careful in the matter of entering one another's homes.

The worst vice of all is the habit of pederasty, practised mostly, however, only by the well-to-do classes, who can afford several pages for the purpose. In the matter of domestic fidelity, they are very stern, for a husband catching his wife untrue to him, is obliged by *adat* to kill both the man and the woman. Should he neglect his obligation and for any reason spare his own wife he may himself be killed by his own relatives for this regrettable oversight and squeamishness.

The whole Atchinese attitude toward women seems to spring from a complete lack of affection between individuals. They do not seem to love their wives in the way that Westerners understand the word. The men are content and kind to their wives so long as the women continue to satisfy them physically and bear them children. They make good husbands and fathers, however, and are very sharp in trade and personally economical.

Intellectually as a whole the Atchinese do not rank high among Eastern peoples, but they are sly and not altogether trustworthy. They do not seem easily to forget their forceful submission by the Dutch, and are seeking always for some means of revenge. The men of the country are very industrious and courageous, and what remains to them of the very mixed religions of the region has tended to make them fatalistic in their attitude toward life and the spirit-filled supernatural.

ONE of their ancient customs, now fortunately out of practice, was that of burying a live youth on the spot where a new house was to be erected. This custom obtained among many other Indonesian tribes, but since the advent of

Western influence, it has gone out of date everywhere, as have also head-hunting in Borneo, the *suttee* in Bali and similar blood-thirsty customs. Today houses are built in the Atchinese land without benefit of human sacrifice.

Their houses are, even apart from this feature, very distinctive, and are built on stiles anywhere from four to six feet high. The roofs are covered with *rumbia* or *nipah* leaves and the houses are divided into three main compartments: the foregallery for social use, the *djurai* for sleeping purposes and the *seramoi likut*, or household department where the kitchen is.

Like practically all the various peoples of the Dutch East Indian islands, they live in numberless large and small villages, each with its headman, and each its *selangkee* and its representatives of the four native divisions. In many places Dutch residencies are established, and, in general, the northern part of Sumatra—in fact, practically the entire island—is accessible by roads, and other means of transportation, so that almost nowhere does there exist that state of near savagery that one is apt to find, say, in Borneo.

But the fact that geographically Sumatra has been well explored does not necessarily indicate that its riches in natural and agricultural resources have been fully exploited. But so far, Sumatra is among the world leaders in rubber and tobacco, this power being one of the reasons for the tensity of the rubber situation throughout the entire world.

The Atchinese territory specializes in rubber and tobacco, and the entire island produces, in large quantities, rubber, kina, tobacco, palm oil, tea, coffee, gambir, petroleum oil, coal, gold, silver, pepper and tin.

All along the east coast of the island runs, today, a perfectly efficient railroad, by which it is possible to travel from one end of Sumatra to the other. I caught it at Langsa, on the east coast, a little more than half-way between Kota-

Radja and Medan Deli, and went on to this metropolis of
Sumatra.

Medan Deli is a shipping centre for a vast number of
products, and is the capital of the east coast division of the
island. From the city run several railway lines up and down
the coast, and across the island through the land of the Bataks.

The town of Medan Deli, in its capacity of leading city
of the island of Sumatra, contains offices of all the leading
rubber and tobacco companies which deal in the produce of
the island. A feature of Medan is the Hotel de Boer, where
come all the planters from miles about at least once a month,
on Hari Besar, to work off the energy for pleasure-seeking
that is virtually denied them on their plantations. Here are
to be seen the white-clad figures of men important in plantation life coming and going, intent on various missions to do
with social life before they hurry back to their headquarters.
They come from Bunut and Kisaran, located inland, where
are the plantations of the United States Rubber Company, or
from Arnhemia and other points in hordes of Dutch, British,
German, American, Belgian, Swiss and other nationalities—a
real polyglot gathering.

Only forty-seven miles from Medan is Brastagi, the
chief resort from heat of the island. Nestled on the 4,500
metres high Karo plateau, it is a veritable colony of cottages
in the European style, filled not only with Americans from
the United States Rubber plantations, but also with people
from other plantations and of other nationalities. It lies in
the shadow of the Sibajak volcano. Here also is the Hotel
Brastagi, where come all the detached men for a visit.

But all around, despite the veneer of Europeanism and
Americanism that has been overlaid, the native Bataks live
on serenely in their own way. Sometimes, as we sat on the
porch within hearing of the sounds of the hotel dance orches-

tra, from the compounds a little distance away would be heard fragmentary strains from a *kutjapi*, a characteristic Batak stringed instrument.

But Caucasians are not the only ones to patronize Brastagi. Here, during one of my many visits, I met some of the Malay Peninsula's native millionaires. These were Chinese, and they came accompanied by vast retinues of servants, valets, cooks, chauffeurs. One was Sir Loke Yen who came from China to Malaya as a contract coolie, and, a year or so after I first met him, died a millionaire several times over.

The other was En Tong Sen whose wealth, like that of Sir Loke Yen, came from tin mining. Both had brought up their children in true European fashion, and I have enjoyed frequent dances with their attractive young daughters.

I grew to know Sir Loke Yen quite well at Brastagi, and later visited En Tong Sen in his palatial homes at Kuala Lumpur and Ipoh. Here before me were two, out of many possible examples of poor immigrants rising to immense wealth and power. Such things, it is assumed, happen only in the United States. But apparently not. The difference is merely that in the East not so much fuss is made about it. From neither of these men did I ever hear a word of self-praise. Like true Chinese, they were self-effacing.

It was from here that I started on my trip through the Batak territory, passing through Karo land in a southerly direction and entering strictly Batak regions about the centre of Sumatra. My trip among the Bataks took me into the jungle land of Sumatra under the guidance of a young native and accompanied by my *djonges*, the Javanese boy who stayed with me during my entire East Indian sojourn. We rode first through country densely grown with coco palms, interspersed with a multitudinous variety of trees running through every shade of green. Our road led up and down through a fairly mountainous territory, and at every turn in the way, new vistas of mountains and valleys, covered by thick green vegetation, opened themselves before my eyes.

Native houses of the Bataks were visible here and there, in the shade of steep verdure-clad mountain sides. At other times, when we crept along the edge of an almost perpendicular mountain, we could see far below us different Batak *hutas*, or villages, well nigh perfectly hidden from view by the towering tops of tall trees. As we came more and more into the heart of the Batak country, the native life gained ever more in its own picturesqueness. Here and there by the road we found large wheels, not unlike those used on old-fashioned windmills in Europe, which were relics of Hindu times and are today used to assist in the irrigation of the rice *sawahs*. On both sides of the road now, attesting to the agricultural industry of the Bataks of this region, were well-planted fields indicating fertile crops. The whole was set off by the steaming tops of distant volcanoes.

My guide told me on the way that the Bataks had at one time in the past been cannibals, but that the practice, like the burial of youths on house sites among the Atchinese, and the head-hunting of the Dyaks, had been given up in recent years. He further informed me that their cannibalism, as distinguished from that of other Polynesian races which fed on their enemies, specialized in the consumption as food of their own celebrated personages who came to natural ends. It appears that they ate the flesh off the bones much as we do the meat of a chicken, and that the hands and part of the scalp were considered the greatest delicacies. He finally informed me that the custom was distinctly dead today.

Almost without warning, as we rode along, the character of the landscape changed. Its aspect now was entirely different. The hills were somewhat lower and connected in undulating ridges, covered with grass instead of the thick tree forests we had passed through some miles back. Swift, foaming mountain streams rushed across our path and tumbled on through the country in deepening ravines. The sides of these were densely grown with vegetation and now we found more villages. On either side of us were sloping mountains, while in the distance we could still easily see the much higher volcanoes. The colouring of the whole was brilliant in the extreme, with a clear bright blue sky, the scenery in all shades of green flecked with the burning hues of jungle flowers.

The quickly changing character of the scenery and terrain amazed me, for very soon we plunged again into huge areas of thick jungle, not so beautiful now, but with patches of dry and open land appearing now and again to relieve us of the fetid heat of the oppressive forest. The trees here were perfectly tremendous, shooting up out of the shadows of the ground to the sunshine far above our sweating heads. The ground, in places, was a carpet of big fallen flowers, while the interstices of the forest were a mass of creepers, bushes, lianas, and other vegetation, so that it was impossible for a breeze to get going.

The sound of birds was in our ears steadily, and I recognized the mywah, a pigeon-sized bird with a forked tail, and sharply coloured with black and yellow plumes. Kingfishers swooped from the trees to bask in the dry sun of the open patches we crossed. Monkeys there were galore, apes peered at us from tall trees, and the tiny shapes of mouse deer, those curious little creatures not more than fifteen inches in height, flitted athwart our road at times. Now and again we wallowed in mud, and at the same time struggled to cut thick creeping vegetation out of the way.

At many spots we passed bunches of wild bananas, and my boys gathered up some of the leaves and herbs which, they claimed, possessed medicinal properties. Several times I saw flowers nearly as large as the huge Rafflesia Arnoldi. There were vast stretches of alang alang and glaga, both herbaceous plants several feet in height which wrap themselves around trees and stifle them. There were many redwood trees, and thousands of the Maranti, from which the natives make their *praus;* and the nangkat, or bread tree, which the natives of this region use to make trays. Likewise we passed through veritable orchards of aren palms, from which the Bataks derive and concoct their intoxicating aren palm wine.

Those who have never travelled through an East Indian jungle will have a difficult time visualizing its appearance. Even illustrations cannot convey the atmosphere of luxuriant wild life, of the bountiful plenty of natural fertility—always with that sinister undertone that makes a jungle trip exciting. For there are a myriad agencies waiting to trap the careless traveller, especially the Westerner, who falls an easy prey to the effects of the heat, of the insects, of the gruelling trekking.

On entering this jungle, which extends almost uninterrupted from the north to the south of the island, travelling over mountains and through swamps, over rocky cliff edges, and through almost impenetrable forests, it was possible for us to make headway only by sticking to trails already made. Some of these were the work of Bataks, but these fall easily into a state of disuse, for the Batak does not travel more than he can help. Other paths we used were the swaths cut through the bushes by the bulk of rhinoceri, these apparently being the only big wild animals which roam the jungle in Sumatra. Elephants, of which there are a great number, stick to the higher and drier ground.

We marched along with difficulty, toiling in dimness, for so thick is the growth, so well do the lianas and other creepers knit the tree-tops together for miles upon miles, that the brightest sunshine is cut in half. Only in the swampy sections was the air really hot, for otherwise in these cool corridors of the forest, the air had a refreshing quality. And everywhere, when for some inscrutable reason all the birds and animals of the jungle became quiet as if listening, there reigned a perfect stillness. Then we heard only the muffled tramp of our own feet on the moss and flower-strewn carpet of the jungle. We hesitated then to speak, for the slightest whisper seemed to echo for miles, and would wake into screaming activity the millions of birds and chattering monkeys. At times this din became deafening, particularly when we disturbed a band of apes in their own travels.

Orchids there were in plenty, their vari-coloured petals languishing on tall stalks or around tree-trunks in the dim shadows of the jungle. No leaves on the trees moved, until suddenly one palm frond would wave lazily to and fro, and then stop, and then another, until perhaps hundreds moved gently. I asked our guide what caused that, since there seemed to be no vagrant breeze. He didn't know exactly, nor did I ever find out. But seeing this, it was easy for me to understand how and why the natives populate their jungle homes with imaginary demons and spirits, who brush against the trees as they whisk invisibly through the forest on their nefarious or benevolent missions.

Both my boys called my attention to the little *patjet*, or jungle bloodsucker. But I had already made the acquaintance of this charming jungle denizen on one of my trips in Borneo, and this time, without outside advice, I had taken the necessary precaution to put salt on my shoes, puttees, breeches, jacket, sleeves and helmet. Thus I was able to avoid the torment caused by these tiny animals, which live in the trees, but are invariably prepared to drop with a catapulting motion on the unwary traveller and sneakily pierce his skin. There they lay their eggs and breed and it is possible to get rid of them only by cutting them out when they are discovered.

After having travelled in this manner for many days, we finally arrived at the first Batak village of importance we had come to. Here I wanted to stop, to obtain some interesting glimpses into these strange habits and customs. The moment we set foot within the confines of the *huta*, we were met by the *pangkulu*—chief—whose countenance betrayed that he was flattered by our visit—a visit from a *blanda*, white man. As a token of his wish to be hospitable in the true Batak manner, he presented me with a couple of cocks and a small bag of rice. The rice I accepted with ostensible pleasure, but the cocks were more than I could cope with. In order not to hurt the feelings of our host at this early stage, I told him in suitably involved language that it was absolutely impossible for me to accept his gift of the fighting cocks. First, said I, it was not my wish to deplete his own supply of these valuable specimens, and secondly, my own gods would be deeply offended were I to accept it, since my acceptance would be directly contrary to the laws of my religion. My main reason, kept to myself, was a mental picture of my small expedition, trailing through the jungle with a couple of fighting cocks. The chief believed me, and with gracious smiles and a few apologetic words for having even unwittingly offended my Lares and Penates, returned them to his flock.

It occurred to our new friend that we were thirsty. Accordingly he sent two of his men up the nearest coco palm, and gave me one of the nuts they brought down, opened with his own knife. After our arduous travel that day, the coconut milk was decidedly refreshing. As we sat on the open fore part of the chief's house, I discovered myself the centre of attraction of many pairs of eyes. Perhaps, thought I, they are supposing what excellent chops I would make. But their curiosity really centred on my being a white man who had taken the trouble to visit them, for in all the Bataks appear a very gentle lot. I stayed in the care of this very hospitable chief for more than a week, and got my initial insight into Batak life.

IN Batak life, it was easy to see, women occupy the most
important position, beginning when they are children,
and ending when they pass from life as old and worn crones.
As children they come into the world on a bench, for Batak

obstetrics believe that the best results for children newly born are obtained by placing mother and child on a bench over a slow fire. This warms them and by dint of the thick smoke keeps evil spirits away.

Fire in the Batak tongue is *api*, and *di gindjang api* means: "above the fire." Thus they speak in this latter term of a child not yet named and under seven days of age. Batak women are careful and solicitous mothers, and suffer torments of shame and humiliation if they remain childless. Like nearly every other Indonesian race, the Batakkers regard barrenness as the most heinous of all possible crimes. They prefer girls to boys, for the same reason as elsewhere, that girls have market value. The husband having paid good cash for his wife, he would rather enjoy getting that outlay back in marrying off daughters. The more daughters the greater the prosperity of a Batak household.

When a child is born, they not only keep a smoke fire going under the bench on which the mother and child lie, but they also feed one constantly under the house, for the same reason: to keep away malicious demons. Bataks are very careful of the feelings of their spirits, and when, for example, a woman throws a bowl of water off her veranda and it splashes loudly on the ground, she believes that she struck a spirit. In order to convince the spirit that no harm was meant, she will toss out another bowl of water. All this is part of their many superstitious beliefs. Another example: when a child falls ill, evil spirits are blamed for its sickness, and when the child recovers if it does, they change its name.

The Bataks have a lot of small prohibitions, like the *pemalis* of the Toradjas of Celebes. The Bataks call them *pantangan*. When a man sows rice, he must not have an empty stomach. They must not speak of a tiger by that name; it must be called "master of the jungle." When chewing sugar-cane, they must first break off a little piece and put it behind their ears. Otherwise the father or mother of the chewer will die.

On the positive side, they believe blindly in the power of specific acts and objects to accomplish certain desired ends. Should a newly planted tree fail to grow, the Batak will plant beside it a stick taller than the tree, convinced that the tree will be stimulated to grow by envy, or shame at being out-done. They carry these beliefs into almost every daily act, and cannot by any means be made to see that there is no con-nection between what they do and what they want. When these remedies fail, as they lamentably do sometimes, the failure is blamed on evil spirits.

Their customs in the general regulation of their individ-ual lives are as rigid as are the *pantangan*. Girls, who are carefully watched from birth up to marriageable age, leave their own homes at the age of eleven or twelve, going nights to sleep in the care of an older trusted woman. Boys also leave their homes at night at the same age and spend thier sleeping hours in the *Soppo,* community hall. It is at this time also that the courting period arrives in young peoples' lives, and the Batak boy begins to cast about him for a suit-able mate.

The priest in this village, when telling me some of these customs, told me also what qualifications the Batak girl must have in order to measure up to the demands of a Batak youth. Her hair must be as black as night. Her skin must be brown-ish yellow like the skin of a lanjat fruit. Her eyebrows must be arched like the artificial spear used at cockfights. Her eyes must glitter like Chinese mirrors. Her teeth must be as even and as equal in size as the pits of a granate apple, and her nose must be graciously formed like a white onion. Her lips must be as red as a mangga fruit and her body must be well formed and smooth like a rice kernel. My friend the priest added that many times the young men lowered this standard somewhat. From sheer necessity, I surmised, after a series of careful looks at the young ladies of this and other villages. Otherwise there should be few marriages.

The Bataks, as well as the Atchinese, are devoted to love philtres, and employ them freely when they fail to win the love of the one they desire. The most frequently used potion is one prepared with the juice of the *djerook* (lemon) with various other more recondite brews added. When this mixture is sifted, the boy will try to get the girl to drink; or, failing that, will use the juice as one of the ingredients of a cake. I had one such potation offered me—not, I hasten to add, for amorous purposes, but purely for scientific reasons— but lacked the courage to quaff it. I take the word of the Bataks that it is efficacious.

As the Atchin people are divided into *kuams*, so are the Batakkers divided into *margas*, or *mergas*, corresponding to tribal sections. They are, in a stricter sense, genealogical units, all the members of each *marga* supposedly de-

scending from the same set of ancestors. This relationship
is a very tangible thing to the Batak, and as a consequence of
it marriage between *margas* is forbidden. The members of
each tribe keep more or less severely to themselves, residing
separately in villages (*hutas*), all of which are governed by a
radja, whose will is law for all Bataks.

Next to the radja in importance is the *pangkulu*, one of
whom is in every *huta*, and he is assisted by a *perpahaan* and
his minions. Under Dutch rule as much local government
as possible is left in the hands of the native officials, so that
really the ordinary Batak comes very little in contact with
white men. His trade is his chief source of contact.

The *hutas* all appear to be well kept villages, for the
houses are of a neat and rustic type. The graceful roofs give
the structures a solid appearance, being of thatch made of
aren palm fronds, while the outsides of the buildings are
decorated with excellent carvings and motives done in the
Batak national colours of white, red and black. I observed
that many of these motives showed definite traces of Hindu
origin, such as the lion's head. The ordinary house is built
up on stiles, and consists of several inside rooms divided off
from each other, as well as a veranda. Some of these houses
are very large and contain more than one family. Each such
group has a master, who inhabits the room in the right front
corner of the building, and to him are addressed all commands or instructions from the head of the *huta*. Thus the
house master is the lowest rung in the ladder of social organization among the Bataks.

The first *huta* I visited, as well as most of the rest I
stopped in, were built on high terraces, and were surrounded
by bamboo palisades. Entrance to most *hutas* is gained by a
small door in the palisade, inside which is a canal running all
around the village just inside the defense system. On the
banks of this little moat are planted rows of palm trees.

As each village is isolated, and the sense of ancestorship is very strong, so in turn the entire body of Bataks have for centuries been cut off from outside influences to a considerable degree. The native character and ingenuity of the Bataks, coupled with the impenetrable nature of the surrounding territory, have all tended to this end, and have produced a nation of men extremely narrow-minded and uncultured, particularly so as compared with the advanced state of the Javans and Balinese. One result of this isolation has been the long reign of cruelty, which outlasted similar practices elsewhere by some time.

On the other side, Bataks are conservative, independent by nature, artistically inclined, as witnessed by the amount of excellent, though completely untrained, craftsmanship exhibited in the products of their ingenuity. In many ways Dutch intervention has been an excellent thing, and on the whole the Bataks have been in a cooperative mood, though the early years of Dutch presence in the Batak regions of Sumatra were marked by many bitter and bloody struggles. Nowadays, however, the Bataks show their best characteristics in their willingness to learn. I was told that every effort is made by the native parents to send their children to the government schools, and further—that they make excellent pupils. They are excellent chess players and I put in many a game of chess with my newly made friends in Batak land.

On the religious side of the picture the Bataks present rather a curious picture. They are, as may have been suspected, animists, but they differ greatly from the heathendoms of other similarly primitive peoples. Their beliefs are much better organized than most animistic creeds, and show definitely the traces of the scientific arrangement of Hinduism. This evidence is confirmed by the fact that the names of their gods, and the names in their astrology and mythology,

are all definitely Hindu. The knowledge of their religion
is vested in the *guru*, who is much of an astrologer. He
makes frequent use of his Poestaka, or ancient astrology
books.[1] The people themselves have little knowledge of the
higher realms of mysticism, and for daily use devote themselves more to the souls of their ancestors. It is only in rare
and dire emergencies, therefore, that the common man has
recourse to the *gurus*.

In general the Batak animism resembles that of other
peoples, having the chief distinguishing factor, as I said, more
consistent and scientific assembly. *Sjamanism* exists among
them, as among other peoples of the Netherlands East Indies, and every yillage has its *sjaman*, who will go into a
trance at specified occasions. In a spiritistic sense the Bataks
recognize the beginning of life, and attach a great deal of
importance to the spirits of the dead. These, called *begus*,
are greatly feared, and are believed to lead a transient,
ghostly existence after death. It is well for the living to preserve the friendship of the *begus*, for they may be of considerable assistance in times of stress or disaster. There is
also another class of disembodied spirits called *hantu*, which
may roughly be characterized as spirits of the forests. These
are virtually all the ordinary man has direct acquaintance
with, for intercourse with the *debata*, or mythological persons, is reserved for the *gurus*.

Without wishing to seem in the least to deplore the condition of the Atchinese, or the Bataks, it is to be regretted
that so few people in this section of the world offer to the
inquisitive ethnographer the fund of lore found among the
Javanese for example. I have hinted at, and explained to
the limit of my space, the reasons why the Bataks, as a good

[1] These Poestakas are harmonica-like contraptions full of Sanskrit words
that bespeak Hindu influence, and are very rare.

example, have been isolated, and consequently have lost the chance at a wider culture, if not improved fortunes.

One remnant of an early Batak custom can, I think, be referred to here without fear of an accusation of flippancy. This is the dog market. It seems perhaps incongruous to bring this in here, immediately following a discourse on the Bataks and their isolation, but the persistence of the dog bazaar seems a strange hangover from other times.

It was at a place near Harangaul at Lake Toba that I found myself, all unwittingly, at one of these bizarre *Basars* or markets; Harangaul being, by the way, near Lake Toba where in 1837 two American missionaries were killed by the natives. From different roads and paths there arrived hurrying Bataks with burdens of varying sizes. Once arrived, they entered into lively trading, bargaining and selling, displaying meats to admiring gazes. But the pieces of animal flesh for sale were of curious size. They came not, I knew, from the caribou, nor from any one or other of a multitude of staple animals. I moved closer to one little fellow who was doing a roaring business.

From this closer view of the cutlets, chops and tenderloins held in the air momentarily, only to be snatched away by an eager purchaser, I derived the disquieting suspicion that these came from dogs. I observed yet more closely, and saw that it was so. The little fellow must have left behind in his native *kampong* a litter of canine carcasses of the best description. Dog chops, indeed!

I never ate any dog chops, or canine cutlets—knowingly. But they might be good.

IN the immediately previous chapters I have pointed out
the curious tribal structure of the Sumatran peoples, particularly the Bataks. They, as I have said, formed themselves in tribes based on ancestorship, each *marga* tracing, or

presuming to trace, its origin from the same set of forefathers. This is in direct contrast to the tribal and community division common among other Indonesian peoples, whose grouping is more or less haphazard. In other words, while the coastal tribes, with the major exception of the Buginese, have led stationary existences, the Sumatran peoples have been of a more nomadic character. Thus they had nothing but their common ancestry to hold them together, and in times of even the slightest stress this bond became of the highest importance. That it has held over into continued periods of living in villages and larger and more firmly established communities is not, under the circumstances, surprising, for now the *marga*, instead of being an institution of self-defense, has become a social unit with its definite purpose in the regulation of governmental and tribal life.

A natural consequence of a social order built on genealogical lines is the problem of exogamy, a very real one among the major and minor peoples of the island of Sumatra. Endogamy, or marriage within the tribe and family, reaches its highest form among the Dyaks of Borneo and the Alfurs of Celebes, and at times achieves the character of incest. However that may be, marriage outside the tribe is not forbidden by *adat* among those people, but is merely not the custom.

Among the majority of endogamous tribes, descent is traced on the patriarchal side; in some rare cases on the matriarchal side, but the outstanding example of an exogamous tribe tracing descent on the matriarchal side is the Minangkabau of southern Sumatra. These people, with certain divisions of the French and Spanish Basques, are the only matriarchates remaining in the world, at least to common knowledge.

Among the Minangkabau, not only is the tribal establishment and marriage regulated by the matriarchal system, it also has full mastery over name-giving, rights of legal descent, legacy and governmental organization, though the full effect of this last has been somewhat lessened since the advent of the Dutch rule. But in all other matters matriarchy is still the supreme power among the Minangkabau, and holds full sway in every detail of life.

The great part of what I put down here is the fruit of my own intensive observation, but I have taken pains to buttress my conclusions by reference to the works of some excellent Dutch authorities, including that of Lekkerkerker of the Bali Institute, whose work on the subject may be considered among the best available.

The fundamental characteristic of the Minangkabau matriarchate is the *negeri*, consisting of part jungle, part cultivated land, altogether corresponding to a communal organization. Over the whole the community government exercises complete control, while really the Dutch colonial government has interfered very little with this kind of organization. Thus, in the mind of the ordinary Minangkabau native, the power of the Dutch rule is very amorphous.

In this *negeri* unit there is a *kotta*, or village, composed of various groups of houses, all built in the extremely characteristic Minangkabau style, of concave roofs decorated at the eaves with pairs of caribou horns. Also, in the *kotta*, are included warehouses, and other structures. According to *adat*, no *negeri* is complete without its own roadway, an open city hall and a *Masdjid*,[1] where Moslem services are held every Friday afternoon.

The *kotta* is not, as I at first supposed, one large enclosed compound, but consists of numerous small compounds, one for each communion house, called *rumah gadang*, or for each larger building, called *rumah adat*. Originally each house

---

[1] Masdjid: mosque, or Moslem prayer house.

consisted of but one main compartment, but as the families grew, the houses have been added to repeatedly, and at the same time the compounds extended. In one place I found *rumah adats* of sixteen compartments. In connection with each compound are its own rice *godowns*, all built up from the ground to keep vermin out. In fact, all the houses, like those of the Bataks, are built upon stiles to keep the floors clear of crawling and creeping things.

Each family unit, thus constructed, is known as a *suku*, and these *sukus* have among themselves—that is, within a village consisting of many *sukus*—the right to marry from one to the other. But a newly married couple does not, in their view, constitute a new family, for the husband remains in the bosom of his *suku*, and his wife in hers. He visits her every night and returns home in the morning for his labours. Thus one *rumah gadang* contains several generations of the female side of the family, the men pertaining thereto all spending their nights in other *sukus* with their wives.

This extremely complicated family arrangement has made the types of houses described here very necessary, and they are built to accommodate the demands of their *adat*. One half of every house is kept for common use by all members of the family, while the other half is divided into a number of rooms, one or more for each female member of the family and her small children. Young boys usually spend their nights, before marriage outside of the house anyway, usually in the Koran school building or in the *godowns*. It will be remembered that this same custom of the men spending their sleeping time outside their homes is prevalent also among the Atchinese and Bataks, though for different reasons.

Another corollary of this kind of matriarchal system is the law that no male Minangkabau may own property in the way of houses, stores, land or anything of that description. All such items descend from family to family, by which is indicated the female side of the genealogical group. This, however, does not prevent a normal Minangkabau father from desiring his own children to profit by his lifelong toils. At the same time the women are extremely anxious that nothing shall pass from the female half of the family. Hence Minangkabau private life is one long succession of bitter internecine quarrels, ending invariably with victory perching on the banners of the ladies, as is so frequently the case even outside Sumatra in non-matriarchal lands.

But I was compelled to admire some of the indubitable advantages of this matriarchal system, for by it no woman or child may starve or be left in want. Theirs is the property, theirs is the possession of all worldly goods and chattels, and no man may leave them in the lurch. Should a male Minangkabau be seized by the wanderlust, and decide to emigrate, he takes nothing with him, but leaves everything in the possession of his wife and probably his mother-in-law.

And it must be realized that the number of Minangkabau men who depart for other parts of Sumatra, the Malay states and the Indies is far from small. Their *adat* prescribes that the men shall labour in the fields and help the women. But few men there have sufficient fortitude of soul to toil on and on, year after year, knowing that it profits them nothing in the end. So they go, leaving on the shoulders of their overworked wives the burdens of the fields and the household.

Here are, then, some consequences of this matriarchal system: the women marry afterwards without bothering to learn the fate of the fathers of their first children. This, even in Minangkabau land, is polygamy, but sheer necessity overcomes the *adat* ruling on the point. Further, the excess labour dumped on the shoulders of the women turns them into gnarled crones at an early age, when they should under normal circumstances be in the prime of life. They are able to bear fewer children, and there is nothing but work in their lives. I have no data on the point, but I suspect that matriarchy is from the physical point of view less of a success with the women than from the angle of pure power. But perhaps the sense of power makes up for whatever disadvantage there may be.

The above practically exhausts the limits of the Minangkabau matriarchy. The bulk of that part of government and administration which comes in contact with outside peoples is left in the hands of men, appointed however, by *adat*.

Each house has a headman, the oldest resident male, called the *Mamak*. He administrates the family goods, and supervises the raising of the children. Over him is the head of the *susu*, called the *Pengkulu Susu*, who has a host of assistants, and the governing power of a district lies in the convention of *pengkulus*. Carrying the same idea further along, many of these bodies, representing various *negeris*, meet and deliberate upon such matters as commerce. Such a confederation is known as a *Laras*, and the chairman of one is one of the *pengkulus* appointed to the position because of his wisdom or power.

I was soon curious to discover what effect the advent of Dutch colonial rule has had on this complex family governmental and social order.

The first discovery made by early Dutch officials was that cooperation between an ordinarily constituted colonial government and such a people organized purely on ancestral lines was not feasible. There were too many people to deal with, for the number of individuals with power among the Minangkabau is past all reckoning. Hence a system of centralization was installed, by which a body of governing chiefs was created to work side by side with the local rulers, but in such a way that they had more concentrated power. These governing chiefs are really the lowest salaried officials of the Dutch local government, but they rejoice in the position and power.

A NATURAL curiosity arises in everyone as to the origin of the Minangkabau matriarchal system, for such a thing is rare in the world as we know it today, or as I conceive it to have been in the past. It is, obviously, a remnant of almost prehistoric times, though a moment's thought will show that prehistoric times in Sumatra do not go back as far as we think of them in relation, say, to Egypt. For here we have available no such records replete with ancient information.

Wilken and Bachofen have expressed themselves—and I tend to the same belief—to the effect that in these early days marriage between couples, between two specific persons, was totally unknown. There were crowds of women and many men. Therefore group marriages were arranged, probably by purchase, so that a body of fifty women would belong to as many men—or perhaps more. Naturally children were born, but—and also naturally—the exact father of each child was a difficult man to identify. But about the mothers there was, even then, small doubt, so that they easily came to attach the children to the mother, and to trace descent down the female side.

From there, passing through the transition stage to specific marriages between specific couples, it is not difficult to see why, under these circumstances, a strong matriarchy developed. Couple this with the beliefs of many Indonesian tribes that the father is responsible for the soul of the child, and the mother only for the bodily parts, and we can see how the man came to occupy a subordinate position. Precisely why and how matriarchy has lasted so well and so long here —a spot really surrounded on every side by millions who consider women of very small importance—is a question not so easily answered. We are able to grasp fairly well the reasons for the origin of matriarchy, but the source of its continuance is entirely another matter.

It is strange to reflect that there are known but three or four matriarchates in the world: the Minangkabau of Sumatra, certain portions of the French and Spanish Basques, and the Khasia tribes in Assam on the border country between India and Burma.

It is odd also to reflect that matriarchy—avowed matriarchy—flourishes only among Orientals and Latins: both of which racial divisions are known, everywhere else in the world, for their extremely material and scornful attitude toward womanhood in general and women in particular. How much longer it will last among the Minangkabau, in the face of the interpenetration of outside influences resulting from foreign rule, is a question interesting to speculate upon.

I N touching on the three most interesting tribes, there is a
great deal about Sumatra I must leave unsaid here. It
must not be supposed that these are the only tribes on this
large island. Not at all, for there are many others scattered

up and down on its rich surface. But these three I have discussed in comparative detail are the most numerous, and by far the most interesting in an ethnological and in a human way.

The Minangkabau are the most southerly located of the three, and my passage among them brought me eventually below them, and down into the southern and western part of the island, where, in its glory, the volcano Merapi rises from the plains near Fort de Kock, one of Sumatra's most picturesque towns with its widely known "Karbouwen gat" (caribou cleft).

This volcano is always active, and emits a strong dark vapour without cessation. It had very severe eruptions in 1918 and 1926, causing heavy damage to property and life.

Its ascent forms an interesting trip, and offers climbing of the steepest kind. The long way to it leads from Fort de Kock, whence I started after luncheon one warm day on horseback. Steady riding brought me, shortly after dark, to the *pasangrahan* at Pagolean some six thousand feet above sea level. There we ate and slept, and arose at five in the morning in order to get an early start, and also to assure us a view of the crater at that clear and beautiful hour. At that altitude the cold was intense at so early an hour and we donned coats thankfully.

Soon after leaving the rest house the incline becomes very steep, and as we ascended we passed through a dense and virginal forest. Once out of this we came immediately to the last and most difficult part of the ascent: the crater wall, which is thickly covered with stones and cinders. It took us two-and-a-half hours, roughly, to make this, and at the same time we picked up some three thousand feet in altitude. On the edge of the crater wall we took a breather, and stared across a vast field of stones at the crater itself, identifiable only by the clouds of whitish vapour pouring from it.

It is a funnel-shape, and is the innermost of three, the others being extinct for who knows how long. Back of us we had a view of the country, while before us, a little further on, stretched a sand sea surrounding one of the extinct crater walls, the Kapoundan, with a clear lake inside.

Back of us was a vista of southern Sumatra visible for miles around from our eminence of almost ten thousand feet: the Indian Ocean, lake of Sing Harab, the peak of Korintji and Tanah Datar, and everywhere the undulating green sweep of the jungle lands, with native villages dotting the panorama, and in the far distance the white clot that was Fort de Kock.

Under the sun that had now risen almost to the zenith it all seemed asleep, dozing in a perennial heat that had no end. Yet underneath it all was a hint of vast energy, of undented powers and resources as yet untapped by the hand of man. That seemingly endless view, stretching away to the sea on all sides, suggested a giant asleep, but destined for great fortune on his awakening.

That awakening is to come, for though Sumatra is practically the youngest of the jewels in the crown of Mother Insulinde it has the potentialities of almost any one of the others. It is the key to a dominant position, because of its future in world commodities. Yet it is still untested and remains a reservoir of strength to be tapped at will—or at the first opportunity—by the tiny country that nestles cleanly on the Zuider Zee.

From there, and from all over the civilized world, men are journeying to help in the development of Sumatra, for there are riches there, to be had by white man or by native.

Those riches will soon be had.

V

BALI

Manik asta gina—Handicraft bears fruit

ONE night the Captain said to me matter-of-factly: "You will undoubtedly meet Mak Patimah—the Princess." Java lay behind us, for we were coming up to North Bali, which showed ahead of us through the pearly haze of the morning. It was early, and the first gleam of the sun struck fire from the volcanic hills that break the surface of Bali into a wilderness of enchanted, flowered rills. Bali *is* enchanted, destined to be a place apart by the force of its civilization of gentle unyielding strength.

The Captain had said, in a tone ever so matter-of-fact, that I would undoubtedly meet the Princess Patimah. As he said it he regarded me in friendly fashion, at times permitting his extremely blue eyes to wander to the preparations for entering the harbour that were going forward on the foredeck. This ship is known as "the pigs' express" (*babi* express) because on its trips from Buleleng to Surabaja it carries a squealing cargo of little pigs, temporarily imprisoned in bamboo cages.

Java lay behind us, and I knew what Princesses were like: many times quite ordinary people, oft times not preferable to the villager eating his polished rice (*nasi*) in a shady corner of the *kampong*. But Bali, with its rapt existence, surely must offer something different in the way of Princesses!

"What is she like?" I asked cautiously.

"Mak Patimah," answered the Captain in a tone tinged emphatically with awe, "is one of the cleverest business women I ever knew!"

"Business women!" I exclaimed. "In Bali?"

The Captain's very blue eyes, set in his pink fat flesh in such a way as to produce an effect of coyness, twinkled with secret amusement. "She is not," he declared as he left me to ascend to the bridge, "at all what you expect."

We anchored outside the harbour of Buleleng. The sun was high now. Far in the distance of a pale blue sky raced a tiny white cloud. The air blew softly and steadily, carrying on it faint jumbled noises from the shore, where tiled roofs of Dutch style houses and steep thatched roofs stood apart aloofly. Colours of every hue contrasted sharply, yet not jarringly. Tufted green hills broke the sky line, and the water reflected the pale blue sky.

When the anchor hawser rattled through the pipes, a cluster of *praus* (*prahus*, prows) darted from the shore— from a low jetty that carried the end of a white narrow street out onto the water. Bronze men in brilliantly-coloured *sarongs* paddled furiously, but one drew ahead: one slightly longer and wider than the rest, propelled across the waveless harbour surface by four men. In the centre sat a very small figure. I watched, knowing that the cluster of *praus* were headed for our ship; that each one, in all probability, bore a hopeful small-wares merchant, intent on selling images, gold and silver work, silks, woven cloths and batiks to the passengers. The largest *prau* won the race by at least a hundred feet, but at the moment it arrived under the Jacob's ladder I had to take a run down to my cabin, having suddenly recollected that I had forgotten to pack a pair of shoes left under the bunk.

I came up the companion and emerged on deck, almost bumping into the Captain, who stood talking to a native woman. I apologized hastily and started to pass by, when he detained me:

"This is the Princess I told you of—Mak Patimah." He spoke in Dutch. I saw a medium-size woman, perhaps forty years old, though I didn't form an accurate estimate of her age until much later. She regarded me—I must have looked ludicrously astonished—with amused black eyes. Her skin was a light bronze of clear unblemished tone. I greeted her and she returned the greeting. She said in not very good Dutch:

"I am glad that you have come to visit our island."

I replied that it was a pleasure to be so welcomed. We began a conversation in Javanese which she spoke with great fluency, couched in the flowery terminology of that language.

Her voice was soft, her gestures few but graceful, though I noticed with great distress that she was a chewer of *sirih*: the betel-nut-chew which stains the teeth, producing a red juice which is swallowed. It has a narcotic effect, though it is not powerful. She interrupted our chat from time to time to admonish her four paddlers, who had ascended to the deck and were offering assorted wares to the different passengers. With apologies for the interruptions she returned to our talk, and finally suggested that I visit her curio shop. I might, she suggested subtly, be interested.

A few minutes later I leaned over the rail, watching her large *prau* bear her small figure in *slendang* and jewelled silk jacket back to the low jetty. A Princess, a business woman, and the proprietress of a curio shop! Decidedly I was intrigued!

But first something about the island of Bali as a whole. We had had fourteen hours on "the pig's express" since leaving Surabaja. Bali might be called the pearl of the Sunda islands, and it is said in ancient legends that once Java and Bali were one, having been connected at a point now known as Banjuwangi, now the eastermost point of Java, and west of Buleleng. The narrow space between the two islands is now known as the Strait of Bali, though formerly, according to the same legend, a volcano existed there. The island is about 4,050 square miles in area, of volcanic origin. The broken hills I saw from the ship were the torn chalk of lava, and their steepness came sharply down to the water on this north shore of the island. Flat plains predominate in the south, while the southern extremities of the island are of coral limestone. A string of volcanoes runs unbroken from west to east, and up into the north, some of these peaks— the Bratan, Batur, Abang, Agung and Batu Kau—rising to 4,500 or 9,000 feet. These are really a continuation of the east Java chain. Of these only the Batur is still active. It lies in the south-east section of the island—where later I went. There are many rivers on Bali, springing from the volcanic lakes and springs, but it is strange, despite this, that only one, the Prantjak, is navigable. It was on this stream that Cornelius de Houtman, the Dutch navigator, anchored his tiny ships in 1594. Two of the crew stayed behind to live two years in Bali. Old Amsterdam was scandalized by a rumour that this effort at colonization was only a screen for amorous activities.

Undoubtedly the volcanoes have in the past been responsible for vast and cruel destruction—tales of it are told —but they have to their credit something which practically outweighs their bloodthirstiness. As in Java, the rain of their ashes has converted the land into one great bed of fertility in which well-distributed water is all that has been necessary to turn the island into a natural garden. Java has enjoyed a similar fate.

Everywhere I went in Bali I observed this: in the comparatively thickly populated districts of the southeast around Den Pasar, Klungkung and Bangli; and in the north, where formerly existed the Empire of Buleleng.

Sampans came to take us off the *Van Wyck*, "the pig's express," at a charge of thirty-five cents per passenger and four cents per piece of luggage. I spent little time in Buleleng, for it is distressingly European. In the roads outside the harbour there swayed at anchor an Australian packet and other smaller ships bound to Surabaja from Macassar in Celebes. American automobiles took us to Singaradja along a seaside road. The pale blue sea on the right, and the steep slopes of volcanic hills on the left, covered profusely with thick growth—flowers, palm trees, cultivated fields—all combined to present an air of great difference from the larger Java to the West. While physically the natives of Bali do not greatly differ from the Javans, they seemed—those bronze, dignified chaps we passed on the road—happier, more contented, more innately sensitive. Only after months spent in constant company with the Balinese did I come to appreciate the fine distinction of their racial and personal culture; their delicately adjusted modes of living, thinking, and dealing with one another and with the white man who finally overcame them.

It is only two short miles from Buleleng to Singaradja— the seat of the Dutch Bali Government.

A short ride brought us to Singaradja, but on the way we passed many things that interested me at once. For instance, something about the great rice cultivation on Bali fits admirably at this point.

Naturally a tropical island like Bali grows a wide variety of fruits, vegetables, flowers, trees, et cetera, some known to our Western eyes; others as strange and sometimes absurd looking as an umbrella on a sunny day. But there is nothing outlandish about rice growing, which is conducted along highly scientific lines. As we spun along the Buleleng-Singaradja road, on our left were frequent flooded rice fields. Here and there groups of small bronze figures waded in the water; only a few turned to stare, curiously and courteously, at our vehicle filled with Europeans.

I wondered, having already considerable knowledge of the geographic formation of Bali, how they managed so ably to have the water they need for the flooded fields. Later I found that many years ago rice field owners situated at any appreciable distance from any of the chief rivers, went without water. They then developed irrigation systems, but these systems caused differences—sometimes extremely acrimonious—something like the great disputes which rage in the United States over distribution of dammed water. The result was the Sékéhé Subak, a kind of communistic organization consisting of all the rice cultivators who needed irrigation supply in a certain district. This organization is ruled over by one of the *Klian Subak* whose function it is to enforce the regulations previously agreed upon, to police the system and to keep accounts. The association regulates the distribution of water. This worked very well for a time, until the result of irrigation was what it has always been: to extend the field of operation. It thus came about that several *Subaks* drew upon the same natural drain for their water supplies. So dams or weirs were built—so ingeniously constructed that many European engineers have studied them with care and wonder—from which, in many cases, led tunnels for many miles, thus transporting ample water to *sawahs*, rice fields, far distant. This method of procedure in Balinese rice cultivation is in force today, and is rarely interfered with, for any reason whatever, by the Dutch Colonial Government, for the simple reason that it works, and works well.

On the same Buleleng-Singaradja road we passed a few small temples, called *kahyangan* (*hyang* means deity, hence —place for deity), dedicated to Siva, and typical of those which dot the villages and main thoroughfares of the island. Later, I visited some of the chief temples, one of them at Karang Asem. I will dwell upon the matter of religion later on in these pages, having had as time progressed greater personal contact with the meaning of religion in their lives.

Arrived in Singaradja, we put up at the *pasangrahan* (Government Rest-house), which was modern, cool and pleasant. The town teems, comparatively speaking, with Dutch Government officials, for, as I mentioned before, Singaradja is the headquarters of the Dutch Colonial Government in Bali. Likewise, a multitude of Surabaja commercial import and export firms maintain extensive offices or correspondents here, for the many exportable objects and products of this marvellous isle. A few German firms are represented, but tourists, beyond writers, artists, photogra-

phers, scientists, students, et cetera, are discouraged by unofficial, and sometimes official, pressure.   Eventually, of
course, Bali will be overrun by tourists of the see-and-run
type, the type that has made certain spots in Europe and elsewhere an abomination to the serious traveller.   This is a
shame, for the riches of Bali, physical, mental, spiritual and
visual, should be tasted by those with proper appreciation of
their real meaning.   It will be a sad day when every other
Balinese has learned to speak English!

ARRANGING my luggage, getting settled in my hotel room,
a visit or two to friends connected with Javanese firms,
and luncheon sufficed to bring the morning to an end. It became warm after luncheon, so that it was impractical to go

through the streets much before four o'clock. When that time came, I went in search of the curio shop of Mak Patimah: an errand I was destined to repeat many times on this and other stays in Singaradja. When, after many months, I returned to Buleleng, and visited her there, in her white stucco house, I was astonished at the division of the entrance. On one side is the shop, while the wall dividing the shop from the house was covered with photographs of well-known Dutch and foreign personalities.

I found her in her shop, a large, airy establishment, filled, but not crowded, with small images, woven cloths, silks, tissues, such as *songkets, endeks,* richly coloured *plangi, tenganan, prada kains* and batiks. Metal objects of forged or raised work vied with gold and silver trays and cups to hold my attention. Carved wood, ivory, brasswork—too much to take in at one or two glances. She told me with a smile that all that was the work of Balinese from different parts of the island. It was extraordinary (as I discovered on trips throughout the island) how the instinct and first-rate ability to draw, paint, or indulge in one or another form of artistic handicraft, exists in almost every Balinese. Nothing in the house, or in personal raiment or objects of daily use, goes unadorned. Houses, temples, leathern objects, metal, everything, bears the work of some delicate, painstaking touch.

Mak Patimah is the richest woman in Bali. She has houses in Buleleng, Singaradja, interests in every chief city, and also in Surabaja. In Singaradja she has a weaving establishment where she now employs one hundred and twenty people!

She didn't tell me all this herself. Much I heard outside, from Europeans and from Balinese, but I shall put it down here with some attempt at chronology.

Her history really begins when she was fourteen and one of the wives of the Rajah of Klungkung in the south. The

Rajah died, and she was faced with the traditional alternative of being burned alive on the pyre of her royal husband or permitting herself to be mutilated cruelly. She chose another course not provided for in her *adat* (customs of her forefathers). She ran away into the bush and placed herself under the protection of the Dutch. Soon after she became the wife of an enormously wealthy Arab, whose wife she is to this day. She had, of course, followed the Balinese Brahmin religion, but on marrying the rich Arab, whom I met only once, she became a Moslem. Once the wife of the Arab, she opened her first curio shop in Singaradja, where her husband made his home, and by dint of the exercise of her great natural business talents, has since won the respect of the entire island, and of those who know her, either personally or by reputation, in Java. By the Arab she has had two children, both girls, whom I came to know well. Ni Wajam Lila and Ni Kadek Raoeh were their names. *Ni* denotes feminine, while *wajam* means first and *kadek* second. No chance for confusion in such a system!

She sent them both to the Dutch Colonial schools, and is proud of them, as well she may be. To this day Mak Patimah, probably between forty and forty-five years old, is a beautiful woman. Her soft bronze colour, black, piercing eyes and well-formed figure made her most attractive. She is about five feet four in height, and her almost black hair was always perfectly coiffured. She wore a jacket, the buttons of which were of platinum and diamonds, and in her hair I frequently saw a big pin set in rubies, diamonds and Balinese gold of from twenty to twenty-two karats.

I cannot resist putting down that I always detested her habit, like that of all the Balinese, of chewing *sirih*, or betel-nut. One day, as an experiment I gave some sticks of American chewing gum to Mak Patimah and her two daughters.

Soon after they complained of having been made extremely ill!

Frequent visits to the curio shop gave me an amazing insight into the vastness of her activities. Besides her shops and weaving establishment, she runs an auto service all over the island in heated competition with Minas, an Armenian who is also a butcher. Also, she exhibits at the annual exposition of the Dutch East Indies Industries (the United States also exhibits) at Bandung, seat of the Dutch East Indies Government. She proudly showed me many medals and awards she had won at these exhibits, to which sometimes she sends as much as forty thousand dollars' worth of silks, weavings, wood-carvings, gold and silver plate, et cetera.

A few paragraphs back, I spoke of the alternative the fourteen-year-old Patimah faced when her first husband, the aged Rajah of Klungkung, died. It was the alternative of going to *Indraloka* (Balinese Heaven) with her husband, whom, probably, she had never cared about particularly, or subjecting herself to the cruelest mutilation.

I asked her one time: "Why did you not wish to go to *Indraloka* with your husband and the sixteen other wives?"

She laughed, and said: "I hate the fire." An excellent reason, and as cogent as any other possible.

From others I had heard stories that, in reality, she ran away from the *suttee* with a young Dutch soldier; again with a priest of her own people. Neither of these stories was true.

She spoke little of this old custom of burning the widows, though no one I met in Bali, European or Balinese, told me more about the island, its people, its *adat*, than she.

From other sources I learned about the burning of the widows.

This custom prevailed only among rulers, for it was not permitted to the wives of others than rulers that they should go to *Indraloka* directly with their husbands. But when a ruler died, and his body had been carefully embalmed and placed in the *bale bale* (The House of the Dead) his wives at once fling themselves at the feet of the *pedanda,* priest, to beg for permission to be burned with their royal consort. Permission was denied to none, excepting those who were pregnant and those who had had smallpox.

Those to whom permission had been granted were from that day on regarded as sacred. They were attired in special garments, and their feet were not permitted to touch the ground. An interim always occurred between the actual death and the cremation of the husband. All Balinese wish to be cremated, and when money is lacking, the body is often embalmed and buried, later to be disinterred and burned when funds are no longer lacking. In the case of the Rajah, the *pedanda* had to wait until the signs in the sky and in all nature indicated that the conditions were favourable for the passage of the royal soul to *Indraloka.*

When the day arrived, a scaffold, *bade,* was built on the cremation field. A bridge of oiled sticks led to the *bade* from a house, the last resting place of the wives to be burned. In there they wore the white *slendang* which also covered the breasts. Below the scaffold was a structure of masonry three feet high, containing the funeral pyre and the Rajah's body. The flames were augmented fiercely by quantities of oil poured on by zealous assistants. At a signal the wives passed over the slippery bridge to the edge of the scaffold. A dove was placed on each of their heads, while below the field was filled by delighted subjects of the dead ruler, and by the relatives of the honoured wives, who turned joyous faces upward. One might suspect here that the priests excited the wives to the pitches of frenzy necessary for this extraordinary act of immolation by doses of hasheesh, though there is no fact record to substantiate this.

The exact details of this custom varied in different parts of the island. Thus, in some cases the widows were stripped of their clothing piece by piece as they poised on the edge of the *bade*. The dove on the head was intended to guide the soul to *Indraloka*, and the moment it flew, a priest delivered a blow in the shoulder-blade with a kris. At that moment the widow leapt down into the flames with a cry. Oil sent up clouds of dark smoke in evil billows, so that suffocation was instant. In other cases, differing from the above, the widows were not stripped before the populace, nor were they krissed. When the dove flew, they jumped.

This was the glorious fate of the widows who chose to accompany their husband and master to heaven, but the fate of those who shirked, or were afraid, was perhaps worse. They were subjected to mutilation, in which the ears, tip of the nose, fingers, toes and nipples were cut off.

Both of these alternatives Patimah escaped, later to become the richest woman in Bali. It might be thought, from the general strictness of the Balinese *adat*, that because of her defection (which was well-known) she might have been looked down upon as unworthy of even an Arab for a husband. But no; she is admired for her courage; a courage which, perhaps, many a young and beautiful Balinese widow wished for as she plunged with a frenzied shriek into a cauldron of black suffocating flames.

One afternoon I had had tea with Patimah, when we had discussed in small conversation the marriage of a well-known native. This had led her to explain to me some of the marriage customs of Bali. These are always of the most intense and revelatory interest in studying a people, so that I was doubly attentive. I knew already that ordinary marriage was contracted under a sort of kidnap or capture system, which is not nearly so bad as it sounds, but means merely a custom of elopement sanctioned by society and the Balinese *adat.* There is also what is known, literally translated, as a "forefather-customs-marriage," or *adat* marriage. This is a ceremony performed precisely, traditionally, as in old Bali, with much religious symbolism, and only takes place under what we would regard as the most extraordinary circumstances. I mention this here because it figures in what followed that same afternoon and night.

But getting back for the moment to marriage customs and their influence upon family relationships, Mak Patimah explained to me that the Balinese regards his father's full nephew (corresponding to our cousinship) as his uncle. His grandfather, in turn, he regards in the capacity of a cousin. And the child of his brother is as his own child, materially and spiritually. But there are also strong spiritual relationships between individuals where there is no blood tie of any description.

For example, to state the facts negatively for the sake of emphasis, a Balinese may not marry the female relatives of his house priest (*pedanda*), nor the female relatives of the teacher (*guru*) of his house priest. He may not marry the sisters of his business associates, nor the pupils of the same house priest or *guru*. Any transgression of these customs is considered incestuous, and belongs to the gravest possible transgressions of the *adat*. Such are drastically punished; in olden times by the most exquisite tortures; now rather by exile. Exile to the Balinese is a ghastly matter, for he bears a great love for his land and the nucleus of community life it forms. Hence, a village ten miles from his home is the other end of the world, and consequently, a journey of a hundred miles and return is to him what a round-the-world voyage was to Magellan.

In connection with the marriage customs outlined above, it is, however, interesting to note that the word incest has in addition exactly the same meaning as in English. With them it is merely widened to include the other violations of the *adat*.

Mak Patimah told me, after answering many questions about the foregoing, that at sundown, at the edge of the town, there was to be a *balians* or *sjaman*, festival. This was an example of a fairly frequent Balinese custom, in which groups of the people called on a male or female *sjaman* (species of priest or priestess) to answer questions in oracle fashion. I was, of course, greatly intrigued.

Accordingly, at the proper time, we set out. On the way Patimah munched a *durian*, that fruit which at first tastes like a weird combination of garlic, vanilla beans, Limburger cheese and— After a twenty minutes' walk, we came to an open space at the inland side of the town. Townsmen and women arrived singly and in groups, walking gravely and in silence, saluting one another and seating themselves in a wide ring in front of a large structure at the left. Torches of resinous palm shoots lit the scene with a soft flickering light, serving also to keep away mosquitoes and other insects. At one side was a group of musicians, differing from most Balinese orchestras in the resonance of the drums, which soon began a heavy, slow sensuous rhythm which beat on the brain with torturing insistence. There must have been fully a hundred and fifty men and women seated in the circles; they paid no attention to me, the only white present.

A girl appeared before the circle from the large structure. She was dressed ordinarily, in a vividly coloured *sarong* and *kubaja* and she seemed about twenty years old. She was the *balian*, a type of female *sjaman* or priestess, which undoubtedly correspond identically with the *sjamans* of the Dyaks of central Kahajan in central Borneo, south and east Borneo and of central Celebes. The foundation of the belief in the validity and power of *sjamans* among the Balinese, as among all people primitive in their religious beliefs, lies in their con-

viction that disease or sickness enters the body only when the
soul has temporarily left the body. Or, in other words, that
a demon (*buta*) has taken possession of the body. From this
it is but a short step to the belief that certain individuals are
"possessed" by ghosts or demons, which speak oracle-fashion
through their mouths, under favourable circumstances. This
may also be traced back to the belief of all peoples at one
time or another that lunatics, or all persons abnormal in one
way or another were "touched by God." These were, as
reference to Indian, American Indian, Asiatic, European and
early American histories will show, held in high esteem, or
at worst regarded with fear and never to be offended or hurt
in any way. Compare this also with the historical incident
of Ivan the Terrible's meeting with an idiot on the road to
Pskow. This so frightened the warrior-ruler, and so impressed him as an evil portent, that he and his whole army
turned back.

The light of modern study has now given rise to the very
natural suspicion that some of these "touched" in all parts
of the world and their frequently parallel, if not concurrent,
civilizations were not as abnormal as they seemed. They
were not "as crazy as they looked." It is not too much to
suspect also, that in certain cases, abnormality was deliberately
assumed, much as the cloth of sanctity may be assumed today.
And we may suppose ironically that it is not a whit more
difficult today than before to get away with it.

Hence the *sjamans* of Bali. The *balians* (female
sjamans) are, in addition to being an order of priestesses,
likewise prostitutes, for which reason their dress differs from
that of the ordinary Balinese woman in that the upper part
of the body is covered by a jacket or *sarong*. Balinese
women uniformly wear the *sarong* (and *slendang* around the
waist) which reaches from the navel to the ground, leaving
the bust exposed. This may be attributed not only to the

warmth of the climate, but also to the belief that a virtuous woman has, literally, nothing to hide. This is substantiated by the custom that women engaged in prostitution must have the breasts covered. Thus the *balians*, being prostitutes in addition to oracles, wear an upper garment.

The drums had begun; darkness had fallen. The girl sat down cross-legged. Her body began to tremble all over, gently quivering. The music became heavier; a tremor convulsed her body in a wave-like progression. This went on for many minutes. Suddenly she jumped up wildly, her black hair flying loose, and she cried out in a soft, long-drawn nasal tone that the demons had entered her body. She was in a trance. Then the orchestra began a terrific uproar lasting a long time, while the girl's head revolved on her shoulders, twisting from side to side so that I thought it would surely fly off. Offerings were pushed forward from different groups among the spectators. *Sirih*, boiled yellow, red and blue rice, flowers, oil-lamps, or palm and lontar leaves. These offerings, Patimah whispered to me, were not to the *sjaman*, but to the demons to placate them. Unintelligible words began to stream from the girl's lips. I could catch no meaning in them, nor could my companion. The impressiveness of this jargon was thereby heightened. I saw two big glistening tears run down the girl's cheeks; her face was now distorted into an expression of the utmost ferocity.

At that moment questions began to rain on her, shot forth from the impressed spectators. Her answers came, couched in oracle-like terms, open to many interpretations. In moments of silence, the *sjaman* emitted a wide variety of astonishing vocal sounds, sometimes screaming her answers at the top of her over-worked lungs, or muttering them so that the questioners had to lean forward, their faces straining anxiously, the torch light falling on them. Grotesque shadows danced on the ground, and surprised murmurs made an undertone to the whole affair. The music kept on, now very loud, now lapsing into complete, almost apathetic silence. Looking about, I saw one man on the outskirts munching a handful of rice. It must have been intended for an offering, but there were many offerings already in the open space before the entranced *sjaman*. And—every gathering contains at least one irreverent soul.

This procedure went on uninterruptedly for hours. The difficulty I had in understanding all that was said and in comprehending many of the movements, or remarks of the *sjaman*, wearied me physically. But I stuck it out, chiefly to see how it would end. It must have been about two o'clock in the morning when the *sjaman* suddenly grow rigid, then fell back on the ground. Convulsive tremors shot through her slim young body, and after a few minutes she got up, and walked without a sound, almost disdainfully, into the house. Mak Patimah told me that after such a siege, the *sjamans* do not recall one item of all that happened during the trance state.

The spectators arose, and a sudden change came over them. A group of six village guards preceded the line of march. They beat loudly on hollow bamboo poles, a reverberating noise resulting, to keep away the evil spirits who frequent the roads at night. The men and women laughed, sang, and chatted with great gaiety, and the torches flared up in greater numbers. We paraded along behind, watching family groups vanish rapidly into their own *kampongs*, until at last I left Mak Patimah at her home and returned to the *pasangrahan*.

There was much about the *sjaman* affair that captured my interest and I made it my business, when possible, to learn more about it.

Sjamans were, originally, recruited from among the lunatics or abnormal individuals in the community subject to

convulsions, hysterics, epilepsy, catalepsy, lethargy, somnambulism and those easily influenced by hypnosis. Weak-
minded and neurotic types were led into the *sjaman* class,
and generally, all those who in early life showed signs of
nervous disorders were looked upon by the priests of this
class as suitable material.

It is probable that priests singled out these individuals as children, and took them away for training. It must
have been easy to do, for on the one hand the people believed
that such abnormals were under the personal protection of
the gods, while on the other, as a derivative, it was considered
an honour for a girl in the family to become a *balian*. But
there are cases on record of brothers deliberately killing their
balian sisters, possibly being over-sensitive because of the
prostitution practised as a side-line by the honoured priestesses, whom above all it was an offense to offend.

There was one case I heard of which shows the peculiar
things which do undoubtedly occur among this strange class.
A certain female *sjaman*, suffering from somnambulism complicated probably by other nervous derangements, lived for
some time with a Christian missionary. She was his housekeeper. Later, when in a somnambulistic state, she would
recite whole passages of the Bible both in English and in
Hebrew. It was found that consciously she had never
learned the languages. This may be compared with similar
examples cited in modern psychoanalysis.

The male division of the *sjaman* class is even more astonishing, and throws an amazing light on a problem which
modern Western civilization seems just to have discovered:
that of homosexuality among men.

The male *sjamans* are called *basir*, the word meaning
literally, "unfruitful." Many are likewise impotent and because of this are permitted access, in their combined guise of
priest and male prostitute, to the most private chambers. As

a rule, they have uncouth voices, extremely weak eyesight, and frail general appearance, symptoms common to this unfortunate class of human being everywhere. Though in fairness to them it should be pointed out that the Balinese men are as a whole somewhat effeminate in habit and appearance; they do not, as do many natural peoples the world over, make a fetich of physical prowess and achievement, though they are innately very brave and proud. Though also, and curiously, the word Bali implies heroism! Balinese men dress in a style which equals in gaiety that of the women; flowers in the hair and *sarongs* of flamboyant colours. Their women massage and anoint them after the bath!

The *basir*, like the entire *sjaman* group, are recruited from among those with nervous disorders, though the priests are probably able, because of their specific knowledge, to single out homosexual youths at an early age. They prefer, I was told, tall boys, probably because of the added impressiveness of the height in religious ceremonies.

A Balinese friend of mine described to me, in response to my questioning, an occasion on which a *basir* acts as a sort of medicine man. A *basir* may be asked for advice on the condition of a sick man. He will first demand that plentiful offerings be placed before him on the ground. He may get fruit, or a sum as large as two hundred kepangs of Balinese coins (the kepang is of Chinese origin) roughly equal to eight cents in American money. The drums and accompanying orchestra are present, as in the case of the *balian* festival, for the drums make it easier for the *sjamans* to work themselves into a trance. When the drum and music have subsided a trifle, the *basir* rings a small temple bell, as if calling his rapt audience to absolute attention. Then he begins to mumble words of an unintelligible jargon, as incomprehensible to himself as to his audience. Little by little his eyes become glassier, his body trembles, the trembling increasing until he is in a frenzy. His hair flies, his body quivers in a sort of obscene ecstacy, his head rolls on his shoulders. At the moment, known to the audience from previous experience, when the frenzy is acute, the question is shot at the *basir*. His answer may be mouthed out ferociously, or screamed forth suddenly and awfully.

A further fact of astonishing character is that the *basir* are, in certain cases, dressed like women and married to men according to *adat*. This means that the ceremony is elaborately performed, in the exact manner used by their forefathers, though this "marriage" need not last long. Likewise, in many circles throughout Bali, the services of the *basir* are more highly regarded and more highly paid than those of women!

THE word *Pura*, frequently used in these pages, means
simply temple, and applies to the many such buildings
which almost literally line the roads and form the nuclei of
hamlets and village communities. Besides these larger tem-

ples there are many smaller shrines called Kahyangan of
which I saw a number on the two mile road from Buleleng
to Singaradja. But the main temples are impressive, both
visually and for what they represent.

In Bali, religion rules the people. It is the foundation
of the duties of man and friend, and tolerance, from which
Western lands may well profit, reigns calmly among them.
Jew, Christian, Mahometan, Confucian, may all preach and
practise their beliefs and creeds. The Balinese do not interfere. True, foreign missionaries have not found this en-
couraging. They have not found a people easy to frighten
into believing that eternal damnation menaces them
should they not at once adopt one or another brand
of Christianity. An illuminating tale is told, confiden-
tially, although it is a public secret, and though it is
actually true, of two Dutch Christian missionaries who came
to the island of Bali. They spent several months in preach-
ing, exhortation and sermonizing. They were courteously
and tolerantly heard, but only one convert resulted; they
named him Nicodemus. One of these missionaries observed
that the Balinese religion, into which I am going within a
few pages, served the people well. It had made and kept
them dignified, honest, courteous, tolerant, sensitive, loyal.
Nicodemus, far from achieving a superior plan of spiritual
life, became most unhappy. Shortly thereafter, in the excess
of his feelings, he killed both missionaries. Balinese justice
took care of him swiftly, and he soon expiated the murders
with his own death. Since that disastrous time the Dutch
Colonial Government has not encouraged missionarying of
any sort.

The Pura Sangsit is constructed on the same plan as the
other larger temples throughout the island. It is three-
walled, with connecting courts. Smaller buildings and sheds
are contained within for conducting ceremonies. I entered

through a cleaved gate (*Tjandi Bentar*) without a roof, and came into an outer court devoid of life. All I saw were a few sheds, *bales* or offering places, and from there I passed on into an inner court through a covered gate with a heavy wooden door. This second court is used for ceremonious meetings, the taking of oaths. It also houses a *bale agung*, a special place for the reception of offerings, and a bell tower (*sangsak*) for the officials of the Dewas.

From this solemn court I passed on into the third most sacred court through another covered gate. In here, along the walks, are the houses of the gods, with little offering niches. Directly opposite the gate through which I had entered was another, leading in the other direction.

The gods' houses presented a strange sight. Those of the lesser gods are simple wooden structures on stone foundations, with rush roofs. For the more sacred gods are provided more magnificent *merus* on sculptured stone foundations, flights of stone steps, and uneven numbers of roofs, anywhere from three to eleven, like Chinese pagodas. These roofs are made of *idjuk*, dried aren palm fibre, resting on wooden frames.

In various of the offering niches I saw little heaps of different-coloured rices on palm or lontar leaves. Silent men and women passed to and fro, uttering no sounds. I visited the Pura Sangsit at a time of day when no ceremonies were in progress, a circumstance I regret, but I had excellent occasion to see a full-size religious ceremony later on in another of the larger temples on the island.

The religion of Bali is interesting, though it was not in its essentials new to me, who had been previously throughout the far East. It resembles the chief creed of India in many ways.

There, according to popular belief, Brahma, Vishnu and Siva, or the Trimurty, are the principal gods, but the Brah-

mins of India pay them but little honour. The Vedas placed
other gods above them, leaving Vishnu and Siva in subordinate positions.

The popular creed of Bali is divided into two great sects:
one worshipping Siva and the other Vishnu. Brahma is
ignored. It is quite certain, strangely enough, that no Vish-
nuites ever came to ancient Java nor to Bali, although their
Vishnu embodies all the characteristics, attributes and names
of the Indian god; he combines in himself the powers of all
the gods. Siva, who is the all-highest and is invisible, dwells
alone in the heart. Brahma was said to be fire, the smoke of
which became water, or Vishnu.

Brahmandapurana, the teachings of the Brahmin religion,
plays an important part in Balinese life, being merely slightly
divided on the score of Vishnu and Siva. The Brahmandapurana teaches that the world was created from an egg, out
of which came four beings because of the penance performed
by Brahma. This was followed by the creation of heaven,
the seas, mountains and plants.

It is worth putting down here, for better understanding
of the Balinese life and character (as it helped me), the
principal precepts forming the doctrine of a Brahmin:

First, Brahmachan is he who lives as a pupil with his
guru or teacher. Second, Grehasta is he who heads the
family. He is the married man, whose duty it is to exercise
the *darma* (sometimes spelled *dharma*) or right of religion,
which consists principally in raising sons, making offerings
for his forefathers (*pitara*) and in being surpassingly hospitable. Third is the Wekanasa, or hermit, who inhabits the forests for the purposes of meditation. Fourth is the Yati, the
ascetic who has in himself brought into subjection all that is
sensuous and worldly. He occupies himself exclusively with
meditation (*yoga*). These are called in India, *Saniassi,* or
saints.

While the Balinese religion cannot be called true, some of it being a remnant and admixture of the Polynesian age, the island of Bali is, in the Dutch Indies, the only bulwark of the old Hindu creed of golden age—the Javanese-Hindu empire of Modjopah... ...en before the followers of the Prophet in the beginning of the Fifteenth Century—which elsewhere had succumbed to aggressive Islam. Here it has been preserved, practically, in all its entirety.

The chief Balinese places of worship are the Sad-Kahyangan, all dedicated under various names and titles to Siva. The oldest and chief of these is at Basuki, at the foot of the Gunung Agung, or Holy Mountain, in Karang Asem. The name of the deity here is Sang-Purnajaya. Next comes the Watu Kahu at the foot of the peak at Tabanan, in central Bali; followed by Kluwatu, on the point of the table land in Badoeng, picturesquely situated on projecting rock by the sea. There is also Jeh Jeruk in Giangiar in the south, another in the village of Narangkana in the interior, and finally Giralawa in Klungkung in the south-east. There are also temples called Puras and Pangastanan, the first for those of the highest rank, the latter for the people, in which Siva is worshipped.

I have already spoken of the wayside shrines and small temples, but must not overlook the small shrines in every house, and the house temples of the Balinese princes, which are completely of stone in pyramidal shapes.

The architecture of Balinese temples is of the same style and class as those of the Javan empire of Modjopahit of the third period. It is only in the most ancient temples, such as the Pura Sangsit that stone carvings are found. Apparently this is one of the few arts not as far advanced in Bali as in other parts of the East.

Religious ceremonies and feasts are of course of various

types: the general feasts, the foundation-day feasts, called Wedalan, the expiatory feasts, et cetera. There are many non-religious feasts: pregnancy festival during a woman's first pregnancy; the Kjumunin Tjamah, or festival of first menstruation, when a young girl is first thought marriageable.

The general feasts of the gods are celebrated on Galungsan and the five weeks following. During this period the gods are said to dwell on Earth, hence constant offerings to them during this time. The preparations for the feasts and the offerings which shall be made during them are most minutely prescribed for each deity and for each temple. Expiatory feasts, called *prayaehitta* (literally: doing penance) the same word applying to the purification of a house in which a corpse has lain, are not celebrated in the chief temples, but in the inner part of the temple-houses. Two of these special feasts, called *Bayakala* and *Pauchawalikrama*, are the foremost of expiatory feasts. At these it is deemed strictly necessary that five *pedandas* should be present, one facing each of the four cardinal points of the compass, and one, perforce a Buddhistic priest, facing south. Let me repeat, however, that Buddha plays a small part in these festivals.

The *pedandas*, by their life and constant study of the Vedas, are identified both spiritually and materially with the supreme Siva. The *pedanda* alone, by mumbling passages from the Vedas, is able to call down the various gods.

Next in rank to the *pedanda* comes the *mangku*, or temple watcher, who superintends the temple and conducts the preparation of offerings according to the strict code.

He must know certain *mantras*, rituals, and employ them when offerings are made. The order of *mangkus* may not be achieved until the deities, or a special deity, has passed into the body of the candidate and has spoken therefrom. This invisible something, said to be the gods, is called *taksu,* which implies oracular powers, such as at ancient Delphi.

Once a day, ordinarily, the *pedandas* mumble the Vedas, when offerings are made, usually by the women of the community. On great occasions it is not sufficient to make the offerings only with the help of the *mantras,* the unspoken ritual prayers, but dances are imperative. Dances, *tandakken,* are frequently coupled with the kris, or dagger, by those inspired directly by the deities, as a sign that the offerer is ready to sacrifice his life. Those inspired by the deities are called *prakulit.* Human sacrifices are a thing of the past, as a result of the foreign control, but to satisfy certain necessary blood requisites, such as at feasts to *Durga* and *butas,* the underworld gods, cockfights are now arranged.

Later I will describe the temple feast and dagger dances that I saw in south Bali. These suggested to me the link that exists between this highly civilized and cultured people and the crudities of a Malay-Polynesian existence of former times that depended for its life on a harsh, unbending realism. Such dances as these, as an example of these links, are the few vestiges of a former racial frame of mind that has since grown into a complex, in some respects sophisticated, tradition. Every civilization has retained some such vestiges, to remind itself that a cruel undertone to life still exists, despite the cushions that philosophers, minstrels and respect for the past have created.

I LEFT Singaradja one early morning in a large touring
car with the top up, American manufacture, hired out
at the regular rate of sixteen dollars per day for from one
to three persons. The road left the coast and went on to

Bubunan. On either side were the rice fields, with many wayside shrines interspersed. In great, sharp irregular waves the volcanic hills rose up, or fell away to reveal small valleys of entrancing, brilliantly coloured beauty. Dark green was contrasted again and again with the yellow and red of extraordinary flowers. On the road we passed of course many people: lithe, slow-moving men, with *sarongs* and *slendangs* of green, orange and violet batik, which is the only raiment fabric on the island. The superb Balinese women, naked above the waist, moving statuesquely along with vast loads on their heads, stood out as amazing examples of balance, strength, sheer natural beauty. Their clear bronze skins shone in the sun, contrasting sharply, yet harmoniously, with the gay colours and designs of their batik garments. We passed on through and beyond Bubunan and were on the stretch to Tabanan, on the way to which I could see, off to the east, the high peak of Tabanan. We passed through small hamlets past temples, *kampongs*, official buildings of the local governments. Everywhere the gay colours, the genial life, of the Balinese. Men with flowers in their hair, or perhaps, in a small stream near the road a cluster of women, nude, bathing unashamedly. And any man passing would not dare to look.

We stopped in a *pasangrahan* on the road between Tabanan and Den Pasar, on the southern portion of the island and almost directly south of Buleleng and Singaradja.

It was the next day that I set out on foot from the *pasangrahan* to enjoy a closer view of the countryside. Bright sunlight fell on everything, not blindingly, nor too hot, but with a softness that blended all the view into a constantly harmonious whole. Dogs yapped at me. Thousands, untold thousands of dogs, infest the island, and bark unceasingly, day and night. They are sacred animals because they are said to contain the souls of as yet unburied persons and may not be killed. They are mongrels of course, yellow-

ish, black-spotted, with red-rimmed eyes and present a de-
jected appearance, not because they are starved, which they
are not, nor because they are homeless; but rather because
they are a sort of public charge. They have the entire
island, yet can lay no claim to any one *kampong* for a home.
So they bark, and are a confounded nuisance.

As I walked, looking about me, yet not feeling myself
a centre of outraged disapproval nor of uncontrollable curiosity, I was approached by a slightly more than middle-aged
Balinese woman, who wanted me to buy some of her wooden
carvings, statuettes or silverware. I dismissed her courteously, for one would not think of being impolite to anyone
in this enchanted place. I walked on, spying small temples
and houses for the gods, the gates of which had open niches
for offerings. These little houses with their niches were a
part and parcel of the walls which surround each home, or
kampong. In one wall I saw bits of porcelain plates, saucers,
cups and other household utensils embedded in strange designs.

I walked on, taken up entirely by the activity of the life
going on about me. Children playing in the *kampongs*, into
which I could see as I tramped by. More of the women,
beautifully formed, walking sedately by with large astonishing loads on their heads, supported by one soft rounded arm.
Balinese women are truly beautiful. They have a serenity of
expression, a general calmness of behaviour, that bespeaks
an inner dignity. They are greatly respected, though they
are not awarded a very high place in the organization of
society. As marriage is contracted by capture or purchase,
they become the property of the husband upon marriage.
Their comparatively low social status, as apart from the
respect accorded them, is due of course to polygamy.

The means of contracting marriage is most surprising.
A young man whom I came to know in Tabanan wished to

marry the daughter of a certain man who lived nearby. Of
the same caste of course. The girl seemed agreeable to the
idea, and accordingly the two frankly eloped, vanishing suddenly from the village to a previously arranged refuge. The
girl's father declared that his feelings and the sanctity of
his home had been outraged when he received an embassy
(*Pedjali*) from the groom. I trembled for the young man,
for the father vowed most horrible vengeance.

The young man and his beloved had been gone several
hours, but I was amazed to observe that despite his threats
and statements concerning his affronted honour, the father
made no haste. He went from house to house of his nearest
friends and described to them the state of affairs. At his
request the *pedanda* beat solemnly on the bamboo gong,
(*kentongan*) the same which is used when a man runs *amok*.
They too were greatly exercised and vowed that this outrage
upon the feelings and honour of their friend should be
righted forthwith. Accordingly, many hours after the young
couple has secretly and discreetly vanished, the father headed
a band of his friends out in pursuit of his daughter. I
thought to myself that this lack of haste was not going to
produce any impressively respectable results.

Many hours later the entire cohort paraded, jovially,
back into the village. Preparations for a festival were immediately begun. I sought out my young friend, the one
who had made this coup, and asked him if he was not afraid.

He replied, in a tone of aggrieved astonishment, that
all had fallen out precisely as it should.

"You are going to marry the girl?" I asked. "Her
father is no longer angry?"

"He never was," replied the happy young man, and went
off to join the feast.

This is the accepted method of marriage. The girl's
father, on discovering, much to his astonishment, that his

daughter has been carried off willy-nilly, pretends great fury. But the lack of haste is deliberate. So is the "hot" pursuit. It is purposely and traditionally so in order to permit time for the young couple to consummate their as yet unofficial wedding. The father and his posse, on discovering that the wedding has already been consummated in advance, make the best of it. In other words, he escorts the couple back to the home *dessah*, orders a celebration and gravely accepts from the young man, or the young man's father, an agreed price for the girl. She at once becomes the property of her husband, lives in his compound, and loses all rights to the heritage of her own family.

The price of a woman may be paid in *sirih* or any other equally desirable kind. Of course, less fiery-blooded swains may obtain wives for themselves without the above doubtless pleasurable travail. Wives may be purchased by direct negotiation followed by festivities, but romance has its way with sufficient frequency.

After marriage women became highly important industrially and agriculturally. They do most of the work in the fields, and are greatly respected in the home. They are as a whole far from stupid and like almost every man, woman and child of the Balinese race, can read and draw passably. If not able to draw, almost every Balinese woman can exercise her native talent in some art of decoration. They dress in the universal *sarong* and *kabaja* of red, orange, yellow, green, purple, blue indigo, violet and designed batik. This *sarong* is one reaching from the navel to the ground, while the *kimbang* or *kabaja* is the upper garment. As a rule, as I mentioned before, virtuous women leave the busts exposed, covering them only on special occasions, such as entering a Sultan's palace or a temple. An unmarried woman leaves one lock of hair loose.

Curiously, despite the nature of women's status after

marriage, they enjoy such a position in Balinese life that no man dares to scrape up acquaintance with them. A Balinese man will not stare at a pretty girl on the road; he will not sit where she has sat before many minutes elapse; he will not tread in the same dust nor will he peep at women bathing in a stream. Women really hold in their hands, as in Western civilization, the power to start or stop incipient romances. Contrarily enough, however, Balinese women are quite without vanity, and take no pains to enhance their natural beauty. This they leave to the men, who parade the village streets in brilliant *slendangs,* flowers in their long curly hair, and with long curved nails tipping their fingers to show that they are aristocrats who do not work.

This gentleness pervades all Balinese life. They regard and converse with natural objects as they would with friends. I have seen a man about to climb a lontar tree, but before doing so he spoke to it in soothing tones, then embraced it. Finally he climbed, having, so to speak, obtained its consent. This same gentleness forbids their haggling over price. This I have never known them to do. Fixed price it is, and it is no more questioned than is the price of a diamond in a Fifth Avenue jeweller's.

But should this great gentless and consideration in private life ever relax, the Balinese wife has redress by applying to the Court for a divorce for which, when granted, she must pay an indemnity to the husband. Buy her way out, as it were. This regularly constituted Court, the Council of Kertas, consists of two *pedandas* and is presided over by an official of the Dutch Colonial Government.

I remained several days in Tabanan, and one afternoon was most fortunate in finding myself on the road not far from the village as a temple feast was about to begin.

Past me on the road streamed crowds of villagers: the men in their gay-hued raiment, the women, who predominated in number, moving in single file. I had occasion then, as many times before and later, to admire the superb grace of their carriage, the smooth muscles in leg, back, neck and breasts developed by the carrying of fabulously heavy loads. Many carried baskets, held in precarious balance by one arm held high. Others wore in their hair the *tjempaka,* or white and red oleander, very plentiful on the island, which the men also wear a great deal. The women's *slendangs* were of purple, green, violet and blood-crimson.

The men's clothes do not differ greatly from the male attire of Java. Here they wear krisses, daggers, in back, so that half projects above and half below the waistline. A little boy trotted complacently by without a kris. I walked along and enquired of him, in elaborately courteous language, why he had no dagger. Gravely he replied that he was not permitted to carry that arm because he had not yet reached a marriageable age.

The road filled with people bathed in soft sunshine suggested, by the rhythmic flow of their strides and the even dignified tread of every individual, the meticulous rehearsing of a great pageant. In nothing in Balinese life does this slightly theatric touch quite disappear. Do not for one moment think that the people are posy, or that they exaggerate their movements in any histrionic manner. Surely not. But the very dignity, graciousness, of the life strikes that note in the eyes of us Westerners, who are used to placing a premium, not on dignity, but on its very absence.

The road we followed led through long avenues of plantain and lontar palms which shaded the road. Beyond the trees on either side of the road was scenery very like that of eastern Java. On distantly seen slopes I recognized the teak, *djati,* tree, while nearer at hand, the lontar trees cast delicately purple shadows on our heads. The lontar not only provides the modern Balinese, as it did his forefathers, with material on which to write his books and letters, but it also grows a singularly luscious and nourishing fruit. Cultivated patches in the near distance grew oranges, bananas, of which there are ninety varieties on the island, mangos, bread fruit, barley, pomegranate, and other fruit and grains. Many of these grow naturally; others must be tended.

As I gazed about me, meantime keeping up with the informal procession, I fell into step beside a middle-aged man. A red and blue *slendang* surrounded his slender waist, and peeping from its tight fold in the back I saw the gleaming blade of his kris. In his thinning curly hair was a white oleander. He addressed me politely, asking if I were on my way to attend the feast.

I replied that I was indeed, but that I had been greatly fascinated on the way by the fields and the neat careful appearance they presented. He expressed courteous surprise on learning that by profession I was an agriculturist and therefore took a keen interest in such matters.

"You should know, then, our proverb," said he, "which declares: *wong desa angertanin gumin ida batara*. The villagers work in the fields: they are, however, the property of the gods."

"I shall bear that in mind," I told him.

He left me then, with a smiling inclination of his head, to join his family some strides ahead.

Frequently as we went along I saw numerous coco palms waving their fronds, which account for the large copra export of the island. Likewise, the *banyan*, or fig tree, abounds, as does also the large-leafed *casuari* in the forests of the mountains north of us. This tree had great dark-green leaves which project a gracious shade. The *kapok* or cotton tree may be seen in many places, while the aren palm furnishes native sugar and from it a liquor is concocted. The latter tree also provides a fibre which is used for house and temple roofs. Off to our left I saw fields of *djagung* or maize. Where irrigation is not possible in the mountain regions, this *djagung* is grown in place of rice.

Ahead then I spied the pagoda of the temple of Watu Kahu rising in sharp silhouette against the pale blue cloudless sky.

My accelerated pace had brought me to the outer wall of the temple (a three-walled construction similar to the one I have already described at Sangsit) ahead of most of the worshippers. Gift bearers came with roast sucklings, sweetmeats, nuts, onions, melons, the evil-tasting durians, mangasteens, *ayams* or chickens. Some carried on their heads great baskets filled with brightly mingled flowers and fruit. I saw hibiscus, oleanders, and many varieties unfamiliar to me. Others arrived with less imposing offerings, as befitted their lower stations. They all climbed the stone steps into the court, where they at once camped in family and friendly circles. They had brought mats and food for themselves.

I asked a woman why they camped in this manner and she told me that they were the guests of the gods during a week of blessing and merry-making, instead of sacrifice.

I wound my way through the clusters of chatting, eating people to a position of vantage beneath the scaffold whereon sat the *pedanda*, ready to bless the assemblage. From there I could see more worshippers, priestesses and the men of the orchestra arrive. Then the *pedanda* began the ceremony of purification.

While his wife carefully washed his feet, he himself washed his own body in water, to prepare himself for the entrance of the spirit of Siva, whose agent he was. He brushed his teeth with pulverized ashes, and then facing eastward, mumbled a prayer with tremendous speed. That done, he picked up a temple bell and rang it, at the same time making ceremonial ritual gestures with his free hand. These are called *mudras* and are used at all Brahmin ceremonies.

This was late afternoon, and the feasting went on uninterruptedly until sundown. I joined a group of friends I found, whose acquaintance I had made in the village of Tanbanan. They freely gave me fruit and meats to eat, and we chatted comfortably. In no wise was I stared at, nor regarded curiously. Either the persons near me were too polite to demonstrate their curiosity or they saw nothing wonderful in a white's wishing to witness their festival. Either supposition is creditable.

The real feast and *tandakken* started at sundown when unexpectedly, to me at least, the *gamelan* clanged out stirring, emotional music. This was the beginning of the kris dance.

A group of flower-decked girls issued from an inner court and danced only a moment. They then retired to a shed at one side, and were followed by girl-children, about fifteen in number. My friend whispered to me that they were only ten years old. The *gamelan* changed in quality to a more clangorous, less harmonious rhythm and the girls seemed to float about in a circle, their high golden crowns and brocades of silver and gold glinted with the light of the palm torches that had now been lit.

I cast a look around. No one ate any more. The flickering light reminded me for a flash of the extraordinary *sjaman* festival I had seen weeks before. But here there was no sinister undertone; no indefinable feeling of deadening tension. Here was rather real engrossment in an absorbing, religious, dramatic spectacle.

The little girls subsided into a seated circle, upon which an old man leapt into the circle with a sharp yell. In his right hand he brandished a gleaming kris. The prelude to the *tandakken* was over.

The *pedanda* gave a signal by raising his hand and another troupe of girls, older this time, emerged from behind the scaffold. They walked in single file and were dressed in *slendangs* of a uniformly worked dull red. It was difficult, however, to make out the colour in the deceptive unsteady light. They were beautiful creatures, chosen for this apparently by age and physical charm.

In the right hand of each was a kris. They walked slowly in a circle for what seemed many minutes, while the *gamelan* music beat louder and more clamorously. Gradually their faces assumed a dreamy look, though not sleepy. They seemed to come under a hypnotic spell. From those pressing forward about me I could hear quickened breathing.

One girl paused in her walk, her slim body writhing at the hips. Another paused, stopped, then another. One suddenly fell prone. When one girl fell, temple guardians rushed into the circle and carried her away. A kris rose in a girl's hand and swept down, slashing her body. Others became possessed, and soon everyone was dancing, writhing, swaying, frequently administering slithering cuts to their naked sweating bodies. Blood streamed; weakened exhausted bodies pitched to the ground. The frenzy spread. Now and then an older man leaped from the nearest fringes of the spectators, wrested a bloody kris from a nerveless hand and joined the wild spectacle. Women's voices cried out piercingly from the crowd. The *pedanda* watched with impassive face. Figures, too enthusiastic, jumped forth to wrestle for a kris. Others fell and lay, gasping, unheeded, almost trampled on.

I had seen enough. And besides, it grew late, so that at a time that must have been after eleven, I left, and went back to my room in the *pasangrahan* in Tabanan.

Much later, when I came back to Singaradja, and was

discussing this festival with Mak Patimah, she told me that the girls were given hasheesh, or some other drug stimulant, before entering the dance. Similar drug stimulation is employed, it is well known, in the ecstasies of the whirling dervishes.

From Tabanan I went on to Den Pasar by way of Tegal
Sempsen, Seset, Kota Beach and Benoa, which is a cir-
cuitous route along the south shore for a while, then across
the neck of a short thick peninsula, and then directly north

into Den Pasar. Near here is the temple at Badun, a large temple very similar to the ones at Sangsit and the Pura Watu Kahu.

Den Pasar enjoys today a privileged position from a European point of view because it is the head seat of the Dutch Colonial Government of Bali, while it is also the residence of the Assistant Resident, who is the foremost Dutch official of southern Bali. There is a comparatively large European settlement here, with a Dutch bank, branches of Surabaja export houses, and the Balinese High Court, consisting of the Assistant Resident and two Balinese. This court adjudicates cases arising between natives and others which directly affect either foreign interests or the relationships between the Europeans and the Balinese. Otherwise the Balinese are permitted to settle their own affairs, as is only right.

Den Pasar is a town of between ten and twelve thousand Balinese and about one hundred whites, who are chiefly Dutch and German. Most of these were well acclimated, happy and contented. In the *pasangrahan* I met a young German, whose name is of no consequence here, who on being employed by the home office of a Surabaja firm, had been sent direct to Bali without a breaking-in period, say in Java or one of the other more Westernized cities of Dutch East India. To one unaccustomed to the East, Bali, or any other similarly "different" place is a difficult one in which to adjust oneself. It resulted that the young German was most frightfully unhappy. He could not, unfortunately, bring himself to order his life to jibe with local customs. He envied and almost resented my departure. I envied his staying.

Den Pasar has seen dramatic times in the history of Bali. Prior to 1906 it was one of the first important places to fall into the hands of the conquering Dutch. It was from there that European troops marched against the kingdom of Tabanan. The ruler of that place was convinced aforetime of the futility of resistance, since he had witnessed, or heard about, the disasters which had befallen his countrymen in other parts of the island. He went bravely to meet the troops and placed himself fearlessly in their hands. He was rushed to Den Pasar, being considered a prize catch. The Government Commissioner, bent upon imposing on a defenseless race the will of a government not yet learned in the ways of treating these people, imprisoned the ruler and deprived him of his kris, a great insult. At the same time he sentenced the man to banishment on Lombok, an island not far from the south coast of Bali. The severity of this punishment may be judged by my past reference to the Balinese idea of home, and the terrifying possibilities of absence from it. Thus humiliated after a noble surrender, insulted and banished, the ruler and his son lay in prison. He managed to cut his throat by hacking at it with a rough piece of iron. His son poisoned himself.

They tell also the following, almost legends now, that illustrate aptly the difference between the gentility of these people and the cynical cruelty of Western minds. History is replete with instances of this sort occurring during conflicts between Western conquerors and primitive peoples of the central latitudes. The Spaniards and the Incas, Aztecs and Indians of Central America furnish many examples.

In 1894 a military expedition was undertaken from Batavia against the island of Lombok, whose people are practically Balinese and are called Balier. The expedition was a rank and disastrous failure, and the remnant of a company with its officers was captured in the western part of the tiny island. They were brought before the Rajah, who ordered the officers to be treated as visitors of noble rank and the common soldiers to be given rice and cool water. At the expiration of six days they were sent back to their boats, which bore them back, astonished, to Java.

In biting contrast to that episode is this, which happened in 1904, when a small sailing ship, owned by a Chinese trader and allegedly carrying five thousand guilders in silver, stranded on the Bali south coast. The Chinaman at once accused the resident people of having, so to speak, salvaged his silver. He went to the Rajah and in irate language demanded repayment in full. The Rajah told him that either his silver was still there, or else it had never been there.

But the Chinaman was not convinced. He brought the affair to the notice of the Dutch Government, which thereby deemed itself affronted, and forthwith sent out a punitive expedition. Two years later in 1906, troops were landed and the inland villages bombarded. The invisible missiles hurtling through the air impressed the uselessness of their resistance on the peaceful Balinese. They put down their weapons and returned to the cultivation of their fields. But such an easy way out was not permitted the ruler by the *adat*. He therefore, with his wives and servants, decided to die in the *puputan*, a kind of deliberate self-immolation before an enemy in the case of defeat. A similar custom prevailed among the Amoncos of Malabar.

The sovereign and his small retinue left the palace, having first put to the kris the old and sick unable to move of their own accord. They came within sight of the Dutch troops, and the Rajah gave the signal for the firing of an old bronze gun. It exploded, killing its bearer. But the detonation was the signal for them all to throw themselves into the path of the flying bullets. The Rajah leaped down from his gold chair borne by four attendants. At the sudden slaughter which resulted, the troops stopped firing, appalled. A priest sprang up and began to plunge his kris into the breasts of those nearest him.   A solitary bullet stopped him.   Another filled his place.

The troops refused to fire.   Back of the line a Christian priest turned away in physical revulsion at the sight: A few women ran forward from the group about the dying ruler and scornfully threw handfuls of gold pieces toward the troops, crying out: "This is the money for which you came to kill us!"

An ironic gesture of supreme scorn.   The Chinaman did not recover his silver, because the Balinese did not have it. Enough.

From Den Pasar I went on to Gianjar, where I met the Regent, a Balinese official, descendant of the family which formerly ruled the district before the advent of the Europeans. He is now an official of the Dutch Government.

He was a man of about forty, very energetic in manner and thought and stately in bearing. He dressed on all occasions like the popular conception of an Eastern ruler: a *slendang, sarong,* large silk turban of subdued colours, with the buttons and ornaments of his clothes consisting of rubies, diamonds, topazes and sapphires. I saw one of his twenty wives; she was an exalted beauty, and was his preferred consort.

I had entered his place which was of somewhat Moorish style, through a courtyard, into which all rooms gave. It was one story high, the rear quarters being devoted to the women. At no time is a stranger ever permitted to enter the women's quarters in the home of a Balinese ruler.

This man was of very high caste, and was very formal in his ways. I dined with him the second day and was amazed at the splendour of his household. It was more like India than the simplicity I had become accustomed to in Bali. On his table were crystal and silver from Europe, and he was the only ruler I met in Dutch East India, except the Sultan of Djocjakarta, who owned and used a white damask tablecloth. While we discoursed upon topics of mutual interest, his beautiful head wife sat quietly attentive, scrupulously so, at the foot of the table. She spoke only when addressed by her spouse. It was this man who related to me, in simple language, the stories of Dutch conquest I have told just now. One might think them to be coloured favourably to the Balinese, but I doubt it.

It was just outside Gianjar that I was so extremely fortunate as to witness a burial and cremation feast. These are particularly interesting, since they vividly exemplify the doctrine of transmigration of souls which prevails in Bali. I have already described the now extinct custom of the *suttee* or burning of the widows. It is believed, too, that cremation and the consequent offerings to the gods effectively exempt a soul from returning to earth in any other shape. Dogs, I have said already, contain the souls of uncremated low-caste people and are therefore not to be harmed. So, when a soul has gone to *Indraloka* where it remains for a certain time in this Heaven of the Dewas, it is entitled to the worship and offerings of surviving relatives.

Not every family is able to do full honour to its dead by means of proper cremation. In the north I had already witnessed the burial of a poor man. His body was enclosed in bamboo, and when it was brought by a procession of relatives to the edge of the grave, all clothes were stripped from the body, which was then replaced in the bamboo coffin and lowered into the open grave. The relatives threw in a few coins, intended for the dead man to provide himself with food for the hereafter. The grave was covered up. Near the grave a bamboo pole bearing on its summit a three-cornered hatch of lattice work was stuck into the ground. In this offerings of rice, flowers and fruit were placed periodically to drive away the evil spirits, *butas*, which are said to infest burial places. But the soul of the buried man may not enter *Indraloka*. The son of the dead man told me that it became his duty to accumulate sufficient funds for a decent cremation, for which he would, of course, have to exhume the bones. This is done whenever necessary and possible, though sometimes it is years before bodies can be, financially speaking, cremated. Of course, there are no remains then. So the body is burnt in effigy: the figure is cut out of lontar leaf in diminutive size. This same custom prevails in the case of Balinese who die outside Bali.

In the case of the cremation feast I witnessed through the courtesy of the Regent of Gianjar, there were nine departed souls about to make their journey to *Indraloka* in company. This number included two high officials, deceased.

The *pedanda* had received permission from the Dutch

East Indies Government for the festival, having also consulted the stars for the propitious day. But in order to confound the evil spirits ever ready to hamper the desires of man, the *pedanda* keeps the date a secret from all except those immediately concerned.

But during this period of waiting I attended the embalming ceremony of one of the officials who was to be cremated. The *pedanda* engaged himself actively in this task in the *Ruma Mati,* or "dead house." My friend the Regent and I stood at one side, hidden in shadows. The *pedanda* busied himself, deliberately oblivious of our presence. There were present only the four of us: the priest, the Regent, myself and the dead man. The priest rubbed the body all over in the juice of special unidentifiable spices, which are dictated by the *adat.* In the stiff nostrils he placed a lily bud; he put small coins in the hands, a tiny mirror on each closed eye, and in the mouth he inserted a golden ring set with a ruby. This extensive preparation is to ward off the demons.

He then wrapped the body in pale yellow silk and bound split bamboo around the outside. The body left in this state, I was told at first, would completely dry up in a few months, were such a wait necessary between death and cremation. But I later learned that this was not so, and that this sort of embalming would not protect the body from partial decomposition. The emanations were therefore collected in a vessel placed under the bench on which the remains rested.

The morning of the third day before cremation, these coverings were stripped off to permit the surviving relatives to have a last look. At the same time the *pedanda* removed the gold ring and ruby from the mouth and inserted five small metal plates, each inscribed with the word *Ong* and a mystic formula. Each was of a different metal: gold, silver, copper, iron and lead, and represented the five principal gods of the Balinese religion: Siva, Vishnu, Brahma, Indra and Yama.

In this connection, I might outline the family: Indra is the god of Heaven, or *Indraloka;* Yama, of the underworld; Warana, of the sea; Suria, of the sun; Durja, of death and Cri of Laksmi, who is also the wife of Vishnu, of agriculture.

For the last three days before cremation the body of the official was under the protection of the six deities, as above.

The morning of the cremation I took my place in the procession behind the *bade,* or movable funeral pyre. I had thought to stay by the *pedanda,* but the Regent advised me to follow the procession. Accordingly I joined the out-skirts of the ranks. They consisted chiefly of near and dis-tant relatives, with friends, dependants, et cetera, swelling the number. They did not wear a downcast mien, for the mourning in our sense is practically unknown. A dead man is not unfortunate; he is, rather, better off, since he is going to *Indraloka.*

The *pedanda* wore a special dress, decorated in a some-what Javanese fashion. The construction of his ordinary *sarong* did not differ from the ones for daily usage, his up-per body being bare and the white *sarong* hanging down from his hips. On his head was a wide red hat, divided into thirteen parts, demarcated by narrow strips of gold, with a cluster of precious stones on top. Across his forehead ran a hair-band, covered with gold and precious stones of crystal in two varieties: one from the sun, the other from the moon. In the centre of the forehead, from this band, hung a little ball, which showed the connection between the Indian Buddhism, and Balinese Sivaism. Ear-rings and a rosary of three-fold string passing over his left shoulder completed his dress. At the point where the rosary joined over his shoulder I saw three more little balls, or *linggas,* one decorated with a red stone for Brahma, the second with a white for Siva and the third with a black or dark blue for Vishnu.

The *bade* fascinated me. It was really a float, since its large bamboo base, concealed by hangings, also concealed a troupe of bearers, who propelled it along the road at a dignified pace. Five stories, called *tumpang*, brought the upper part, the *triwangsa*, pretty high up. The tiers, in somewhat pyramidal form, were composed of bamboo or wood.

The number of tiers in a *bade* is religiously significant, like the pyramidal Buddhistic buildings and their philosophical meanings. The number of tiers is always uneven, and varies according to the station of the deceased in life. For example, the Dewa Agungs, princes of the onetime kingdom of Klungkung, were permitted eleven tiers. The ornamentation of this *bade* was imposing, consisting of elephant heads on the four corners, with the sides scatteringly covered with little balls of cotton in the popular Balinese colours: red, dark blue and yellow. The outer sides were also decorated with red-painted tinsel and mirrors. Inside I could see many small mirrors and some odd pieces of furniture.

Back of us in the procession were the *bades* of the other deceased to be cremated that day. The nearest one was of a *satriya*, second in rank of caste, and his *bade* was similar in structure and design to the one I was following, though in addition it was fastened to a float in the shape of a serpent-like animal with short narrow wings. In other *bades*, different animals, including their mythical bird, the *garuda*, appeared in the decorations. These variations denote differences in caste.

We started. While silence prevailed for the most part, short conversations frequently broke out among the followers. The faces were grave but not sad. Directly ahead of us was a large group of women carrying gold and silver vases and trays laden profusely with flowers, yellow and black rice, incense, coins, batik shawls, jewelry—all to be offered in a spirit of propitiation to the gods of the underworld headed by Yama.

Behind them marched many men, regal in bearing, and armed with spears and krisses. *Gamelan* players were also included and among this troupe I saw two young boys holding aloft, with prideful demeanour, bamboo poles from which were suspended old and faded garments. This was to attract the souls of relatives long deceased and to induce them to aid the most recently deceased. Then came large puppets, manipulated by boys, which danced crazily about and emitted fearsome growls and roars. Those walking near me shrank repeatedly in fear at a more terrible blast than usual. These puppets represented the good spirits who were protecting the procession from demons.

We stopped three times, once in the market place, to give the deceased a chance to have a last moment near their homes. Dead do not give up live associations so easily. At last we arrived before the *pedanda* in his temple. The nine floats with their fantastic animals came to a stop in front of him. He gazed at them stolidly, muttering litanies in an undertone. Prayer bells rang thinly, incense floated skywards in tiny blue puffs. This purified everyone. His hands lifted up and his body shuddered; he was in direct contact with the deity. A priestess came toward him, bearing a small puppet in her arms as a mother holds a small baby. She reached down and touched the puppet to the priest's foot.

The great dragon, or serpent-like animal which had led the first *bade*, faced him. He advanced solemnly toward it, taking at the same time a golden bow and arrow from an attendant. In the hollow end of the arrow he placed a white flower, and then shot the arrow in the air toward the dragon. He did the same to all four cardinal points of the compass, and then once each to Heaven and earth. After that the procession moved again, this time direct to the cremation field.

The cremation field was flat, buff in colour, while overhead the afternoon sun beat down solidly. Greyish-white clouds floated immovably to the West. Nine funeral pyres rose starkly before us.

At once the entire procession ran in formation three times around the pyres, the floats rocking crazily on the bearers' shoulders. Bamboo poles swayed weirdly, like the masts of foundering ships. The *bades* were put down and the bodies brought to earth by stairways. Then the bodies were borne three times around their individual pyres, to signify symbolically the struggle between the forces of Heaven and of earth, the departed finally winning their way to Heaven. The bodies were then placed in bamboo coffins, some shaped like cows, others like lions. These coffins were then thrown, with a strange effect of dignity and the end of all things, into the erratically jumping, tall flames of the lighted pyres.

Late afternoon shadows scampered across the smooth ground. Strange cries, half-glad, half-demented, rang in a subdued, respectful way over the swiftly moving heads of the crowd. Flames leapt up on the *bades* while small boys climbed hurriedly to retrieve the ornaments, leaving a chicken in a cage on the top of each *bade* to guide that particular soul to Heaven, like the dove in the former *suttees*.

We watched, awe-struck. The flames roared, crackled and flared in sudden unpredictable bursts, driving back incautious spectators and watchers. It grew darker, and the fantastic shadows became darker, almost tangible, mixing with the figures which flitted by in ghostly fashion in the purplish dusk.

The crowds thinned, until only appointed guards were

left. But I waited, for soon the women of the family came
back for the ashes. These were taken to be thrown into the
sea, so that when the departed soul does return in another
and superior incarnation, no trace of the former incarnation
shall turn up to disconcert him.

I WENT on to Karang Asem, where I was to meet the *Stede-houder*, Ida Gusti Bagus Djilantik. I passed through Klungkung, Kosamb, on the southeastern coast, Edjune and so to Karang Asem not far from the eastermost tip of the island. Ida Gusti Bagus Djilantik is a much respected and admired man.   He is a *Stedehouder* (or city holder) and draws three thousand guilders a month.   I was much astonished, later, to learn that he and his son, Ida Bagus Oka, had collaborated on a book on Balinese laws, in codified form. He is the Blackstone of Bali.   The book is in High Balinese, and a copy of it lies in the New York Public Library at Forty-second Street and Fifth Avenue.   A long jump, and I regret not having been able to tell the Gusti of his extended renown.   Even if there are only a few in this country able to read Balinese script.

He resided in a cluster of buildings which served him as a home and also as his administration buildings.   I called on him, and a respectful attendant said that the Gusti was in Amsterdam.

"In Amsterdam?" I repeated in amazement.

"Yes.   Over there."   I looked and saw that the man indicated another building about fifty feet away.   It was the fancy of the Gusti to call all his buildings by the names of European cities.   So I went over to Amsterdam and met the Gusti.

He was a short man with the bronze tone of his facial skin obscured somewhat by the grey of his whiskers.   He had a soldierly appearance, as much because of his bearing as because of the dark blue uniform he had on.   Though in this and many subsequent meetings he always wore a uniform, I have reason to believe that he would willingly have thrown it off and squatted comfortably on the floor.

We met in Amsterdam, which was elaborately furnished with marble tables and red upholstered furniture.   A broad veranda kept us cool.   After a short chat in Malay, we went to Berlin, the conference hall.   His wives and concubines— very beautiful ones, too—he kept in London.   He was not, it is only fair to say, an ironic man.

We had tea in Berlin and discussed irrigation, rice, crops, condition of pigs (for Bali is proud of its pig-export trade, as witness the ship I had come in on: the "pigs' express"), taxes, and the change of money. It was at that time that the Dutch Colonial Government wished to change from Balinese copper to Dutch East Indies currency, denominated the same as Dutch money for Bali.

We sat at tea and discussed many things. He was a man of about fifty, of strong personality, though not so quick in mental action as the Regent of Gianjar. It was easy for me to understand, sitting opposite this man, how difficult it was for the Dutch to overcome the Balinese, who were the last people of the Dutch East Indies to be subdued. The father of this Gusti and a contemporaneous Regent of Klungkung, twenty-five miles in a south-east direction, were the last hold-outs against the Dutch in 1906.

He told me that his son had been sent to Europe to study, as are the sons of most wealthy Javanese and Malayan princes. He demonstrated a keen, intelligent interest in everything European, as evidenced by his constant drawing-room manner in his home when receiving foreign visitors, and especially by his interest in things American. He owned an American automobile of up-to-date model.

That first day he made me a present of a sheet of leather, cunningly embossed in gold in his own workshop, which is still in my possession.

On one of many subsequent visits to this end of the island, during which I called repeatedly on my friend the Gusti, we went to his "summer home" at Udjan, a few miles away. Imagine a summer home in the tropics!

But here I had another surprise as the Gusti had permitted his imagination, coupled with his extensive fancy, to guide him. It was very Japanese in style. Tiny pagodas, bridged lagoons, an architecture of combined Indian and

Balinese style—only lacking tiny saffron Geisha girls! His
artistic temperament had led the Gusti to plant a vast number of diminutive citrus trees. Thickly verdant slopes led to
a large one-story house. The landscape was a perfect job,
done under the direction of the Gusti and his advisers. European landscape artists, visiting Bali, make a point of visiting
the Gusti's estate at Udjan in order to learn. And yet it
was done without the complicated science that has grown up
about such European work. The Gusti had no formulas nor
modernistic designs, whereby to lay out his walks, plant his
trees, build his bridges and enclose his lagoons. But every
vista was perfect, fringed with red, yellow, blue, green flowers and bushes. Pinkish white blossoms gave the trees a
misty outline, while lontar and aren palms gave dignified
shade, standing among the tiny citruses like so many thin but
haughty giants.

I T was on one of these late trips that I settled in Klungkung for some months. While there I attended many
sessions of the court in the Kerta Goose, or Court House.
This is in the form of a pavilion-like temple or *pendoppo*:

verandas on all four sides, its floor elevated on piles to about eight or ten feet in height, and the roof supported by four pillars. The ceiling and walls are decorated with painted friezes, depicting the traditional punishments for certain standard crimes. But many of these punishments were executed in the olden days exactly as they are shown here in the Court House. Some of the painted figures represent Siva, Vishnu and Brahma.

The punishments depicted here are particularly horrible. One panel shows women, who had been prostitutes, having their sexual organs burned with torches; in another tigers chewed rapaciously on the hands, feet and sexual organs of men. Some culprits were being boiled slowly in great vats. Other wrongdoers were impaled on the spikes of trees; snakes ate the breasts of women, while those who had tortured or maltreated women lay face down on the ground while officers hacked at their defenseless bodies with double-edged swords. Above the scene hovered birds of prey and carrion, to feast on the mangled remains.

In all, a worthy rival, in punishments, for the contrivances of the ancient Chinese and the Inquisitorial Venetians and Spaniards.

One case I attended in this Court was that of a man who had settled on a plot of ground without first obtaining the permission of the local *Subak*, or communal economic organization. The land, therefore, was to be sold, at the decree of the Court, in the interests of the community, the *Subak* having much to say in the matter.

Another trial resulted in the death penalty being passed upon the culprit.

For the execution he was led indirectly to the cremation field, where previously I had attended the strange cremation festival. He was dressed completely in white, with white flowers behind his ears. From the Court House he was led first to the temple of the dead, and during the entire way there he prayed to himself in a low, steady mutter. In the temple the judge, *Kantja*, read aloud the judgment which was written on a lontar leaf. After that the leaf was folded and inserted in the criminal's waistband. During this procedure the man gazed about him tranquilly, not visibly concerned. The executioner appeared before him, an oversized kris in his right hand. According to custom, since no man may be executed by the law without first giving his permission, the executioner requested this permission now. The man nodded and the kris plunged at once into his bare breast with great force. The man fell, writhed, his face contorted with pain, blood covered his chest, his hands clawed at the wound, then suddenly he lay still.

In Bali no distinction is made between civil and criminal actions and in the event that no verdict is reached, the plaintiff must defray all costs and pay the penalty.

In Balinese court procedure, much stress is laid on oath-taking. When a man takes an oath he must bring with him two other men, to act as his guarantors. Should he be unable to find the necessary pair within the prescribed time of thirty-five days, the Court accepts that fact at face value as (prima facie) evidence of guilt. But there are qualifications which these oath-helpers must fill:

They must be married, have children, be in perfect mental and physical condition, and be no more than a friend or acquaintance of the man who takes the oath. The two must not be related.

I was present at an oath-taking ceremony. It was most interesting. The judge had the man and his two guarantors appear before him. The judge wrote on a lontar leaf the sacramental oath formulae, after which the man read it aloud to the judge. Then it was placed in a vase full of water and the man took a drink from it. I have such a lontar leaf, and it specifies fifty-one different punishments to be meted out, to the man or his oath-helpers, at the discretion of the Court should perjury be committed.

This same man whose oath ceremony I saw, later refused to abide by the decision the Court rendered in his case. This refusal the Court avenged by declaring the man "dead": no one must speak to him, no one might enter his house, and the use of the cremation ground and the temples were denied him. The judge confided to me that there were only two decisions open to him: leave the village or abide by the ruling of the Court. Unfortunately, I left Klungkung before I found out the man's decision, but I am confident, from what I have seen of the Balinese character that after a short taste of being "dead" he abided by the Court ruling. Exile is far too great and crushing a punishment to be borne.

ANOTHER time, when I was in Badung, in the eastern
part of Bali, I attended a ceremony on the twenty-first
day of the Balinese year, when all princes and grandees worship in the temple there, the holiness of which is ascribed to

a legend that the ship of Deva Danu, a goddess, stopped there on her way from India, and turned into stone.

A word about the Balinese calendar. It is a combination, really, of the Polynesian week of five days, called Pahing, Puan, Wage, Kaliwon and Manis, and the Indian seven-day week consisting of Rediti, Soma, Anggara, Budda, Wrehaspati, Sukra and Sanes-Chara. The combination gives periods of thirty-five days, occurring six times a year, so that the Balinese year is two hundred and ten days. The first, eleventh and twenty-first days of each thirty-five are sacred. Each thirty-five day period has its constellation, but their constellations differ radically from ours; with the exception of Orion and the Pleiades their signs are quite arbitrary.

From Karang Asem I went on toward the centre of the island through Bangli and then turning almost directly north to Kintamani, near which is the Batur crater, a great natural wonder and scenic beauty.

As we travelled through the valleys, I felt repeated delight in the multitude of little *dessahs* (villages) with their active market-places and temples, beside which towered dignified and wide-spreading waringin trees. Between the villages I had frequent views of the marvellously irrigated *sawahs,* their glistening surfaces stretching away down the slopes behind us, for we were climbing up toward Kintamani. Here and there, around *dessahs,* were thick clumps of tall trees, while beyond, I beheld long narrow belts of gleaming silver water under the soft sun. When the road finally arrived among the hills north of Bangli, the steep sides were covered with planted *paddi,* giving the effect of even smooth grass. Behind these slopes were terraces piling one above the other into the distance, until back of them rose the steep majestic slopes of the mountain range that intersects Bali from east to west. The roads were hardly ever empty of people coming to and fro: men leading the ugly little Balinese horse, or lowering caribou, men with fighting cocks in cages, women with fruit and vegetable-filled bamboo baskets on their heads.

At a height of some twenty-five hundred feet the road left the *dessahs* and *sawahs* and planted slopes behind and entered the jungle of palms and the predominant *casuari*, which rustles whisperingly at the slightest puff of breeze. Here and there we passed coffee plantations, surrounded by the dark green of the forest.

We came at last to the *pasangrahan* at Kintamani, where my friend Schirmer is in command. This man, of German blood, had been in Bali since just after the last *puputan*, or self-immolation of the Balinese, in 1906. He had married a half-caste woman and they had a pleasant son. Both Schirmer, a tall burly man with a hooked nose, pepper-and-salt hair, and bright greyish-blue eyes, and his silent, but nice dark-skinned wife, were most hospitable. Schirmer was about forty-eight years old, and his son, named Fritz, was then about seventeen.

The *pasangrahan* there is a one-story stucco building. Schirmer had placed an old Dutch grandfather-clock inside the entrance for a strange touch. He has a group of these rest houses, and made his own headquarters in Den Pasar a few miles away. He had a hand also in native industries, besides running an automobile line, in competition with Mak Patimah and the Armenian Minas' firm, from Kintamani to Singaradja.

The astute German left the *pasangrahan* at Kintamani chiefly in the hands of the Balinese *mandur*, manager, who it is said had many years before appropriated some money from him. Instead of jailing the luckless chap, Schirmer made him work off the theft over a period of twelve years. A hint

of extended enforced labour was all that was needed from
Schirmer to redouble the *mandur's* zeal. The house staff
was: Balinese *mandur,* Malay waiter and Chinese cook.
Kintamani is fifty-five hundred feet above sea level; roses
bloom in the garden; I picked strawberries, and I slept every
night under a blanket.

Five miles away, from my bedroom window, I could see
Batur, its smoke columns rising slowly and mixing with the
snowy-white clouds always around its wide summit.

A few months before I came there, Batur had erupted,
throwing down its slopes in furious streams a vast quantity
of fluid lava. The lava flowed in fiery tongues directly toward a village near the foot of the mountain, Dessah Batur.
The inhabitants fled, panic-stricken, to the slopes on the opposite side of a little valley. The licking, demolishing
streams of steaming lava, they saw, reached the walls of the
temple on that side of the village nearest the crater. But
the lava did not destroy it, nor the village. Inexplicably, the
evil stream switched to one side and the only damage was a
slight injury to the wall where the lava had touched the
temple.

One morning, with a guide furnished me by Schirmer and
his *mandur,* I set out for Batur. This man told me that in
1918 there had been a tremendous eruption, which the villagers of Dessah Batur interpreted as a warning to bring more
offerings to the temple. That the offerings had been successful was attested by the escape of the temple and the village
from the next eruption. We climbed steadily for over two
hours, along well-worn paths, very steep, surrounded on
every hand by thinning vegetation.

At last we reached the edge of the cone. I faced the interior. The cone within was covered on all sides by layer
upon layer of hardened lava, which gave back the rays of the
sun in irridescent beams. Back of me, the crater seemed to

be enclosed in a vast cup, thirty miles in circumference, the remains of an ancient crater-lip. Many villages dotted the great dark-green expanse. The crater cone above us showed many holes and crevices, from which the smoke and lava burst forth during its eruptions. I had seen the Smeru, Merapi and Bromo volcanoes in Java, but this of Batur is the most impressive, in size and colour, of any on the island of Bali. A tiny lake glinted in the sun; the thin, dazzling colour-rays of the lava, the deep-green mountain slopes outside, combined to produce an effect of unequalled grandeur.

We returned to the *pasangrahan*, where I would have liked to stay even longer than I did. Its cool atmosphere was a most agreeable change from the sometimes suffocating heat of the lowlands.

In the nearby village of Dessa Batur there were held, twice a week, extensive bazaars, where Arabs, Chinamen, and Balinese congregated to barter wares and produce. No whites ever mixed in these, though Schirmer, I suspected would have liked to. He invariably plunged himself into Balinese affairs in Kintamani, thinking that it would give him greater renown. It did.

In the *kampong* at Kintamani I became very friendly with a young Balinese who offered to put on a cricket fight for me one night. I went down at the appointed time. My friend had produced two men, each the owner of a fighting cricket, which he had in a small cylindrical cage. Spectators ringed us in, and the fight was begun by placing the cages together, then opening their doors. Thus the crickets were left face to face. These little animals are called *jankriks*, and the same word is used for the fights. There are rounds in these fights, and time is kept by permitting water to trickle through a hole in the bottom of a half coco-nut shell. The cricket owners urged on their beasts with cries of encouragement in staccato tones, at the same time prodding the excited animals in the backside with pointed sticks. The crickets leapt upon one another, and fought heroically. Betting ran fast and furious around the ring of watchers, who cried out in enthusiasm or disappointment as one or another cricket gained an advantage. One cricket lost a forearm; the other a leg, until finally one lay, dismembered and lifeless, on the floor of the cage. The other hopped about victoriously but almost at once, overcome either by his own prowess or by the severe drubbing he had taken even in winning, he too dropped dead.

THE next day I telephoned Mak Patimah; she sent her
chauffeur, Ithi, for me in a car, and in a few hours I
was again in Singaradja. I was welcomed back pleasurably
by my friend the Princess. We exchanged gifts, and I fre-

quently wear the ring she gave me. We talked long about the many things I had seen, as was our custom on my many journeys to and around Bali.

I have talked little of caste in Bali, but something must be said about it here. Among this people, descending from heathens who were Hinduized under the influence of Javanese refugees fleeing before the Islam onslaught on the fall of the ancient Empire of Modjopahit, caste plays a very important part, even influencing the language very definitely. It influences the attitude of the people toward the ruler, for whom everything exists, though there is a proverb: *saking bukin alite*: The ruler must know always that he owes his might to the people.

But to the ruler goes everything of the best: he may choose the prettiest girls, the finest rice is sent him, and so on. His house is built for him, he is provided with guards.

The influence of caste on the language shows in that there are two dialects: one spoken by the lower to the higher orders and the other by the high to the low. The high dialect is almost pure Javanese, while the low tongue is a crude Polynesian dialect resembling the Malay and Sundanese tongues.

Four hundred and fifty years ago, the Balinese were practically savages, without an elaborate language, written or spoken. But the Hindus and Hindu-Brahmins coming from Java brought with them the Sanskrit in their sacred writings. They may also, I think, have carried along a Prakrit dialect. Thus a direct derivative of Sanskrit is kept alive in Bali, though it has been dead, for all practical and creative purposes, in India for hundreds of years.

The Balinese language has eighteen letters, and all writing is done on lontar and waringin leaves.

Coming back to caste. There are four: the Brahamana, titled Ida; the Satriya, called Deva; the Sutra, otherwise called kahnea or orang. The first caste are the *pedandas,* tracing their descent from a certain Wahu Rawu, who came from Java. The second caste, the Satriya, are said to be the rulers and warriors. Any one of them may become a king. The third, the Wesya, are most numerous and important. Many princes belong to this class, though it was originally intended to include only merchants, farmers and artisans. The fourth caste consists of working men and servants.

When meeting another on the road, the Balinese will address him as Djro, friend. But when he finds out what the man's caste is, he will switch to the proper dialect.

In Singaradja I spent much time visiting friends, both Balinese and Dutch. One night in nearby Buleleng, a young German and I went to an opium den. There is an opium factory in Java, and opium is exported from there under special permit. Patimah's chauffeur Ithi guided us to the den through interminable dark alleys, where we fell over the inescapable dogs, who yelped. The den, when we reached it, was hardly worth the effort. I have seen more exciting ones in Chinese ports and even in London. Here were all Balinese men, except two young girls, who lay, heavy-lidded, their garments in disarray, their young breasts rising and falling in uneasy breathing, on dirty couches.

We left hastily.

The final effect of Bali is harmony: a life undisturbed by the cosmic reflections to no purpose that hound us in the rest of the world. Such problems are settled for them by a consoling religion developed especially for them. What is the result? What I have tried to show: that the effect upon the people, and upon him who comes to see, is one of moving along with the feet just off the ground in an atmosphere of sparkling, brilliant colour.

No clanging factories belch up clouds of evil-hued smoke to blemish the sky. It is no wonder that Bali has enchanted countless people. And yet, where is the written record of that enchantment?

I have made my contribution, and hope sincerely that it does justice to an island that gave me, not only times of a peace unknown on earth, but memories that have helped to smooth out of the rough sections of a road leading over the rocky hills of other lands.

BIBLIOGRAPHY

Abd Al-Humaid ibn Muhammad Ali, A Religious Treatise on the Birth of Mahomet.

Abendanon, Eduard Cornelius, Midden Celebes Expeditie, Leiden, E. J. Brill, 1915-1919 (with Ministery of Colonies' support.)

Abendanon, Jacques Henry, Las Indias Neerlandesas, Indicaciones, Relative a su historia, su politica, sus leyes, su administracion, su cultura y su estado economica, Real Academia de jurisprudencia y legislacion, Madrid, 1921.

Adriani, Nicolaus, Mededeelingen Omtrent de Toradja's, Batavia Tydschrift voor Indische Taal, Land en Volkenkunde, volume 44, 1901.

Ameer, Ali, Islamic Culture in India, Hyderabad, Deccan, 1927, in "Islamic Culture," Hyderabad.

Bateson, William, Mendel's Principles of Heredity, Cambridge University Press, 1902.

Bauduin, Dominique Chretien Marie, Het Indische Leven, denHaag, H. P. Leopold, 1927.

Beauvoir, Marquis de Ludovic, Java Siam, Canton, Paris, H. Plon, 1870.

Blink, Prof. Dr. Hendrik, De Bewonders der Vreemde Wereld-deelen, Amsterdam, Elsevier UitgeversMy, 1898.

Blink, Prof. Dr. Hendrik, Ned. Oost en West-Indie, Leiden, E. J. Brill, 1905-7.

Blink, Prof. Dr. Hendrik, Opkomst en Ontwikkeling van Sumatra, den Haag, Mouton & Co., 1926.

Boas, Franz, Anthropology, National Academy of Sciences reports.

Borrmann, Martin, Sunda, eine Reise durch Sumatra, Frankfurtam Main, Frankfurter Societäts Druckerei GMBH. 1925.

Brandes, Jan Laurens Andries, Pararatón (Ken-Arok), Batavia, Albrecht & Co., 1896.

Brandes, Jan Laurens Andries, Nagarakrétagama, Batavia, Bataviaansch Genootschap voor Kunsten en Wetenschappen, volume 54, 1902.

Brandes, Jan Laurens Andries, Beschryving Barabudur, Haag, M. Nyhoff, 1904.

Brandes, Jan Laurens Andries, Beschryving der Javaansche-Balineesche en Sasaksche Handschriften in Nalatenschap Dr. H. N. van der Tuuk, Batavia Landsdrukkery, 1901-15.

Brandstetter, R., Die Geschichte von Djajalaukan. Ein Makassarische Roman Geschw. Doleschal, Luzern, 1898.

Brandstetter, R., An Introduction to Indonesian Linguistics, London Royal Asiatic Society, 1916.

Broek, Ingenieur J. van der, Tinmynbouw, Haarlem, H. D. Tjeenk-Willink, 1921.

Broek, Dr. W. Palmer van de, Javáansche vertellingen bevattende de lotgevallen van een kantjil, een reebok en andere dieren. den Haag, M. Nyhoff, 1878.

343

Broersma, Dr. R., OOSTKUST VAN SUMATRA. Batavia, Javaansche Boekhandel en Drukkery, 1919.

Brooke, Sir James, NARRATIVE OF EVENTS IN BORNEO AND CELEBES, Journals by Capt. Mundy, London, 1848.

Bruce, Charles, TWENTY YEARS IN BORNEO, London, Cassell & Co., Ltd., 1924.

Bruckner, Gottlob, PROEVE EENER JAVAANSCHE SPRAAKKUNST, Serampore, 1830.

Bruin, Cornelis de, REIZEN OVER MOSKOVIE, PERSIE EN NEDERLANDSCH-INDIE, Amsterdam, R. & G. Welstein, 1714.

Bunzek, Alois, AUS DEN PARADIS DES OSTEN, Leipzig, Xenien Verlag, 1926.

Bybel-Genootschap, GENESIS BATAK. DE SCHEPPINGSGESCHIEDENIS IN DE TAAL DER BATAKS, door H. N. van der Tuuk, by Nederlandsch Bybel-genootschap, Amsterdam, 1853.

Campbell, Donald Maclaine, JAVA PAST AND PRESENT, London, W. Heinemann, 1915.

Childe, THE MOST ANCIENT EAST, London, Paul, Trench, Trübner & Co., Ltd., 1928.

Clifford, Sir Hugh Charles, BUSHWACKING AND OTHER ASIATIC TALES, London, W. Heinemann, Ltd., 1929.

Collet, J. A. Octave, TERRES ET PEUPLES DE SUMATRA, Amsterdam, Société Elsevier, 1925.

Couperus, Louis, EASTWARD, London, Hurst & Blackett, Ltd., 1924.

Coupland, Reginald, RAFFLES, Oxford University Press, 1926.

Craufurd, Q., RESEARCHES CONCERNING THE LAWS, THEOLOGY, LEARNING, COMMERCE, ETC. OF ANCIENT AND MODERN INDIA. 2 volumes, London, 1817, printed for T. Cadell & W. Davies, Strand.

Crawfurd, John, A SKETCH OF THE GEOGRAPHY OF BORNEO, London, Royal Geographic Society, London, volume 23, 1853.

Darwin, Charles, DESCENT OF MAN, London, J. Murray, 1874.

Dekker, Eduard Douwes, MAX HAVELAAR (MULTATULI), Edinburgh, Edmonston & Douglas, 1868.

Dissel J. S. A. van, HIKAYAT SI MISKIN, Leiden, E. J. Brill, 1897.

Djilantik, Goesti Poetoe & Oka, Ida Bagus, ADA AGAMA, OLD JAVANESE LAWBOOK IN HIGH BALINESE, Batavia, Landsdrukkery, 1909.

Doorn, C. L. van, THE EUROPEAN POPULATION OF THE DUTCH EAST INDIES, The Asiatic Review, July, 1930.

DuLaurier, Ed., DES LANGUES ET DE LA LITTÉRATURE D'ASIE, Paris, Société Géographique.

Dumont, DE JAVAAN IN DE DESSA, Weltevreden, Visser & Co., 1905.

East Indies Dutch Binnenlandsch Bestuur, Afd. Bestuurszaken, Encyclopaedisch Bureau, HET GOUVERNEMENT CELEBE: by L. van Vuuren, Haag, M. Nyhoff, 1920.

East Indies Dutch Department van Belastingen, HET CHINEESCHE ZAKENLEVEN, 1922, Batavia, Java.

East Indies Dutch Department van Mynwezen, JAARBOEK, Batavia, 1926.

Elshout, Dr. J. M., DE KENJA DYAKS UIT HET APO-KAJAN, denHaag, My. Nyhoff, 1926.

Enthoven, J. J. K., BYDRAGEN TOT DE GEOGRAPHIE VAN BORNEO'S WESTERAFDEELING, DEEL, 1-7, Leiden, E. J. Brill, 1903.

Eschelskroon, Adolph, BESCHRYVING VAN HET EILAND SUMATRA, Haarlem, C. H. Bohn & Zoon, 1783.

Evans, AMONG PRIMITIVE PEOPLES IN BORNEO, London, Seeley-Service Co., Ltd., 1922.

Eysinga, P. P. Roorda van, DE KROON ALLER KONINGEN, BOCHÁRI VAN DJÓHOR, Batavia, Landsdrukkery, 1827.

Fairchild, David G., SUMATRA's WEST COAST, National Geographic Magazine, Washington, 1898.

Faure, l'Abbé Pierre Etienne Lazare, DICTIONNAIRE JAVANAIS-FRANÇAIS, Vienna, Buchverlag, 1870.

Friederich, R., AN ACCOUNT OF THE ISLAND OF BALI, in Volume 8, Royal Asiatic Society Journal, London, 1876.

Gaspar, Correa, THE THREE VOYAGES OF VASCO DA GAMA AND HIS VICEROYALTY, London. Printed for the Hakluyt Society.

Geerligs, H. C. Prinse, CANE SUGAR AND ITS MANUFACTURE, Altrincham, England, N. Rodger, 1907.

Gerini, Col. G., RESEARCHES ON PTOLEMY's GEOGRAPHY OF E. ASIA, Royal Geographic Society, 1909, London.

Hakluyt Society, THE VOYAGES AND WORKS OF JOHN DAVIS, THE NAVIGATOR, 1535. London, 1880. Printed for the Society.

Hamilton, H. C., and W. Falconer, THE GEOGRAPHY OF STRABO, 3 volumes, London, Henry G. Bohn, 1854.

Hickson, Sydney J., THE LIFE AND WORK OF GEORGE EVERARD RUMPHIUS, Proceedings, Manchester Literary and Philosophical Society, Manchester, 1927.

Hickson, Sydney John, A NATURALIST IN NORTHERN CELEBES, London, J. Murray, 1889.

Hien, H. A. van, DE JAVAANSCHE GEESTENWERELD, Semarang, G. C. T. van Dorp, 1896.

Hoëvell, Wolter Robert van, REIS OVER JAVA, MADURA EN BALI MIDDEN 1847, Amsterdam, P. N. van Kampen, 1849-1851.

Holtus, W., CELEBES, ONBEKENDE GEBIEDEN, Amsterdam, Scheltema & Holkema, 1926.

Hooyer, G. B., DWERGHERT VERHALEN (KANTJIL FABLES) UIT DEN O. I. ARCHIPEL, in opdracht Raad van Beheer, Koloniaal Instituut, Amsterdam, deBussy, 1921.

Horsting, L. H. C., RAMBLES THRU ISLE OF BALI, Batavia, Sluyters, 1922.

Horsting, L. H. C., VAN LEVEN EN WERKEN IN INDIE, Visser & Co., Weltevreden, 1928.

Horsfield, Dr. Thos., ESSAY ON THE GEOGRAPHY OF JAVA, Batavia, A. H. Hubbard, 1816. (Bataviaansch Genootschap van Kunsten en Wetenschappen deel 8.) ·

Hose, Charles & W. McDougall, THE PAGAN TRIBES OF BORNEO, London, Macmillan & Co., Ltd., 1912.

Hrdlicka, Ale., THE NEANDERTHAL PHASE OF MAN, Smithsonian report for 1928, publication 3002.

Humboldt, Wilhelm Freiher von, UBER DIE KAWI., Torino, R. Academi de Scienze, volume 34, 1899.

Hurgronje, Christiaan Snouck, ATJEHSCHE TAALSTUDIEN, in Tydschrift voor Indische Taal, Land en Volk, volume 42, Batavia, 1900.

Huxley, Thomas, MAN's PLACE IN NATURE, London, Williams & Norgate, 1863.

Irving, Washington, LIFE OF MAHOMET, London, J. M. Dent & Sons, Ltd., 1911.

Jansz, P., NEDERLANDSCH-JAVAANSCH WOORDENBOEK, Semarang, G. C. T., van Dorp & Co., 1898.

Jasper, DE INLANDSCHE KUNSTNYVERHEID, 1 & 2, DIE BATIKKUNST, Haag, Mouton & Co., 1912-1927.

Jongejans, J., UIT DAJAKLAND, Amsterdam, J. M. Meulenhoff, 1922.

Joustra, M., MINANGKABAU, Minangkabau Institute, Leiden, L. H. Becherer, 1921.

Junghuhn, Dr. Franz Wilhelm, LICHT EN SCHADUW BEELDEN, Amsterdam, C. L. Brinkman, 1883.

Juynboll, H. Dr., BYDRAGE TOT DE KENNIS DER OUD JAVAANSCHE LETTERKUNDE IN JAVAANSCH, in Bydragen, Taal Land en Volkenkunde van Nederlandsch Indie, volume 51, Haag, 1900.

Juynboll, H. Dr., HET OUD JAVAANSCHE BRAHMÁNDAPURÁNA, in Javanese, volume 51, 1900.

Juynboll, H. Dr., MAHÁBHÁRATA, ÁDÍPARWA OUD JAVAANSCH PROZAGESCHRIFT, Haag, text in Javanese, M. Nyhoff, 1906.

Kalff, S., EEN DOODE TAAL IN INDIE, Baarn, Hollandia Drukkery, 1915.

Kalff, S., IETS OVER INDISCHE VROUWEN, Indische verlofganger, 1930.

Kaudern Walter, RESULTS OF THE AUTHOR'S EXPEDITION IN CELEBES, 1917-20, Göteborg, Elanders Boktryckeri Aktiebolag, 1925-28.

Keith, Sir Arthur, CONCERNING MAN'S ORIGIN, London, Watts & Co., 1927.

Kern, Prof. Dr. H., VERSPREIDE GESCHRIFTEN, SANSKRIT LITERATURE, OCEANIC LANGUAGES, MALAY LANGUAGE AND DIALECTS, Haag, M. Nyhoff, 1913-1928.

Kern, Prof. Dr. H., RAMAYANA OUD JAVAANSCH HELDENDICHT, Haag, M. Nyhoff, 1900 (in Javanese.)

Kern, Prof. Dr. H., HET AANDEEL VAN INDIE IN DE GESCHIEDENIS DER BESCHAVING EN DE INVLOED DER STUDIE VAN HET SANSKRIT OP DE TAALWETENSCHAP, A. Dissertation, at University Leiden, 1865.

Kern, Prof. Dr. H., WRTTA-SAÚCAYA, OUD JAVAANSCH LEERDICHT IN KAWI TEXT, Nederl. vertaling, Leiden, E. J. Brill, 1875.

Koehler, H. J., HABINSARAN, HET LAND VAN DEN ZONNESTRAAL, Zutphen, W. J. Thieme & Cie, 1926.

Koloniaal Museum Haarlem Holland, by Dr. de Loos, GESTEENTEN, MINERALEN.

Koninklyk Instituut voor de Taal, Land en Volkenkunde van Nederlandsch Indie, Commissie voor Adatrecht; ZUID SUMATRA. ADATBUNDEL.

Koninklyke Vereeniging Koloniaal Instituut, by Rutgers-Pekelharing, VERHALEN OVER INDIE.

Kop, G. G. van der, LIGHT AND SHADOWS ON BALI AND BALINESE, Batavia, in Inter-Ocean, volume 5, 1924.

Kops, George Francis de Bruyn, OVER BALI EN ZYNE BEVOLKING, Baarn, Hollandia Drukkery, 1918.

Kopstein, F., EEN ZOOLOGISHE REIS DOOR DE TROPEN, Batavia, G. Kolff, 1929.

Kraemer, H., DE HOUDING VAN ZENDING EN CHRISTENDOM IN INDIE, Zendingtydschrift de Opwekker, 1930.

Kraemer, Philip, DIE STERBENDEN INSELN, München, G. Müller, 1928.

Krom, Dr. Nicolaas Johannes, BARABUDUR: ARCHAEOLOGICAL DESCRIPTION, the Hague, M. Nyhoff, 1927.

Krom, Dr. Nicolaas Johannes, BESCHRYVING VAN BARABUDUR (Krom and van Erp), Haag, M. Nyhoff, 1920.

Krom, Dr. Nicolaas Johannes, INLEIDING TOT DE HINDU-JAVAANSCHE KUNST, Publication, Koninklyk Instituut voor de Taal, Land en Volkenkunde van Nederlandsch Indie, Haag, M. Nyhoff, 1920.

Kruyt, Albert C., DE ADOPTIE IN VERBAND MET HET MATRIARCHAAT BY DE TORADJAS VAN MIDDEN CELEBES, in volume 41 van Tydschrift voor Indische Taal, Land en Volkenkunde, Batavia, 1899.

Kruyt, A. C., DE BOSCHMENSCHEN OP CELEBES, Nederlandsch Zendingblad, 1930.

Kruyt, A. C., HET WICHELEN VAN DE TORADJAS IN MIDDEN CELEBES, in Volume 44, Batavia, Tydschrift voor Land, Taal en Volkenkunde, 1901.

Kruyt, A. C., with Nic. Adriani. DE BARÉ-E SPREKENDE TORADJA, BATAVIA, Landsdrukkery, 1912-1914.

Kunst, Mr. Jaap, HINDU-JAVAANSCHE MUZIEKINSTRUMENTEN, OOST JAVA, G. Kolff & Co., Weltevreden, Java, 1927.

Labberton, D. van Hinloopen, HET SANSKRTA-ELEMENT IN DE GEOGRAPHISCHE NAMEN VAN DEN INDISCHEN ARCHIPEL.

Lauts, Ulrich Gerhard, HET EILAND BALI EN DE BALINEEZEN, Amsterdam, G. J. A. Beyerinck, 1848.

Leeuw, Hendrik de, BORNEO'S OIL DEVELOPMENT, Houston, Texas, Gulf Publishing Co., volume 54, no. 5; July 19, 1929.

Leeuw, Hendrik de, NATIVE RUBBER CULTIVATION IN DUTCH EAST INDIES, New York, The Rubber Age, volume 26, February 10, 1930.

Leeuw, Hendrik de, OLD JAVANESE BATIK AND ITS TRADITIONS, New York Antiquarian, volume xiv, number 2, February 1930.

Leeuw, Hendrik de, SUMATRA, ECONOMIC AND GEOGRAPHIC, Geographic Society Bulletin, Philadelphia, volume xxviii, no. 1, January 1930.

Leeuw, Hendrik de, THE JAVA CANE SUGAR INDUSTRY, New York, Sugar Publishing Co., June 1929, volume 6.

Leeuw, Hendrik de, TIN MINING AND SMELTING IN THE NETHERLANDS EAST-INDIES, New York, Engineering and Mining Journal, August 9, 1930, McGraw-Hill Co., New York.

Lekkerkerker, C., BALI EN LOMBOK OVERZICHT DER LITERATUR TOT 1919 (for Bali Institute), by Blankwaardt & Schoonhoven, Ryswyk, 1920.

Lekkerkerker, C., IMMIGRATIE IN NEDERLANDSCH INDIE, Haag, Indische Gids, 1930.

Lennep, J. H. van, HET BOEK VOOR DEN ZEEMAN. Uit Davids' Boekekraam. Journaal, 1618. Willem Ysbrandtsz. Bontekoe. Printed in Haarlem 1861, J. J. Weeveringh.

Masturzi, Giovanni, DAS SINGAPORE A HONGKONG ATTRAVERSO LE INDIE OLANDESI (GIAVA-BALI-BORNEO), Firenze, in Universo, 1925.

Mjöberg, Eric, BORNEO DESS LAND OCH FOLK, Stockholm, Ymer, 1929.

Moerman, Jzn. J., IN EN OM DE CHINEESCHE KAMP, Weltevreden; Landsdrukkery, 1926.

Molengraaff, Prof. Dr. G. A. F., BORNEO EXPEDITIE, LEIDEN, E. J. Brill, 1902.

Naeff, Paul, UNTER MALAYISCHER SONNE, Frauenfeld, Huber & Co., 1925.

Nanninga, Dr. A. W., DE THEE CULTUUR OP JAVA, Baarn, Hollandia Drukkery, 1915.

Nederburgh, Sebastiaan Cornelius, JOURNAEL DER REIZE VAN MR. S. C. NEDERBURG LANGS JAVA's NOORDOOSTKUST IN 1798, Amsterdam, W. Holtrop, 1804.

Nederland-Indie Oud & Nieuw, NADPADA KRAMA: HET HUWELYK VAN NADPADA, den Haag, Jaargang 14, 1929.

Nielsen, Aage Krarup, MADS LANGE TIL BALI, Kobenhavn, H. Aschehang & Co., 1925.

Nieuwenhuis, A. W., DE ZENDING EN DE BESCHAVING IN INDIE, Haag, Tropisch-Nederland, III, 1930-1931.

Nieuwenhuis, A. W., DIE DURCHQUERUNG BORNEO's DURCH DIE NIEDERLÄNDISCHE EXPEDITION, Gotha, Petermann's mitteilungen, volume 44, 1898.

Nieuwenhuis, A. W., HET ANIMISME IN NEËRLANDS-INDIE, Amsterdam, Land en Volk, 1913.

Nieuwenhuis, A. W., QUER DURCH BORNEO, Leiden, E. J. Brill, 1904-1907.

Notovitch, UNKNOWN LIFE OF JESUS CHRIST AND VOYAGE TO INDIA, Chicago, Indo-American Book Co., 1907.

Oldenburg, Hermann, ANCIENT INDIA, ITS LANGUAGE AND RELIGION (THE STUDY OF SANSKRIT, translated by A. H. Gunlogsen), Chicago, Open Court Publishing Co., 1896.

Oldenburg, Hermann, BUDDHA, HIS LIFE, HIS DOCTRINE, HIS ORDER, London, Williams & Norgate, 1882.

Parmentier, Jean, DESCRIPTION NOUVELLE DES MERVEILLES DE CE MODE ET DE LA DIGNITÉ ED L'HOMME EN LISLE TABROBANE AULTREMENT DICTE SAMATRA Paris, 1531. Reprinted in Boston, 1920, Massachusetts Historical Society, no. 32, from Bibliothèque Nationale, Paris.

Perrier, Edmond, THE EARTH BEFORE HISTORY, MAN's ORIGIN AND THE ORIGIN OF LIFE, London, Paul, Trench, Trübner & Co., 1925.

Pigafetta, Antonio, MAGELLAN's VOYAGE AROUND THE WORLD, The Arthur H. Clark Co., Cleveland, 1906.

Pleyte, C. M., in Tydschrift voor Indische Taal en Volkenkunde, volume 49, In Sundanese and Dutch, Batavia, 1906. RADEN MOENDING-LAJA DI KOESOEMA, OLD SUNDANESE ROMAN.

Polo, Marco, ACCOUNT OF JAPAN AND JAVA, 1298, Old Southern Leaflets General Series 32.

Polo, Marco, THE BOOK OF SER MARCO POLO, THE VENETIAN, LONDON, J. Murray, 1903.

Polo, Marco, THE FIRST BOOKE OF MARCUS PAULUS VENETUS OR OF MASTER MARCO POLO, A GENTLEMAN OF VENICE, HIS VOYAGES, 1625, 111.

Pratt, Edward Ewing, INTERNATIONAL TRADE IN STAPLE COMMODITIES, New York. McGraw Hill Book Co., Inc., 1928.

Pryohoetomo Mas, MINAHASA, The Hague, Oedaya, 1930.

Radermacher, Jacob Cornelis Matthieu, KORTE BESCHRYVING VAN HET EILAND CELEBES, Rotterdam, R. Arrenberg, 1786.

Raffles, Lady S. H., MEMOIRS OF THE LIFE AND PUBLIC SERVICES OF SIR STAMFORD RAFFLES, London, J. Duncan, 1835.

Raffles, Sir Thomas Stamford, THE HISTORY OF JAVA, London, J. Murray, 1830.

Ramayana, RAMAYANA IM ALT UND NEU, Indische studie no 1, Hamburg, Friedrichsen de Gruyter & Co., GMBH, 1928.

Raynal, Guillaume Thomas Francois, HISTOIRE PHILOSOPHIQUE ET POLITIQUE DES ETABLISSEMENTS ET DU COMMERCE DES EUROPÉENS DANS LES DEUX INDES, Amsterdam, M. Schalekamp, 1773-74.

Ridley, H. N., MALAY PLANT NAMES, (1902 Journal of the Straits Branch of the Royal Asiatic Society), Singapore.

Roelfsema, H. R., EEN JAAR IN DE MOLUKKEN, Haarlem, H. D. Tjeenk-Willink & Zoon, 1917.

Ronkel, Ph. S. van., HERKOMST VAN ENKELE MALEISCHE BASTAARD WOORDEN, Tydschrift voor Indische Taal, land en volkenkunde, Batavia, volume 47, 1904.

Ronkel, Ph. S. van., DE KROON DER KONINGEN, in Tydschrift voor Indische Taal, Land en Volkenkunde, Batavia, 1899, volume 41.

Roorda, Taco, ADJI SÁKÁ, OUDE FABELACHTIGE GESCHIEDENIS VAN JAVA, Amsterdam, F. Muller, 1857 (in Javanese).

Roorda, Taco, BEKNOPTE JAVAANSCHE GRAMMATICA, Zwolle, Tjeenk Willink, 1906.

Roorda, Taco, DE WAJANG VERHALEN VAN PALÁ-SÁRÁ IN JAVANESE, Haag, M. Nyhoff, 1869. (Published for Royal Institute.)

Rosenberg, Karl Benjamin Herman van, DER MALAYISCHE ARCHIPEL., Leipzig, G. Weigel, 1878.

Ross, John Dill, SIXTY YEARS LIFE AND ADVENTURES IN THE FAR EAST, London, Hutchinson & Co., 1911.

Rouffaer, G. P. and H. H. Juynboll, DIE BATIK KUNST IN N. INDIE, Haarlem, H. Kleinmann & Co., 1914.

Rouffaer G. P. and J. W. Yzerman, DE EERSTE SCHEEPVAART NAAR OOST INDIE ONDER CORNELIS DE HOUTMAN. Haag, M. Nyhoff, 1915. (For Account Linschoten Vereeniging.)

Rumphius, RUMPHIUS GEDENKBOEK in Koloniaal Museum, Haarlem, 1702-1902.

Rutgers, Dr. Abraham Arnold Lodewyk, DE TOEKOMST VAN DE BEVOLKINGS-RUBBER-CULTUUR, Amsterdam, deBussy, 1925.

Sarasin, Paul and Fritz, VERZEICHNIS WICHTIGER GESCHRIFTEN ÜBER CELEBES, REISEN IN CELEBES, Wiesbaden, 1905.

Scheltema, Johann Friederich, MONUMENTAL JAVA, London, Macmillan & Co., 1912.

Schotel, Dr. Gilles Dionysius Jacobus, LETTERKUNDIGE BYDRAGEN TOT DE GESCHIEDENIS, ETC., VAN TABAK, KOFFIE EN THEE, Haag, P. H. Noordendorp, 1848.

Schrieke, Bertram Johannes Otto, THE EFFECT OF WESTERN INFLUENCE ON NATIVE CIVILIZATION, Batavia, G. Kolff, 1929.

Scott, Edmund, AN EXACT DISCOURSE OF THE SUBTILITIES, FASHIONS, POLICIES, RELIGION AND CEREMONIES OF THE EAST INDIANS, AND ALSO WHAT HAPPENED AT BANTAN IN THE EAST INDIES, SINCE THE 2ND OF FEBRUARY, 1602. Printed in London, 1606, by W. W. for W. Burre.

Shah, Professor K. T., THE SPLENDOUR THAT WAS 'IND., Bombay, D. B. Taraporevala Son & Co., 1930.

Stamp, Laurence Dudley, ASIA: AN ECONOMIC AND REGIONAL GEOGRAPHY, London, Methuen & Co., Ltd., London, 1929.

Stutterheim, Dr. W. F., CULTUURGESCHIEDENIS VAN JAVA IN BEELD, Weltevreden (for Java Institute), 1926.

Swettenham, Sir Frank Athelstone, BRITISH MALAYA, London, J. Lane, 1929.

Tagore, Sir Rabindranath, LETTERS FROM JAVA, Visva-Bharati Quarterly, Sravan, 1928, volumes 5 and 6.

Thorne, Robert, THE BOOKS MADE BY THE RIGHT WORSHIPFUL ROBERT THORNE IN THE YEARE 1527, East Indies, London, 1598.

Thunberg, Karl Peter, TRAVELS IN EUROPE, AFRICA, ASIA, LONDON. Printed for F. & C. Rivington, 1793-1795.

Tideman, J., SIMELUNGUN, Leiden, L. H. Becherer, 1922.

Tonkes, Hommo, VOLKSKUNDE VAN BALI, Halle-a Saar. Buchdruckerei des Waisenhauses, 1888.

Toorn, J. L. van der, MANDJAU ARI: MINANGKABAUSCHE VERTELLING, Batavia, Albrecht & Russche, 1891.

Treub, Melchior, A TROPICAL BOTANICAL GARDEN, Smithsonian Institute, Report, 1890 pt. 1.

Tuuk, Herman Neubronner van der, KAWI-BALINEESCH-NEDERLANDSCH WOORDENBOEK, Batavia Landsdrukkery, 1897-1912.

Veth, Prof. P. J., MIDDEN SUMATRA, 4 volumes, Leiden, E. J. Brill, 1881-92.

Veth, Prof. P. J., NEDERLANDSCH INDIE, 4 volumes, Haarlem, E. F. Bohn, 1896-07.

Verster, Balbian and M. C. Kooy van Zeggelen, BATAVIA, ONS MOOI INDIE, Amsterdam, J. M. Meulenhoff, 1921.

Viruly, E. W., MET DE CAMERA DOOR NEDERLANDSCH INDIE, Amsterdam, J. H. deBussy, 1923.

Vogel, Prof. J. Ph., BRONNEN TOT DE KENNIS VAN HET OUDE INDIE, Leiden, Dissertation, Ryks Universiteit, 1st April, 1914. Leiden, E. J. Brill, 1914.

Vollbehr, E., WAYANG ORANG IN DJOCJAKARTA, In Tropisch Nederland, volume 3, 1930.

Volz, Wilhelm Theodore August Hermann, IM DÄMMER DES RIMBA, SUMATRA, Breslau, F. Hirt, 1921.

Vreede, Dr. Albert Cornelis, BABAD TANAH DJAWA, Haag, M. Nyhoff, 1899-03. JAVANESE HISTORY UNTIL 1647.

Walbeehm, A. H. J. G., JAVAANSCHE SPRAAKKUNST, Leiden, E. J. Brill, 1915.

Wallace, A. R., THE MALAY ARCHIPELAGO, New York, Harper Bros., 1869.

Wells, Carveth, SIX YEARS IN THE MALAY JUNGLE, Garden City, Doubleday Page, 1925.

Westenenk, L. C., DE MINANGKABAUSCHE NAGARI, Weltevreden, Visser & Co., 1918.

Wilken, Prof. Dr. G. A., PLECHTIGHEDEN AND GEBRUIKEN BY VERLOVINGEN EN HUWELYKEN BY DE VOLKEN VAN DEN INDISCHEN ARCHIPEL. En Andere Bydragen. In Bydragen Tot de Taal, Land en Volkenkunde van Nederlandsch Indie voor Koninklyk Instituut, 1901.

Wilken, Prof. Dr. G. A., THE SOCIOLOGY OF MALAYAN PEOPLE. Published by the Committee for Malay Studies at Kuala Lumpur, 1921.

Winter, the Elder, KAWI-JAVAANSCH WOORDENBOEK, Batavia, Landsdrukkery, 1880.

Winter, C. F., ADJI-SÁKÁ (for Koninklyk Instituut voor Taal land en Volkenkunde), Amsterdam, F. Muller, 1857.

Zwaan, Johannis Pieter Kleiweg de, BYDRAGEN TOT DE ANTHROPOLOGIE DER MENANGKABAU MALEIERS, Amsterdam, J. M. Meulenhoff, 1908.

Date Due

Demco 293-5			